The Garbage Brothers

a novel by Paul Neville

IFD Publishing
P.O. Box 40776, Eugene, Oregon 97404, U.S.A.
www.ifdpublishing.com

The Garbage Brothers
Copyright © 2023 by Paul Neville
All rights reserved. No part of this book may be reproduced or transmitted in any form or by any means, electronic or mechanical, including photocopying, recording, or by any information storage and retrieval system, without the written consent of the publisher, except where permitted by law.

This is a work of fiction. Any resemblance to actual events or locales or persons, living or dead, is entirely coincidental.

Cover art, Copyright © 2023 Julia O'Reilly

ISBN: 979-8-9852827-6-4
Printed in the United States of America

Acknowledgments:

For my wife Candy, the dream keeper. And for the finest writing group on any planet in any universe.

The Garbage Brothers

a novel by Paul Neville

Eugene, Oregon

Chapter 1: Lost in Freedom

Freedom was the least likely small town in the Midwest where a soul could get lost that hot, hazy June afternoon in 1969. But there I was, clueless as a stray dog, my baby blue Chevy Corvair idling at a highway crossroads where a scattering of establishments had sprouted over the years like weeds in sidewalk cracks. I could see most of them: the Greasy Wrench Truck Stop and Cafe, Gary's Grab and Go Market, the Pink Flamingo Motor Inn, the Jaguar Gentlemen's Club, the Liberty Township Hall, and the Tabernacle of the Holy Winds Church. But for the life of me I could not find my destination, Willard Sanitation Service, and I already was 13-minutes-and-counting late for my 3 p.m. job interview with owner Benjamin Willard III.

I uncrumpled the directions, which were scrawled on a piece of notebook paper that had molded to the steering wheel under my sweaty grip. Mr. Willard gave them to me that morning over the pay phone in the lobby of Sydney O. Roxbury High School, where I was a senior teetering on the brink of graduation. But I was distracted by the sight of the lithe, long-legged Lyla Packington, whose attention I arduously and unsuccessfully pursued my entire senior year. I managed to scrawl just a few words of the business owner's directions in the cramped, nearly indecipherable script that had tormented my teachers since I was in grade school: "Wrench. Truck. Trees. Entrance." At the bottom of the page in capital letters and underlined for a reason I could not now remember, was the word: "DON'T."

I dropped the directions on a car floor papered with unfinished homework assignments, fast-food wrappers, and a postcard reminding me that "federal law requires all 18-year-olds to register with their local draft boards," and took geographic inventory. Like most of the kids who lived in Fox Breath Meadow—a subdivision for Chicago commuters built on what until a few years ago had been corn and soybean fields and gravel pits—I passed through Freedom on my way to and from high school each day, stopping only to buy corn dogs and Cokes at Gary's Grab and Go or to gas up at the truck stop. On Friday nights in the fall I'd hung out with my teammates on the football team in the parking lot of the Jaguar Gentlemen's Club gazing at indifferent strippers as they took smoke breaks from their mysterious labors. That was as close as most of us, with the exception of my best friend Brett who at age 18 looked as if he were 35, got to seeing the inside of the Jaguar. Brett Warner, a fellow aspiring writer who had already churned out what he readily conceded was a cataclysmically bad first novel, just grinned when I asked him what he'd seen one night after he strolled into the strip club without even having to use his fake ID. "Such knowledge is dangerous for innocents," he said.

With a rising sense of desperation—I was now 15 minutes late—I pulled my Corvair into the parking lot of the Pink Flamingo. A jaunty pink neon bird with a sword beak, black top hat, and monocle was perched on a sign that informed passers-by when rooms were available, which was most of the time. Directly across Highway 40 I could see the Greasy Wrench Truck Stop and Cafe, a low-slung, gray cinder-block building with a half-dozen gas pumps and an asphalt parking lot where the big rigs parked while their drivers received a Holy Communion of eggs, bacon, hash browns and toast in the cafe. Squinting against the glare of afternoon sun, I made out the mounded top of a Quonset hut 50 yards behind the truck stop.

The confluence of clues was promising and jibed with my half-assed directions. I gunned the Corvair across the two-lane highway and into the truck-stop parking lot, where behind the cafe I saw a narrow gravel drive with a sign that read "Willard Sanitation—Humpin' to Please." But as soon as I entered the drive, my car fishtailed in what I realized too late was a deep road bed of tire-swallowing rock, and after 20 yards my car ground to a stop. I accelerated, causing the tires to smoke and the car to sink deeper. I looked up, and in front of the Quonset hut garage ahead I could see a tall, pear-shaped man standing with one arm akimbo and the other leaning on a push broom. He stared out of the open sliding door of the green building, looking to see what the gravel-grinding commotion was about.

It was then I remembered the meaning of the word "DON'T"—as in "DON'T drive your car down the gravel driveway that leads to the Willard Sanitation garage." Despite my predicament, I cheerfully waved at the man with the broom and tried to open the car door as if I intended to park my car in the middle of the drive. But the door was wedged shut. Left with no dignified option, I crawled out the driver's window, landing on my palms in the gravel and then springing quickly to my feet as if I'd rehearsed such exits several times a day.

"Mr. Willard, sir?" I said as I approached the man. "Sorry I'm late. I got lost."

"I gave you directions," he said.

"Yes sir, you did. And they were excellent directions," I said. "I just didn't follow them."

"Well, you should have at least paid attention to the part where I told you to leave your car at the cafe and walk to the garage. Trucks get down here just fine, but the gravel swallows kiddie cars like yours."

"Yes, sir," I said, as I tried to look like the very picture of a confident, competent summer garbage helper. Where the afternoon sun sliced through the entrance, the garage's interior looked as big as a high school gym. The owner looked to be in his mid-50s, 6 feet tall, pink and plump, and wearing a perfectly pressed khaki uniform and a matching cap that encased his thick head. He extended a soft, moist right hand. "Benjamin Willard III," he said.

"Jesse Wheeler," I answered, shaking his hand and noticing his eyes looked glazed and he was weaving in the late afternoon heat. It appeared that Willard Sanitation's proprietor, the man I hoped would provide me with gainful employment, was under the influence, and I'd had considerable experience discerning that condition in my own father.

I waited for the owner to speak, but he was silent, lifting the cap off his sweating forehead and then pulling it back on again. "We talked on the phone this morning about the summer job I saw advertised in the paper," I prompted.

"Well, you're too late," he said. "I didn't think you were going to show so I just called and hired another young man."

I needed this job more than Benjamin Willard III or God himself could possibly understand. All my friends had summer jobs and were heading to college in the fall. I not only didn't have a job, but so far I'd been rejected by all three colleges to which I'd applied. Even if a school overlooked my cellar-level grades and accepted me, I couldn't afford tuition, since my father's recent and sudden death at age 42 left our family broke. My mother put our house up for sale and planned to move in with her sister in Indianapolis, and she'd readily—far too readily for my comfort—endorsed my half-assed plan to find a summer job and remain behind in Freedom.

"Can you interview me anyway?" I said.

"The job is already filled," he said. "Why would I interview you?"

"I don't know," I said. "Maybe just in case."

He paused for a moment, clearly considering the best way to make me go away. "OK," he said, glancing at his wristwatch to let me know he was a busy man and that the push broom would not tolerate his absence much longer. "I have a couple minutes—tell me about yourself."

It was a predictable question, but I wasn't ready for it—not at a time in my life when I was floundering in a river of disappointments, failures, and uncertainties. My father and I had not been close for years—his work was the focal point of his life, and he'd uprooted us nearly every year to take a new job in a new city where I was always the "new kid" who moved away just as he started to put down roots. Yet his death had profoundly affected me by stripping away my suburban "everything-will-turn-out-OK" security blanket and imposing financial hardships I'd never before experienced.

"You said on the phone that you are about to graduate from Roxbury

High," he said. "How are your grades?"

"Good," I lied. My grades were, as my friend Brett once observed of his own academic performance, "the marks of a gentleman"—mostly Cs and Ds, with occasional As from English teachers who appreciated, as one of them called it, my "fecund imagination." As my high school counselor, Mrs. Manlove, was fond of pointing out, my GPA was mired in "the bottom quartile" of Sidney O. Roxbury High School's graduating class.

"How about college?" he asked. "I like to hire college kids as summer helpers."

"I'm definitely planning to go to college," I said. It was another lie that I immediately compounded with yet another. "I'm still deciding between schools."

The owner nodded and glanced again at his watch. He pulled a small blue spiral notebook from his back pocket and handed it to me along with a pencil. "Here," he said. "Leave your name and your phone number. Just in case."

I scrawled my name and number in the notebook and handed it back. He put it in a front shirt pocket, reached for the broom and started sweeping the garage entrance, making clear it was time for me to leave.

I turned and walked back up the driveway, forgetting in my disappointment that my car was stuck. Then I heard a rumbling, grinding, chain-jangling racket and looked up to see an elephant-sized, cherry red garbage truck approaching. It pulled to a stop in front of my car, and the driver opened the door and jumped down from the cab. He was a short, swarthy man with medicine-ball shoulders and gorilla legs. He raised both thick arms, palms upturned, hairy armpits exposed under a filthy cutoff sweatshirt.

"Tho what the hell? How am I thuppothed to get to the garage?" he said with a heavy lisp that prompted not the slightest trace of self-consciousness. He was just an inch or two over 5 feet, but he was nearly as wide as he was tall. Either he or his truck, perhaps both, exuded a rich, dank, amazing stink that reminded me of driving past the county dump on Highway 40. He looked at once aggravated and amused by my predicament.

"My name ith Billy Bart and I'm the foreman of thith thorry-ath outfit," he said, extending a greasy hand. "Who told you to drive that little piethe of thit on thith road?"

Not wanting to admit I hadn't heeded the owner's warning, I gestured toward the garage. Mr. Willard was doing slow circles with his push broom, keeping his head down and clearly wanting no part of rescuing me from my predicament. It was another lie, but what the hell, I was on a roll.

"Figureth," he said. "Benjie don't know hith athhole from hith belly button." He removed a large, flat-bladed shovel that was hanging from

The Garbage Brothers

a metal hook on the side of the truck. "Here," he said, handing it to me. "Thtart digging."

I gripped the shovel—manfully, I hoped—with both hands, reared back and swung it hard at the gravel that had swallowed my car up to its chassis. But instead of plunging deep into the gravel as I intended, it took a ringing skid across the surface and gashed the car's rear bumper.

"Jeethuth Chritht, you're ath thtuck ath a dog'th dick," he said. Then he hopped back into the truck cab, smoothly shifted into reverse, and backed into the truck-stop parking lot. He then turned the massive truck around, and effortlessly backed it down the narrow driveway a few feet behind my car. He climbed out of the cab and went to the rear of the truck, where he pushed a button that released a thick steel cable from a winch on top of the truck. He released enough cable to reach the back axle of my car, and turned to me: "Gonna pull your car out," he said. "Leth jutht hope there'th thomething left for you to drive."

He picked up the shovel from where I'd dropped it on the roadway, and with a half-dozen pile-driving strokes cleared room to hook the chain to the rear axle. He laid down on his stomach and hooked the thick cable to the axle and then leaped back into the cab and gunned the gas. "Better thtand back," he shouted. "If the cable thnapth, it could take your head off."

He eased the truck into gear and pulled forward, making the cable taut. Then with a demonic "what-the-hell" grin, he accelerated hard. For a second nothing moved. Then slowly, surely my beloved Corvair rose like a dolphin out of a gravel sea. The foreman looked in his side mirror and accelerated again, pulling my fishtailing car another 10 yards out of the driveway and into the asphalt truck-stop parking lot. I ran alongside until my rescuer put on the brakes and jumped out of the truck. "Why are you thtandin' there like a goddamn thombie? Unhook the cable—and thank your Lord and Thavior for thending Billy Bartkowthki to your thorry-ath rethcue."

He watched as I got down on my hands and knees, peered under the bottom of the car as if I'd never seen the underside of a vehicle before, which was close to the truth, and after a few seconds of looking reached up and pulled the cable hook free from the axle. Billy pushed a button on the back of the truck that rewound the cable onto a winch above the truck's rear trough. "Pleathe don't tell me you're the idiot college kid who'th our new thummer helper," he said.

"No, I didn't get hired," I said. "I was late for the job interview, and the owner hired someone else." I paused and decided to tell Billy Bartkowski the truth about my situation. I had nothing to lose; I'd already lost the job, and maybe, just maybe, I could end my brief time at Willard Sanitation with a sliver of self-respect. "I'm not a college kid," I said. "I told Mr. Willard I was, but I'm not. I need the job so bad that I lied about college."

The foreman looked unfazed. "Well, knowing how to lie to the owner ith an exthellent thtart—ethpethially thith owner. Tho what—are you thtill in high thchool?" he asked.

"No, I'm graduating this week," I said. "From Roxbury High"

Billy nodded. "My alma mater," he said. "Graduated in 1959 — I was a five-year man. My girlth—Thuthie, Thandy, Thara, and Thally all are going to thchool there, and I played football there. Coach Kelly Cox thaid I wath the thtrongetht fullback in thtate high thchool hithtory."

"I played football, too," I said, and for once I was telling the truth. "Coach Cox called me the slowest running back in Illinois high school history."

Billy grinned, and I decided to lay the rest of my sorry cards on the table. "Look," I said. "I don't know if you can help, but I need a job. Bad. My dad died last year. My mom's moving and, man, I've got to earn some money."

Billy shook his head. "Thorry about your daddy," he said. "Mine died when I wath a kid—got killed in the Korean War—thot by a thniper ath he got out of his foxhole to take a thit."

"Mine had a heart attack on the couch drinking a martini and watching Johnny Carson," I said.

"Better way to go," Billy said.

I nodded and Billy's gleaming eyes fixed on me. "You know, it'th jutht pothible the college kid the old man hired won't make it patht hith firtht day. Thtrange and dithturbing thingth can happen when thomeone ith humpin' garbage. Tho jutht maybe you'll end up being the one getting the wortht job in town."

Chapter 2: The Mysterious Lyla P.

I drove west on Highway 20 toward the nearby community of Rivergreen, listening to gravel rattle loose from the bumpers and wheel wells where it lodged after Billy Bartkowski dragged my car down the river of gravel. I glanced in the rearview mirror to see if any vital automotive organs—a muffler or transmission—had fallen. But there was just hot, empty pavement.

I was headed to Lyla Packington's house, where I planned to confide my dismay at not getting the job at Willard Sanitation and my uncertainty about the future. Lyla had not yet realized that destiny dictated we would someday become passionate and intricately entwined lovers, but I needed a sympathetic ear. I also harbored a secret hope that my unburdening might unleash the floodgates and Lyla would volunteer comforts of the carnal kind. But that was a futile hope this 18-year-old virgin carried with him in every encounter with the lovely, ever-elusive Lyla P.—and, for that matter, with most other members of the female species.

I was now confronted by a sudden and disorienting deficit of prospects thanks to my long- standing disinterest in all things academic, my subsequent consignment to Mrs. Manlove's "bottom quartile," and my father's passing. My assumption was that everything would turn out fine in my life—that I would go to college, write groundbreaking novels, travel the world, date beautiful and exotic women and maybe someday get married and have a small herd of wild, gifted kids. Here I was newly 18 years old, an age when most young men are supposed to be sowing their seeds, and I already was reaping the whirlwind.

I had two friends who made my senior year at Sydney O. Roxbury High tolerable. One was Brett Warner, who like me had arrived in his senior year. He moved from Southern California where he was a star football player, a surfer, an anarchist poet, and a rebel of epic proportions who managed to get thrown out of four high schools. His family once hired a private tutor to teach him at home—a 28-year-old female doctoral student whose services were deemed no longer necessary when Brett's mother returned home from work one afternoon during the noon hour to find her son and his tutor in a compromising position on the kitchen table, their lunches devolving into something else. "Tuna fish and cookies everywhere," Brett recalled.

Paul Neville

Brett was as schooled in the ways of life as I was inexperienced, and he was as towering and exceptional in appearance as I was average and mundane. While I was 5 foot 10 with an unfortunately prominent nose and a weedy clump of brown hair, Brett stood 6 feet 6 with hawk- like features and sun-bleached blond hair that mesmerized the girls—and, evidently, 28-year-old tutors. His personality was even more striking. Outrageous, spontaneous behavior flowed from Brett like an underground stream emerging from a mountainside. One moment he might be walking down a school hallway and the next he might be wriggling on his stomach, head elevated like a chameleon, tongue flicking in and out with fly-catching speed. Once, he sauntered late into Mr. Elmer Schmidt's English literature class while the teacher was perched on a stool in front of the class reading Chaucer in impenetrable Middle English. Brett strode across the back of the room and peered out the second-floor window. Seeing that it was a brilliantly sunny day—certainly no day to be stuck inside listening to a bald academic read the "The Summoner's Tale" in accentual-syllabic meter—Brett climbed out an open window onto a ledge and jumped 15 feet to the grass. He limped off into a nearby cornfield as I, along with my classmates and Mr. Schmidt, looked on in amazement. For that memorable offense, he earned a three-day suspension, which was nothing to Brett Warner, the master of three-day suspensions.

Lyla Packington was our mutual friend, although I longed for her to be more than a friend to me. I met her nine months earlier on the first morning of school. I was miserable, alone in a sea of strangers, like I was at the start of school in other towns in so many other years. I was always the odd kid out, the boy with the wrong sweater and wrong pants, socks and shoes from some wrong other place. Always the piece that didn't fit in the puzzle. Lyla was in the cafeteria where the seniors gathered before the start of school when I saw her, thin and long-haired and looking, like me, hopelessly out of place. She was sitting alone at a large round table reading a paperback of the collected poems of Pablo Neruda. She raised her head, met my eyes, paused for the slightest of moments and then descended with a maddeningly private smile back into her book.

I didn't know anything then about Lyla, but I was smitten by this fellow stranger. While my life had been spent shuttling from one mundane suburb to another—from places like Cleveland, Indianapolis, St. Louis and Chicago, Lyla clearly seemed to be from elsewhere, somewhere far from the Midwest and its flat roads and rivers and cows and suburbs and high schools located in the middle of corn fields.

Turned out I was right. After we became friends, I learned she had lived in wondrous and faraway places like Martinique, Hong Kong and Nairobi, her father being a researcher for a global fertilizer company. She landed in

Freedom, where she confided in me with a languorous sigh that she would endure a tiresome senior year and then escape to a progressive college where she would study literature, theater and dance.

She was slender with a head of long, thick, black hair, and her arms, legs, feet and loveliest of necks were connected in sensuous ways that other peoples' parts were not. When she walked down the hall, every part of her drifted as a synchronous one. When she read, every part of her immersed itself in whatever book she was devouring at that moment. She was always reading books. As soon as she finished one, she would order me to read it so that we could talk about it—or, more often, so I could listen to her talk about it. She voraciously read—anything and everything she could get her hands on—Dos Passos, Pound, Whitman, Socrates, Blake, Cervantes, Faulkner, Stein, Kerouac—and when she walked down the halls, usually with a book in front of her, she glided through the churning, chaotic sea of students like a clipper ship bound for destinations known only to her.

We hung out together and talked endlessly about books and places and poetry and philosophy—subjects on which I could more or less hold my own—and whenever I tried to steer her, us, in the direction of anything resembling romance, she would flash a look of feigned disbelief that had the maddening effect of making me want her—and her long, knee-socked legs, her Martinique curves and those elusive lips—even more. Once she made the mistake of confessing that, while living on the island of Martinique she had roamed the beaches half naked and barefoot like the other children until she was caught by the nuns in the convent where she went to school. If some evil spirit had conspired to devise a story to drive an 18-year-old more mad with love and lust that summer of 1969, I don't know what it possibly might have been. I couldn't shake that image from my mind, and I wanted nothing more than to some day see Lyla naked—half, full, quarter—it didn't matter—on a beach in Martinique, on the banks of the Seine or even the old blue couch in her basement in Freedom.

I pulled into Lyla's long gravel driveway, which wound through low-lying groves of poplar and birch to a spacious, rambling brick ranch house on a rise overlooking the Fox Breath River. Brett's car, an old white Ford station wagon with a porous muffler that made it sound more like a cabin cruiser than a car, was parked in the driveway. He hadn't told me he was coming by Lyla's after school. Her mother's car was not in the carport but that wasn't unusual. Mrs. Packington was an artist and often traveled to the city for showings of her works—large, fleshy watercolors of birds of paradise were her specialty.

I knocked on the door. No answer. Maybe, I thought, Lyla and Brett were on a walk along the river—or maybe they were in the kitchen making something to eat. I opened the door and called "hello." No answer. I walked

Paul Neville

through the entrance, and everything was still except for—what was that sound—a cough, a rustling? Now through the family room to the kitchen, where the basement door was open. I walked down the wooden steps into the cool dimness, and when rounded the corner at the bottom of the stairs, I saw Brett and Lyla on the couch. They were in a hot, churning embrace, clothing in disarray, shirts lifted and unseen parts of Lyla now exposed in a blur. I turned away, suddenly aware of my own breathing, my own foolish presence, and I walked soundlessly up the stairs.

I left the house. I got into my car and headed back to the highway, where I would drive to my soon-to-be-vacated home, a friendless, jobless, collegeless and deeply morose virgin. My only meaningful possession was a baby blue Corvair that was still kicking up gravel and a future that looked as empty as a prairie horizon.

Chapter 3: A Ray of Light

Rain poured for two days, and the gloom outside matched the darkness that descended upon me after seeing Brett and Lyla doing a torrid tango on the basement couch.

My awareness that Lyla consistently spurned my advances did nothing to ease my sorrow and humiliation. I knew it might take time for her to come to her senses and understand that we were meant for each other in the same way that Guinevere was made for Lancelot and Lara for Dr. Zhivago. It didn't matter that I had never confided the depth of my feelings about Lyla to Brett. I believed a friend should just know such things, at least a true friend, and I now knew with certainty that Brett was not a true friend.

I retreated to my bedroom, where I slumped at my desk writing lengthy, rhymeless poems about darkness, doom and death, pausing now and then to finger the tip of a dagger my father had acquired during his time serving on a Navy minesweeper in World War II. I had appropriated it from his underwear drawer after his passing. I did not know why he had kept a dagger in his underwear drawer, but rationalized that he must have put it there so that his son could find it in the event of his untimely passing. The dagger was sharp and rusty, and those qualities suited my current temperament. I was reflecting that the rust might help ensure death by blood poisoning if I decided to plunge the blade into my heart and my aim proved as bad as my judgment had been in choosing my friends. The phone rang in the kitchen, bringing me back to my senses. I put down the dagger and walked down the hall to the kitchen, wondering if it was Brett calling to confess that he had seen me in the basement and wanted to beg my forgiveness. And I knew, with a hard certainty, that when that happened I would hang the lime-green receiver back on the wall next to the Frigidaire without saying a single word. I picked up the receiver and waited. No answer. After a few seconds, the voice on the other end of the line said, "Hello, is anyone there? Hello?"

"Yes, how can I help you?" I said, with just enough edginess that Brett would know that I knew what he did—and that he would know that these were the last words he would ever hear from his former friend.

"This is Benjamin Willard of Willard Sanitation. Is Jesse Wheeler there?"

"Mr. Willard, sir," I said, scrambling to regain my footing in reality.

"How can I help you?"

"You can have the summer helper job if you still want it. The college kid I hired walked off the job in the middle of the route on the first day. Said he couldn't handle the maggots or my foreman."

"Yes, I want the job," I said. I didn't know what it paid or how long I'd last. I might end up walking off the job, too, but goddamnit I wanted—and needed—that job.

"You sure?" Mr. Willard asked. "The work isn't easy and my crew is a rough bunch."

"Yes, sir," I said. I did not know what terrible acts Billy Bartkowski committed on my behalf and hoped that they did not entail serious physical or emotional damage to the young man in question. I didn't know yet who else I'd be working with beside Billy. I didn't know where I was going to live after my mother moved, and I did not know what life would bring in the fall. But damn it, the kid from the "bottom quartile of his graduating class"—the one who nearly drowned his car in gravel—had the summer-helper job at Willard Sanitation. And in a glorious flash I could picture Lyla's reaction when I told her about the new job and the look on her face upon learning that I'd become a workin' man just like Sal Paradise in "On the Road." And yeah, maybe becoming the summer helper at Willard Sanitation wasn't quite the equivalent of migrant farm labor or railroad work, but it was something.

"OK," Benjamin Willard III said. "Be at the Greasy Wrench Cafe at 5 a.m. on Monday—the crew meets there every morning for breakfast. We'll see how you work out."

"Thank you, sir," I said.

"You don't have to 'sir' me any more. Just call me Benjie."

"Yes, sir."

"Good God," my new employer said. "My crew's going to eat you alive."

Chapter 4: The Greasy Wrench

Two days later, at 4 a.m., my WestBend alarm clock woke me for my first day at Willard Sanitation Service. I pulled on a pair of blue jeans, looking in dismay at their dark stiff rookie newness, put on a white T-shirt with fold marks, two pairs of white cotton socks, and then laced on the high-top work boots I had bought along with the rest of the outfit at the Army surplus store in Wilton.

I arrived at the Greasy Wrench Cafe at 5 a.m., and got out of my car, the unyielding jeans already chafing my thighs. I walked toward the glowing terrarium that was the Greasy Wrench just before dawn. I opened the glass door, and a brace of small bells jangled overhead. I stepped apprehensively into the moist light and a fragrant fog of smells—coffee, hash browns, bacon, sausage, eggs, pancakes, toast, hot butter, and just a whiff of urinal cake.

A half-dozen men sat at a lunch counter, spaced like fat crows on a barbed-wire fence. On the other side of the aisle were six booths lining big windows that looked out on the truck stop's parking lot. In one of the booths sat four men, indifferent to my entrance, their table strewn with food-covered, thick ceramic plates and black plastic ashtrays that contained smoldering cigarettes. I could see Billy talking with both cheeks full of food to my future colleagues at Willard Sanitation.

The waitress, a jerky-thin woman with a precise head of blond hair and a yellow-and-white uniform, stood in front of the booth. She held several blue plastic menus in one hand and a full glass coffee decanter in the other. She watched me hesitate as I approached the booth. "All right, boys," she announced in a loud but not unpleasant voice. "Looks like some fresh meat has arrived. Try not to scare this one away."

I stood in front of the booth, looking at the foreman for a welcome, directions, an introduction—anything. "My, my," Billy said. "Look at you jutht thtanding there, all drethed up in your brand-new jeanth and ready for work. Ain't you jutht the thweetest thight."

"Shut your pie hole, Billy," the waitress said.

The foreman's face gleamed with pleasure at the rebuke. "Tell you what I'd like to do with your pie hole, Mith Deloreth," he said. She ignored him and handed me a menu, gesturing impatiently with a flick of her right hand for the mountainous man sitting across from Billy to move in and give the new kid some room for God's sake.

The giant, who had a mortician's countenance, edged over a few inches at Delores' direction, leaving me less than a foot of red-vinyl-covered bench on which I perched my right buttock and just enough of the left to keep myself from falling to the floor. "Billy—why you've quite forgotten yourself. Wherever are your manners? Proper introductions, please." The falsetto voice—and phony British accent—came from the far end of my side of the booth. I leaned forward and cocked my head to look around the giant between us, and there was a young man with a full-on Jesus beard and full, swept-back head of blond hippie hair that cascaded to his shoulders.

"Oh, pleathe forgive me, ladieth," Billy said with a flourishing wave that landed a middle knuckle in a puddle of egg yolk. He licked it off before continuing. "Thith ith Benjie'th new college kid. Hith name ith Jethie."

"You sure it's Jesse and not Shitheel?" muttered the gray-faced, rail-thin man next to Billy.

Billy ignored the comment and pointed at the far end of the bench on which I was uneasily perched. "That beatnik over there with the long girly hair and the beard ith Jake Callahan—we call him Theuth." I glanced to my right, and Zeus was leaning forward, the fingers of his right hand combing and probing his chest-length beard. He gave me what I hoped was a friendly look and a half wave.

Billy continued: "And the little guy sitting next to you ith Mithter William Peterman, better known ath Pickleth." I looked up, because up was the only way to see Pickles' huge round face. He nodded and gave me a quarter smile that disappeared as quickly as it appeared. Next, Billy jabbed his thumb toward the hard-ass looking, middle-aged man to his left who had sat motionless since my arrival except for long, nicotine-sucking drags on his cigarette. "And thith here ith Merle Japeth, better known around here ath Gritth. He'th a real charmer—jutht a barrel of laughth."

I looked at Grits and then looked away. I had never seen anyone who looked as mean and downright sociopathic as Grits, whose slit eyes looked like two butcher's knives hovering over my tender young ribs.

"And you and I have already met," Billy continued. "I'm Billy Bartkowthki—everyone jutht callth me Billy Bart—and I'm the foreman of this thorry bunch of thad thackth." I nodded and smiled at the man who just a few days earlier had rescued my car from a gravel grave and had somehow, through some mysterious and clearly devious means, gotten rid of my predecessor.

Billy had done me a massive favor, but he remained an unknown and intimidating entity.

The Garbage Brothers

In the silence that followed the foreman's introductions, I was aware that I was being scrutinized, assessed and measured. I searched for a proper response. It was important to make a good first impression. "Well," I said. "It's certainly nice to be here and to meet you all."

The room fell silent, and even the cook in the back ceased the clacking of his spatula on the grill. Grits, the wraith next to Billy, stirred, his lips twisting into a hemorrhoidal smirk. "You gotta be kidding me."

"Did the new college kid just make fun of our foreman?" Zeus said. "I do believe I heard him say 'nithe'?"

I looked for a friendly face but found none. I was appalled. Undone. I knew this misunderstanding had to be remedied before I ended up on the floor with Billy's fork in my left eyeball for mocking his lisp, a sin I had not committed.

"I didn't say nithe," I tried to clarify. "I said nice."

Pickles cocked his head. "No, Zeus is right. I definitely heard you say 'nithe'," he said. "You aren't calling my friend Zeus a liar, are you?"

My head reeled. My chest tightened. Then I felt a light yet steadying touch on my left shoulder. It was Delores, her eyes moving steadily around the table at the crew like a third-grade teacher taking names. "How 'bout a couple nithe eggth, honey?" she said.

Pickles took a deep breath and exhaled. "Well," he said, "I'll give you the benefit of the doubt this time, but I hope Billy here don't take it out on you on the route today."

The crew returned to their eggs and cigarettes, and their conversation mercifully moved on to other topics. Delores poured me a cup of steaming black coffee. I thought about asking Pickles to pass the cream and sugar but decided it was safer to just drink it the way it was. It tasted sharp and bitter—it was the first time I'd ever drank coffee black. I looked out the window, and saw the sky growing lighter over the big Freightliners parked at the far edge of the parking lot. And I wondered what the holy hell I was doing in this cafe with this group of menacing strangers when I could be home safe in bed. I took another sip and thought of Lyla several miles away sleeping in her sweet bed, and wondered if she would ever talk to me again. What would she think if she saw me now, sitting at a table in the Greasy Wrench next to grown men named Pickles, Zeus, Billy and Grits who were talking about. . .what exactly were they talking about?

I adjusted frequencies and heard the crew talking about past summer helpers with names like Little Pete, Big John, Mini Toad, Tall Steve, and Horny Alex. They talked about Little Pete's tumble from the back of the truck turning a corner in downtown Wilton. They guffawed about a truck chain slapping Big John in the back of the head and knocking him permanently cross-eyed. They recalled Mini Toad finding a nudie magazine in a customer's trash and Billy threatening him with castration after he committed the mortal sin of not handing it over to his foreman. They rehashed in detail how a St. Bernard had treed Tall Steve and how Horny Alex had lost several fingers to the compactor blade.

Delores arrived with my eggs—two over easy, hash browns, bacon, and toast. Billy reached over and took one of my bacon strips and the conversation meandered on. The eggs, cooked in butter, were the best I'd ever had. Billy recalled how Little Pete had gone to the rear of a house in the Rivergreen subdivision to pick up the garbage and found a nude woman—"completely naked, mind you—not a goddamn thtich of clothing on her and lying on one of those yellow banana loungerth."

Billy paused, and no one said anything. I stared at my coffee. Everyone at the table seemed to be waiting for me to say something.

"So what happened next?" I said.

Billy considered my question. "Well," he said. "The lady thtood up without covering any of her delicateth, and thaid to Little Pete, 'Thankth for the warm-up act, now thend a real man to pick up my garbage. Thend that magnifithent thpethiman named Billy Bart.'"

"Like hell she said that," Zeus said. "What she really said was. . ." Zeus' voice kicked into falsetto, "Oh thank God it's you, Little Pete, 'cause I run inside and put on a chastity belt and a snowsuit whenever that filthy Billy Bart sneaks back here."

The bells on the front door of the Greasy Wrench jangled and Benjamin Willard III walked in looking plump, pink, and purposeful in his creased khaki uniform pants, shirt and short-brim cap. The crew met his arrival with sighs and muttering. Zeus, in particular, seemed aggravated by his presence. He slapped a hand on the table and stared into the parking lot. Pickles' eyes fixed on a Union Pacific wall calendar that showed a silver passenger train entering a mountain tunnel.

Grits was viper still except for a faint pulsing in his temples. Billy grinned and plucked the last piece of bacon from my plate and happily devoured it.

"G'morning, Benjie," Billy said. "And how are you thith fine day?" The boss responded with a nervous nod. He put on the narrow reading glasses that were dangling around his neck with a slender black chord. "Gentlemen," he said. "Unfortunately we have quite a few complaints this morning." His right hand held a bunch of blue slips of paper with large, scrawled ballpoint writing. He paused, then glanced down at me, looking confused as if he couldn't remember who I was or why I was there.

"Oh, yes," he said after a moment. "You're the new college kid. I wasn't sure you were going to show up."

The Garbage Brothers

Billy rubbed his hands together. "Oh, he thowed up, all right—jutht like a little baby in the nurthery, all ready for Papa Billy," he said.

"Gentlemen," the boss began again. "Unfortunately we have some customer complaints." A collective, silent snarl rose like a gray mist and enveloped the booth. Clearly these were not men who dealt well with authority, and the only smile in the room belonged to Billy, who busied himself poaching food off the plates of the drivers as the boss read the complaints. The first was from a Mrs. Thomas Gleason on Hawthorn Place, who said her garbage man left tissues strewn across her rose bushes for two weeks in a row. "Zeus, I believe that's yours," the boss said, holding out the blue slip for him to take and then placing it on the table when he didn't.

More complaints: A call about missing books and magazines that had been stored in a diaper pail next to the garbage can in their garage. Could someone possibly have mistaken this valuable collection of eros for refuse, and if so, could they please return them to 125 River Loop Terrace with no questions asked? "Billy, I believe that was your stop."

"Yeth, thir," Billy said. "I'll get right on top of that."

The boss continued. A woman at 3225 Mistletoe called to say she and her teenage daughter, Misty, were driving home from the market when they saw a very large man in the bed of his garbage truck behaving in a manner that led her to believe that "defecation might be occurring." Granted, this large man was shielded by a large carrying receptacle, but she and her daughter clearly could see bare buttocks, and surely there were more appropriate places for such activities.

"Well," Billy said with a considered solemnity. "Did thee thay if Pickleth wiped hith butt or not? Becauthe it doethn't thmell like he did thith morning."

Pickles' right arm was a blur. It flew across the table, and the back of his knuckles flicked Billy across the forehead. Then Pickles was holding his coffee cup before the foreman knew what grazed him.

Billy rubbed his forehead, still grinning. "Damn," he said. "That wathn't nithe, Pickleth." He looked up at the boss. "Any more feedback from our valued cuthtomerth, thir?"

The boss sighed and dropped maybe a dozen more blue slips on the table. "Just take care of these, Billy," he said. "I will see you men at the garage. Jesse, you go with Billy this week, and he'll show you the ropes."

"Billy's gonna hang 'em by those ropes," Zeus said.

The boss looked down at me and smiled. "They're just joshing, young man. Never mind them. Billy will take good care of you." The boss started to walk away, then turned back and tipped his camouflage cap. "Always look for proper facilities when nature calls, gentlemen," he said. Then he walked out the door, bells jangling his departure.

Paul Neville

"Well, I think I need to uthe the proper fathilitieth right now," said the foreman, rubbing his forehead with one hand and picking up both our checks with the other as he pronounced the Benediction. "Then it'th time to go to work, boyth. Let'th get humpin'."

Chapter 5: The Thweet Thienthe of Thanitation

After breakfast and the boss's morning briefing, Billy led the crew out of the Greasy Wrench. We walked the gravel drive through an oak grove to the garage. Billy was shorter than I remembered but looked wider and stronger than Pickles, who towered above him. Grits was average height and gaunt, but he had the look of a man who could slap the eyeballs out of your head. Zeus was a couple of inches taller than me, and lean and fit. He nodded to me, his long beard bobbing against his gleaming white T-shirt.

"Nervous?" he asked.

"Yeah," I said.

"Nerves are fine. But don't be scared of any of us drivers," he said. "We may look like British royalty, but we're just normal human beings."

I glanced to see if he was kidding, and Zeus grinned. "You're gonna be fine," he said. "Keep your head low, don't take shit, and don't daydream, especially when the blade's running. We had a summer helper who lost all the fingers on his right hand and had to stop jacking off."

"Something wrong with his left hand?" I asked.

"Ah, a resourceful lad," Zeus said. "You're gonna be fine."

At the garage, Billy hitched up a large key ring on his belt that had dozens of keys on it and inserted one into a fist-sized, brass Yale lock. He pushed open the great sliding wooden doors, which rattled like thunder in the morning stillness. Billy headed for the first truck in line, the cherry-red Ford with a hulking body that nearly reached the ceiling of the garage. Pickles walked toward a battered, mid-sized blue Ford that looked as if it had seen several decades on the road. Grits headed for a black cab-over International Harvester, and Zeus ambled, hands in his pockets, to a vintage green Chevy that looked half the size of the other trucks. As the drivers started their trucks, I stood breathing the sweet-sour smell of decaying garbage mixed with diesel fumes, and I felt dizzy and scared. I was entering a new universe, one for which I had no road map.

Billy pointed at a wooden bin containing a couple of dozen large plastic drums, half of them a grimy pumpkin orange and the rest a gun-metal gray. "Grab a carry can, and put it in the back of the truck," he said. Most of the cans were in clusters of twos and threes, jammed inside each other like stacked

Paul Neville

paper cups. I picked up two of the orange cans that were stuck together—they were surprisingly heavy—and tried to shake the bottom one loose. Nothing budged. I pulled them out of the bin, laid them on their sides and sat on the dirt floor, gripping the lip of the top can and pushing with the soles of my virgin workboots against the top rim of the bottom can. Still nothing.

I looked up to see the drivers standing on the running boards of their trucks or sitting in the cabs, watching with amusement. "Thweet Jethuth," Billy said. He jumped out of the cab, took the cans and smacked them against the hard dirt, and then easily twisted off the top one and dropped it next to me. I put my can in the trough of Billy's truck and climbed into the passenger side of the cab. The inside was surprisingly organized for a man of Billy's disheveled appearance. There was a definite sense of order—a worn but clean spare shirt hanging in the back of the cab and a doorless glove compartment filled with complaint slips. On the floor next to the gearshift was an old tool box filled with girlie magazines. Billy took the complaints he had grabbed off the table in the Greasy Wrench and stuffed them in the glove compartment. He saw me gazing at the magazines. He reached down and flipped open the top one, a Playboy, to a centerfold that showed a brunette lying on her stomach on a bearskin rug. "Thith ith my thweetheart," he said with a radiating, vibrating enthusiasm. "They're all my thweetheartth."

Billy pounded the gas pedal four times and turned the key in the ignition. The truck coughed and then rumbled to life with an impressive roar. He reached under the seat, pulled out two yellow couch cushions with Arabesque tassels, and placed them one on top of the other under his rear end so that his shoulders extended over the top of the wheel. Then he reached down with his left foot, pushed on the clutch and eased the truck into first gear. We rumbled our way out of the garage. Our truck was the first to leave; Benjamin Willard III stood at the entrance, watching his fleet take sail. He was gesturing to Billy, who rolled down the window.

"Listen to me, Billy," the boss shouted. "Don't scare off the new kid."

My introduction to what Billy called "the thweet thienthe of thanitation" was a fragrant blur of garbage, sweat and pain. We pulled into the first neighborhood on the route, a street of vintage and affluent homes in the woods near the Fox Breath River. Billy stopped the truck and grabbed a pair of filthy, torn brown cotton gloves from a shoebox under the driver's seat and tossed them to me. "Let'th get humpin'," he said. He shoved open the driver's door with his big left shoulder and jumped out of the truck, his thick, short legs churning as he hit the ground. I opened my door, gently lowered myself to the ground, and walked to the rear of the truck. By the time I got to Billy he had pulled both carry cans out of the trough, and his was slung over his right shoulder.

26

The Garbage Brothers

"Get movin'—we ain't got all day," he said, and took off running toward a large, red brick ranch house. I picked up my can and chased after him, my new boots slipping on the dewy grass. When I got to the garage, Billy had already yanked the door open and was standing next to two shiny metal garbage cans near the entrance. He tossed the lids on the concrete floor. They clashed like cymbals, then Billy emptied the first container into his carry can, giving the shiny aluminum sides a quick shimmy and rattling it against the sides of his carry can, peering inside afterward to make sure nothing was stuck to the bottom. He repeated the process with the next can, then slammed the lids back on the metal cans. "Alwayth thoftly," he said with a malicious grin. "The little darleength might be thleepin'." He pulled down the garage door, and was off again with his strangely graceful ape run, the half-filled carry can slung over his back.

At the next stop, Billy headed for a two-story, wood-frame house. In the back were two underground cans, and by the time I caught up with him Billy had stomped on the foot pedals next to them, lifting the red metal lids, and pulled the stainless steel cylinders out of their silos. "Empty thethe in your can," he instructed, and he watched intently as I did, stopping me before I dropped the first can back into the ground. "Alwayth mind the tithues," he said, reaching inside to retrieve a pink tissue that had stuck to the bottom of the can. "The little lady here loveth to complain," he said. Then Billy loped off to the next house.

Running with an empty can was difficult for me, but running with one filled with 60 pounds of garbage was nearly impossible. As we moved through the first subdivision, I had to set down my carry can several times and drag it in pursuit of the truck that Billy kept pulling ahead of us. When Billy saw me, he grimaced. "You're gonna wear a hole in the bottom of that can and when it leakth you're going to be thorry," he said. But I wasn't worried about a leaking can; survival was my only concern. By mid-morning, I was in deep pain. My lower neck and right shoulder, the place where Billy had shown me to rest the hard heel of the carry can, were bruised and swollen. My right ear was chafed and raw from rubbing against the side of the can. My spine was on fire from the contortions of wrestling the can from the ground to my shoulder, and my arm, hand and fingers were cramping.

By noon, everything that was hurt and chafed now screamed and pulsated. When I picked up my can for the 150th—or was it the 200th—time, something wet was leaking out of the can and onto my T-shirt and bleeding raw shoulder. I dropped the can on a freshly sodded front lawn, grabbed the wet sleeve of my T-shirt and pulled it to my nose. Pickle juice. On my shirt. In my wounds. Down my side. Into my pants and underwear. Dripping now down my right leg and into my new boots.

I dragged my can down to the truck, where Billy waited.

"Whathamatter little fella—got a boo boo?" he asked.

"I'm soaked with goddamn pickle juice," I said.

Billy leaned over, took a whiff and affirmed my diagnosis. "Definitely dillth," he said.

He picked up his carry can and jogged up the driveway of the next house, shouting over his shoulder. "Didn't ol' Billy Bart warn you not to drag your carry can? He told you it would make it leak and thath exthactly what happened."

I picked up my leaky carry can, slung it over my back, and slogged gingerly after Billy, the container bouncing against my filthy, aching, and now pickled back. The blisters in the heel of my brine-soaked boot burned like a barn fire. Perhaps it would help, I thought, if I ran on my toes. I gave it a try and it helped make the pain slightly less intolerable. I took a few more steps, bounding a little with each one, and looked up to see I had arrived at the side of the house, where Billy was beaming as he watched.

"What?" I asked.

"Tippy Toeth," he said. "That'th the perfect nickname for you."

By early afternoon I was ravenously hungry despite the stench, pain and exhaustion. Billy was on a dead run all morning and showed no signs of slowing, much less stopping to eat, and I didn't want to show weakness by asking when—or if—we would stop for lunch.

I was in too much pain for conversation, but Billy happily filled the verbal void. Driving between subdivisions at mid-morning, he said he had worked for Willard Sanitation for 15 years. After graduating from high school he'd taken welding classes at the local community college but his wife, Serena, got pregnant with twins before he graduated. They had four children in four years—"There wath a lotth of thith going on in the Billy Bart houthehold," he said, moving the middle finger of his right hand in and out a circle created by the thumb and forefinger of his left. Serena had named their children "Thuthie, Thandy, Thara and Thally."

"Really?" I said. "Your wife named your kids Susie, Sandy, Sara and Sally?"

"Lovely nameth, right?"

As we drove to another neighborhood, Billy recalled that he and Benjamin Willard III started working at what was then called Dickoff Sanitation about the same time. "Benjie wath a college kid like you, but he married the owner'th ugly daughter." Billy said. The company's owner and founder, a man with the unfortunate name of Frank Dickoff, died of a heart attack at the Snake Pit Tavern across from the dump during a dispute over his bar tab. Now, his son-in-law ran the renamed Willard Sanitation, even though, as Billy put it, "Benjie don't know hith ath from a hole in the ground."

"Jutht like you, Tippy Toeth," he said.

~ ~ ~

Shortly before 2 p.m., I summoned the courage to ask Billy about a lunch break. We were standing behind the truck as he held down a lever that caused the massive steel compactor blade to descend into the full hopper at the back of the truck, and then ram the garbage into the cavernous truck body. "Are we going to stop for lunch?" I asked, trying not to sound as whiny and desperate as I felt.

Billy looked at me with pitying amusement. "Ith our thweet little Tippy Toe'th tummy rumblin'?" he said. He yanked on the lever to halt the descending blade and gazed into garbage, eyes gleaming like a lizard searching for a sand flea. In a flash his thick right hand plunged down into the garbage, brushing aside a rotten half-head of lettuce and an empty Cheerios box, and grabbing what looked like a grapefruit, dented and lopsided, but still whole and unpeeled.

"Holy thit, mother of God," Billy said. He gripped the grapefruit with both hands, and tore it apart with his filthy claw fingers. He held one jagged half to his face and ground it against his mouth and jaw as if he were a human juicer. He lowered the limp, now meatless rind, jowls wet with juice and pink pulp impaled on his wire-thick stubble.

"Ah Ambrothia," he sighed, closing his eyes and shaking his head with sweet appreciation of what had just slithered down his gullet. He held out the other half to me.

"Want thum?"

~ ~ ~

The crew looked surprised when I limped into the Greasy Wrench on Monday morning after my first week on the job with Billy—everyone except Pickles. He just stared at the wall calendar as if he were at the throttle of the silver train streaking into a mountain tunnel somewhere far from the unrelenting flatness of Freedom. Sensing my presence, the big man ticked the fingernails of his right hand on the lime-green Formica tabletop, sighed, and then scooted over a few inches to leave a bare minimum of perching room on the bench for me.

"Well, our thweet little thummer helper hath rithen from the grave," Billy said. "And how are we feelin' today, Tippy Toeth? Are we a jutht a bit thaddle thore?"

I nodded and winced at the foreman's use of "Tippy Toes," which I knew would be taken up by the other drivers. I would have preferred a more macho name—something like "Night Train" or "Flash" or "Wild Man"—anything but "Tippy Toes."

Billy was right. I was saddle sore. And foot sore. And leg sore. And butt sore. And back, shoulder and neck sore. My right ear was scabbed where it had rubbed raw against the side of my carry can. The blister pain on my heels forced me to exchange my work boots for a pair of old sneakers, and I had abandoned my stiff new jeans for the oldest and most comfortable ones I could find in my closet, a pair with a gaping tear in the right knee. I wore a rumpled old uniform shirt that the boss had stuck in my hands on Friday afternoon after Billy and I had rolled back into the garage. "You made it through your first week, so here's your uniform," the boss had mumbled, and I smelled his bourbon breath as he handed me a gray work shirt with the name "Lester" stitched on the pocket.

"You ought to turn around, go back to your sweet little suburban home and crawl back in your little beddy—you look like a little turd," said Grits, who Billy had informed me on Friday would be my driver for the second week on the job. It was the assignment I dreaded; none of the other drivers radiated danger quite like Grits, who wore a worrisomely large hunting knife in a sheath that hung from his belt.

"No, I take that back," Grits said. "Even turds don't look as bad as you do. Last year's helper—Big John—didn't look this bad after his first week on the job. Big John just skipped in here lookin' like he'd been on a goddam vay-cay-shun in Hawaii."

Other drivers joined in with their own Big John stories, and I ignored them, focusing on the huge plate of hash browns that Delores had delivered with a pat on the shoulder and a "Here you go, sweetheart." I took a bite, savoring the crunch and the crusty confluence of grease and potato and ketchup, and I wondered what Lyla would think if she saw me—a workin' man eating workin'-man food with his workin'-man comrades.

The conversation paused. I looked up, and there was the boss, looking down at me as he stood in front of the table. "Are you OK, young man?" he asked.

"Good morning, Mr. Willard, sir," I said. "I'm a little sore, but I'm OK."

"He'th no Big John, thir—that'th for thertain," Billy said. "But Tippy Toeth here thurvived his firtht week with ol' Billy Bart, and he'th ready for week two with Gritth."

"We'll just see about that," said Grits, sliding a pack of Camels into the left front pocket of a work shirt that draped over his skinny frame like a horse blanket on a sawhorse. "He ain't done a real man's work yet."

Week two, under the terrifying tutelage of Grits, turned out to be both easier and harder than week one with Billy. Easier because even though my 18-year-old body was stiff and sore, it was acclimating to the grinding work. And harder because Grits rarely lifted a rail-thin buttock from the driver's seat of his black cab-over International, the newest truck in the Willard Sanitation

The Garbage Brothers

fleet, and one he apparently believed required his constant tending behind the wheel.

Unlike Billy, Grits left picking up garbage from homes on his routes to me, and he left the yanking and jerking of the stubborn dumpsters behind restaurants, motels, and other businesses to the summer helper. He sat in the uncluttered cab, chain-smoking Camels, shoulders curled against the back of the black leather driver's seat, watching my every move and snapping out directions that invariably began, "Hey, numbnuts. . ."

At each stop, I jumped off the back of the truck to see Grits glaring at me in the big rearview mirror mounted on the driver's door. After I grabbed my carry can and trotted like an obedient Labrador retriever to stand by the driver's window, he informed me where the garbage cans were located: "Hey numbnuts, the cans are behind the fence to the left of the gate. Make sure the Doberman isn't loose in the yard or he'll tear off one of your tiny balls." "Hey numbnuts, get the three underground cans up there next to the chimney and between the lilac bushes. Don't step on the bushes, or the old lady will have a goddamn cow." And, "Hey numbnuts, there are three cans in the garage. Leave the garage door open 6 inches for their asshole cat."

On a couple of occasions, I called down to the truck for help when I couldn't find garbage cans or figure out which house was next. But usually I had to figure it out on my own because Grits liked to crank up the Motorola transistor radio that he kept wedged between the dashboard and windshield. The radio was a prize that Grits had salvaged from the trash. He kept it tuned to WBBR, a country station that played artists like George Jones, Johnny Cash, Roger Miller and Porter Wagoner. When I asked why the tuner was covered with duct tape, Grits replied, "To keep numbnut assholes like you from playing your Beatles and all that rocky-rolly bullshit."

When I asked why the Willard Sanitation trucks weren't equipped with built-in radios, Grits shook his head. "That's because our asshole boss ordered his shit-for-brains foreman Billy to remove the dashboard radios—standard equipment on an International, mind you—so us drivers wouldn't be distracted from our work. Like humpin' garbage is brain surgery."

So began my second week on the job. Barrel after barrel. Home after home. Block after block. Then sometime around noon—I'd pretty much lost track of time and hope—a bony forearm extended from the cab of the truck, summoning me like the Grim Reaper. "Get in the goddamn cab, numbnuts," he said. "I'm hungry and I don't believe it's possible for you to work any slower. We'll dump our load first and stop for lunch."

I entered the cab, and Grits examined my sweaty, filthy, fragrant self with disgust. "You get any of the garbage in the truck—or did you just decide to wear it all?"

Paul Neville

"Yeah," I said, looking down at my clothes. "I'm pretty dirty."

"Pretty ain't the word for it, son," Grits said. My ears perked at the word "son." Perhaps Grits was beginning to regard me as a human being. "On second thought, I don't wanna smell you all the way to the dump," he said. "Get out and ride on the back."

I stood on a 1-foot-square steel-grated platform and clung to a grab bar intended to keep helpers from being thrown to their deaths when drivers took curves too fast, as Grits was fond of doing. As he accelerated through turns, I recalled the story I'd heard at the Greasy Wrench about one of my predecessors—"Little Pete"—tumbling off the back of the truck and hitting his head so hard he thought Billy Bart was his mama. I held on tighter, bent my knees, and prayed what I could remember from Presbyterian Sunday school of the Lord's Prayer. "Our Father, which art in heaven, hallowed be thy name, thy something be done . . ."

Chapter 6: The Snake Pit

Ernie's Snake Pit Tavern was on Highway 40 across from the entrance to the Liberty Township Sanitation Facility. The dump, with its red clay soil and bloated, fermenting—and occasionally burning—waste mounds, was located on the east side of the highway. The Snake Pit was on the west side next to an old gravel pit filled with water tainted by dump seepage. Dozens of reeking dead carp floated belly up in the pond, but that didn't discourage the migrant farmworkers, children and old men who fished from its banks.

The normal lunch routine for sanitation drivers was to empty their bulging trucks at the dump, then snag a receipt for the boss along with,—if their timing was good—nudie mags from Gary the backhoe driver. Then they bounced their rocking, clanging, unburdened trucks back to the highway and crossed to the Snake Pit for chili and cheeseburgers, and more importantly, shots and beers.

The Snake Pit was located in a ramshackle former auto body shop with dim lighting. At the south end of the room were an assortment of beat-to-shit tables and chairs, three pool tables and a jukebox. At the north end were a small kitchen, more tables and chairs, and a curiously elegant bar with scrollwork and hand-carved columns that rose like serpents and stopped a couple of feet short of the water-stained ceiling tiles. The tavern had a gritty concrete floor, and the smells of sour beer, fried meat, sweat, grease and bad teeth permeated the joint to its sagging bones.

A shot of peppermint schnapps and a short glass of Stroh's were waiting for Grits when we reached the bar. He stood as he downed the shot and then reached for the beer. Then he slumped on a barstool and motioned for me to sit. He took a swig and contemplated my presence. "Move your goddamn stool over a couple feet," he said. "You're my helper—you ain't my date."

I took in my surroundings. Zeus had told me that the Snake Pit had two categories of customers. On the bar and kitchen side of the building were the sanitation and dump workers who drank beers and shots, wolfed chili and cheeseburgers, and traded tales of garbage woe. On the pool-table end were the leather-clad members of the Renegades Motorcycle Club, a Chicago-area gang, notorious for its drug dealing and other bad-ass activities. The club had a garage behind the Snake Pit, a reputed den of iniquity that was conveniently out of the Chicago Police Department's jurisdiction.

I glanced over at the far side of the tavern and saw a half-dozen men, most of them wearing leather vests or jackets despite the summer heat. They were drinking beer, smoking cigarettes and playing pool. I spotted the jukebox near the pool tables and took two steps toward it before Grits spoke.

"Where you think you're goin', dumbshit?" he hissed.

"Going to go see what tunes are on the jukebox."

"Sit your stupid ass back down," Grits said. "You don't need to be wandering to that side of the bar. Those guys will cut your lips off before you have a chance to say, 'Gee, hiya, fellas. Love those leather vests. Know where I can get one to wear when I go off to college?"

I returned to my stool. I'd learned that there was no disobeying a Grits edict. At one of the pool tables was a short man with a powerful build, creased face, and coal-black hair slicked back in an Elvis pompadour.

"Who is that tough-looking little guy at the pool table?" I asked.

"His name is Largo, and he's a drug-dealin' mean-ass son of a bitch you don't want to know," Grits said. "Now stop starin' and shut the hell up."

"Where's the menu?" I asked.

"Ain't no goddamn menu," he said. "Snake Pit has chili and cheeseburgers. That's it."

An old man shuffled toward us. He was bone thin—thinner, if possible, than Grits—and he wore a pair of black wool pants held up over a rumpled white dress shirt with a pair of thick black suspenders. The cuffs of his pants hovered just above his skinny ankles, which were encased in sagging white socks and inserted into a pair of fur-lined slippers. In each hand he held a thick white porcelain bowl of chili, his long, gnarled fingers around the sides and his bent, bony thumbs over the edge and dipping into the thick beany redness.

"How they hangin' today, Ernie?" Grits said.

"Not sure," Ernie said. "Ain't checked 'em for some time."

He put one bowl in front of Grits and the second in front of me, studying me through thick, brushy salt-and-pepper eyebrows. "Who's the kid?" he asked.

"Just the latest of Benjie's college kids," Grits said. "Billy calls him Tippy Toes. But I call him 'pain in the ass.'"

The old man extended an arm and gave me a surprisingly strong handshake. "Ernie DePadilla," he said. "I'm the proprietor of this shithole. You gonna eat this chili, or should I use it as rat poison?"

"I'll eat it. Thank you, sir," I said.

"Your helper's got some goddamned manners. More than I can say for you, Grits," Ernie said.

The Garbage Brothers

Grits shrugged and pointed at bar owner's feet. "Where did you get those slippers?" he said. "Looks like they're filled with fur."

"That driver, Sonny, from Ace Sanitation dropped 'em off for me last week. Said they were still in the box when he found 'em in a dumpster. Said they were rabbit fur, but it feels like I'm waltzing with pussy all day long," Ernie said. He looked at me. "What did you do to make Grits so goddamn sour? I heard him hissin' at you all the way across the bar."

Grits answered for me before I could speak. "Kid here was going over there to play him a tune on the jukebox," Grits said.

"Hooo," Ernie said, arching his caterpillar eyebrows. He wiped the chili from his thumb on the apron that dangled from his waist like a ceremonial loincloth. "Son," he said. "Most of them motorcycle fellas don't take to college kids."

"Well, I don't take to 'em, neither," Grits said. He reflected and then amended his statement. "Well, as I recall there were a few college kids down in Joliet who made themselves useful."

"You talkin' Madam Fifi's Charm School?" Ernie said.

"Where else?" Grits said.

Ernie nodded and looked around his establishment. "You know, this place is going to hell," he said. "In fact, I think we may be there already." He turned and walked away.

Grits took a few spoonfuls of chili and slid the bowl away.

"What's Madame Fifi's?" I asked.

"What do you think, dumbshit?" he said. "It's the goddamn state penitentiary. Every state's got a Madame Fifi's Charm School."

"Why were you there?"

Grits took a drag on his cigarette and then answered: "Don't never ask someone why they done time. If they wanna tell you, they will."

I directed my attention to my chili, remembering the first-knuckle depth to which Ernie's thumb had been inserted. I took my first spoonful. It was red-bean-explosive glory, the best chili I had ever eaten. It was for such a mess of pottage that Jacob sold his birthright to Esau, I thought, even though I'd never been sure in Presbyterian Sunday school exactly what "pottage" was. No doubt it was something like the chili at the Snake Pit.

Grits downed the remaining half-glass of beer and started toward the front door. I took several more spoonfuls of chili and followed. We walked through the dusty, cratered parking lot toward Grits' truck. "Hey Grits, you ought to know I'm not really a college kid," I said, hoping that my confession would improve Grits' opinion of me. "The boss thinks I am, but I'm not. So far I haven't found any college that will take me."

"What the hell you talking about?" Grits said. "Billy says you live in that goddamn Fox Breath Meadow development. That means your family's got money, and that means you're going to college. I don't know why you are messin' around with this shit-ass job, but you're going to end up some day sittin' in a goddamn office and tellin' people like me what to do."

"My father died last year," I said. "My mom's broke and is selling our house and moving to Indianapolis. My grades are shitty, no college wants me, and I don't know how I'd pay for school even if I got the chance."

Grits spit on the ground. "Sorry about your daddy," he said. "But I still got you figured for a college kid 'cause you sure as hell ain't one of us. And I don't really give a diddly shit where you come from or whether you go to college. Your sorry ass is humpin' garbage on my route and that's all that matters."

We reached the truck and climbed into the cab. I looked out the window as we pulled out of the parking lot and onto Highway 40, which ran south to Chicago and north to the Wisconsin border and, if you drove far and long enough, to Canada. Grits flipped on the transistor and cranked up the volume on Merle Haggard's "Okie from Muskogee."

Grits flicked his cigarette ash out the driver's window. "Tippy Toes," he said. "How'd you like to meet my niece?"

He looked hard at me, and I knew I had to say yes. I didn't know much about Grits yet, but I knew that a man who had done time in Madam Fifi's Charm School was not a man who would respond well to "No, thank you, I don't want to meet your niece." Plus, my social calendar was not overflowing with commitments, and perhaps this niece of Grits' was an Appalachian beauty.

"I just asked you a question, numbnuts," Grits said.

"Sure," I said. "I'd be honored."

"Honored?" Grits said. "Good God. Don't tell me you're not a goddamn college kid."

Chapter 7: Delores and Zeus

On Monday morning, I rolled up to the Greasy Wrench a half-hour early. Besides Delores, the only people in the cafe were a farmer sitting alone at the counter and wearing overalls and a red John Deere cap, and Lars, the cook, whose spatula was clattering on the grill in the kitchen. Next to the cash register was a Sylvania radio playing the morning farm report. The announcer was saying that corn futures had closed the previous week down 2.7 percent.

I slid into the Willard Sanitation booth, savoring the opportunity to sit for the first time with both butt cheeks on the bench. "G'morning, little sweetheart," Delores said. "You're up bright and early. Coffee?"

"Thank you," I said, and I meant it. Delores liked me. I didn't know why, but I was appreciative, since the rest of the crew, with the possible exception of Zeus, held me in the same regard as a sidewalk turd. Delores set a thick white porcelain cup in front of me. As she filled it with fresh coffee from a full decanter, I noticed her hands were thin and delicate, and smelled like the pink lotion that my mother used when I was a child. Delores looked like she was in her 40s, and her face was prettier than I had noticed before, with high cheekbones and a sprinkling of freckles on a faintly creased forehead. She wore a standard-issue, yellow-and-white waitress dress, nylon stockings and white Keds.

"Hey, Delores," I said, making conversation before the rest of the crew arrived. I'd brought a paperback, the latest collection of Ray Bradbury short stories, to kill the time, and pushed it to the side to signal my interest in discussion.

"Yes, sweetie."

"You got any kids?"

"Two boys," she said. "They're out in Montana with their daddy."

I waited for more, but she said nothing. I primed the pump. "How old are they?"

She stood, holding a pale green order pad in her right hand. "They're 9-and-a-half and just-turned 13," she said. "Their names are Bobby and Darin, and they are the sweetest and squirmiest boys on the face of the Earth. Now what do you want for breakfast?"

"Bobby Darin—I like that."

"I'm more of a country girl, but I liked his style," she said. "What do you want for breakfast, honey?"

I ordered the No. 4—a ham-and-American-cheese omelet with four strips of bacon, hash browns and toast, and she turned to take my order to the kitchen. Then she paused and looked back. "How's it going out there with the boys?" she asked. "They're a spicy group, and I know humpin' garbage ain't easy work—how you holding up?"

I looked at her with gratitude. Someone at the Greasy Wrench actually cared whether I survived my summer job—or at least was kind enough to pretend to care. "It's going OK," I said. "First few weeks were rough, but I think I'll make it through the summer."

"A lot of the college kids walk away," she said. "The crew makes it hard on them."

"I'm not going to walk away," I said.

A minute later I felt a warm hand on my shoulders. It was Delores, who had turned in my order and returned to show me a well-worn, white leather billfold with a photo of two young boys dressed in red blazers and sitting in small blue chairs. They were smiling with intense concentration and had wet-combed hair. The youngest was holding a football, and the oldest a baseball bat.

"My boys," Delores said. "I took them to Sears for a portrait last Easter when they were visiting. That's Darin on the right, Bobby on the left."

"They look like nice boys," I said. "Both good-looking."

"They're nice boys, and their mama's gonna get 'em both back," Delores said. She pulled a bronze coin from the billfold and held it up in a palm just high enough for me, but no one else, to see. "I've been sober for more than a year," she said. "I'm gonna get custody as soon as I find a judge who'll give it to me."

The bells on the front door jangled before I could answer, and Billy entered, stomping his feet like they were covered with snow even though it was July. The billfold disappeared from Delores' hands as if by magic.

"G'morning, Billy," Delores said. "What's the world's biggest asshole want for breakfast this morning?" she said.

"You know what I want, Deloreth," Billy said.

"I do. You want the daily special, and it ain't what you think. Now park your lard butt in that booth with Jesse, and keep everything where it belongs."

"You know where my everything belongth," Billy said.

"Yes, I do," she said. "It belongs right there in your right hand."

Delores poured Billy a cup of coffee and he slid happily into the booth across from me. The smell of axle grease from his rumpled, filthy work shirt wafted across the table and melded in a surprisingly pleasant way with the smell of the coffee.

"And a good morning to you, Mithter Tippy Toeth," he said. "And what got you up and out tho early thith morning."

"Couldn't sleep. Thought I'd do some reading," I said, nodding at the paperback next to me.

It was a lie. The real reason I'd gotten up early wasn't a desire to read. It was the start of my third week at Willard Sanitation, and I was excited to get a chance to work with Zeus. Of all of the drivers, he was closest to my age, maybe 10 or 15 years older. He had an innate sense of garbage grace, a coolness and levitating energy. Zeus also had a swept-back mane of blond hair that ran to his shoulder blades, a biblical beard, and a wit that enabled him to run taunting circles around the other drivers. Zeus was the closest thing to a role model—and I hoped, a friend—to be found at Willard Sanitation.

Zeus was the cleanest garbage man on the crew—and maybe the entire universe. With his freshly laundered jeans and T-shirts and impossibly white high-top Converse sneakers, Zeus was even more fastidious than Benjamin Willard III, who was famous—and reviled—by his crew for refusing to do any work that might soil his boss uniform.

Despite his complete coolness, or perhaps because of it, Zeus was an object of derision among the rest of the crew. They mocked his long hair and the great beard that he combed incessantly with his fingers. They teased him about his epically endowed wife, Totina, who showed up on paydays wearing a mini-skirt and low-cut blouse to get Zeus' check from an appreciative Benjamin Willard III before her husband finished his route.

Zeus drove his beloved black GTO with no bumpers and a mismatching white hood, and parked it across the highway in the Gary's Grab and Go parking lot to protect it from getting hit by a truck at the Greasy Wrench. The rest of the crew rolled their eyes at that, but nobody said anything. Zeus' hair, beard, T-shirts, sneakers and even his wife's breasts were all fair game, but the crew knew his GTO was off limits.

Zeus was usually the last to arrive at work. He caught my eyes, arching his eyebrows in pretend aggravation as he waited for Pickles and me to slide out of the booth and allow him to take his customary window seat. There was no question of us moving in to make room for him to sit on the outside. Each driver had their regular seat—in my case a half-seat. It was the way things were done at the Greasy Wrench.

"Tho today ith your firtht day with Theuth," Billy said to me.

I paused to swallow a mouthful of hash browns before speaking, and then tried to sound casual. "That rings a bell—I think Mr. Willard told me that Friday."

"Billy ain't tryin' to set no damn bells a ringin'," Grits said. "He wants to know if you know you are Zeus' bobo today. Didn't nobody ever teach you how to talk to grown-ups?"

Zeus came to my defense. "Yes, Tippy Toes is coming with me today, Grits," he said. "What do you think? That's what Benjie told us last week, and unless our goddamn boss had a goddamn stroke and lost his goddamn mind then the goddamn kid is coming with me today." He ran his fingers through his beard as Delores leaned over the table to Billy's leering and lip-smacking encouragement. She filled Zeus' coffee cup. Flashing her middle finger at Billy behind her back, Delores straightened and left just as Benjamin Willard III arrived with a stack of blue complaint slips.

After the boss finished his droning recitation of the previous day's sins and omissions, Zeus peered around the stone-faced monolith that was Pickles and gave me a knowing look that seemed to suggest we were members of a different tribe than the rest of the crew. "Tippy Toes, are you ready for the most edifyin' day in your entire shittin' life?"

"Yeah," I said. "I'm ready."

~ ~ ~

Zeus was in a talkative mood during our morning drive to Northgate, a suburb located a dozen miles south of Freedom. He told me about his 4-year-old daughter, Lily, who had long, curly red hair and liked to dance in purple tutus. He talked about his brother, Darnell, who lived in Las Vegas, where Darnell had recently lost his Pontiac Tempest to a German tourist in a poker game. "Can't believe my idiot brother gambled away the car that I helped him rebuild. Gold-flecked paint job. Chrome mags. Rollover bar. Had a V-8 that could drive a hole through a brick wall. Stupid asshole Darnell."

While I humped the garbage of Northgate, Zeus sat in the truck dispensing logistical information, telling me where the cans were located as he sat in the driver's seat sipping coffee from the paper cup that Delores handed him on the way out the door. She did it every morning, and no one else received such a consideration—or dared to inquire why it was bestowed upon Zeus. There were no parting cups for Pickles, Grits or Billy. And certainly none for Benjamin Willard III, who Delores said tipped like a dead man and looked like one, too.

As we drove to the dump at mid-morning, I asked a question that had been nagging at me since Grits had revealed that he had been in prison. "Zeus—do you know why Grits served time?"

Zeus set his cup on the dash and plucked a hair from his beard. "Why don't you ask Grits?" he said, looking amused at my audacity. And cowardice.

"I did. He told me it was none of my business."

Zeus nodded. "Grits is not overly fond of summer helpers who ask questions." He paused, one hand on the wheel and the fingers of the other working away at his beard.

"Ah, what the hell," he said. "I'll tell you. Grits was in the big house for grand theft auto—23 counts."

I nodded as if the answer was what I suspected, although the truth was I had expected something more sinister like murder or kidnapping. Zeus wasn't fooled. "What?" he said. "You wanted something better? The guy stole 23 cars—and those are just the ones he got nailed for. He's probably in the car thief hall of fame in Booger Holler or wherever the hell he's from down in Tennessee."

I tried to look as neutral as I could. I was fast learning that Zeus could pluck my thoughts like a pickpocket.

"No, he ain't the only one," Zeus said.

"What do you mean?"

"Grits ain't the only one—all us drivers have done time."

I paused before asking the question we both knew was coming. "You, too?" I said.

"I did four years in Joliet for armed robbery and another two for drug possession," Zeus said. He gave me a sideways glance. I avoided eye contact, not knowing how to react to the revelation that I, Jesse Wheeler, whose worst offense to date had been swiping a Playboy magazine from a pharmacy, was cruising in a garbage truck with someone who had committed armed robbery and had been busted for drugs.

"So who—or what—did you rob?" I asked, as if such a question was everyday conversation.

"Convenience stores," he said with a grin. "They were my specialty. "Easy in, easy out—and they're everywhere."

"How many stores did you rob?"

"Enough to get caught," he said. "That's all you need to know."

I nodded, and considered asking about the drugs. But I was treading on thin ice and knew it. Time to move on.

"How about Pickles? What did he do?"

"Nosey little shit, aren't you?"

I waited. I knew there was more coming. And it was going to be good.

"Well, your new colleague Pickles shot an insurance salesman dead," Zeus said. "Caught him bonking his wife at the Pink Flamingo Motor Inn. Pickles got his shotgun out of his truck and shot him in the gut. Shot his wife in her bony hip, too, and now she's a cripple living at the township home in Wilton."

"How long was Pickles in prison?"

"Six years," Zeus said. "Pickles was in long enough to stab an inmate in the leg for spitting in his pudding. They gave him two more years for that.

Pickles didn't give a shit. Said the man deserved it for ruining a bowl of butterscotch pudding—his favorite."

"Billy?"

"He's pretty much a Girl Scout these days, and that's why Benjie made him foreman. But he had his wild times, and he did some time in county for breakin' a bouncer's jaw in a fight at a titty bar. That was before he got married and Sheila had him neutered. She is the meanest woman I've ever seen—even meaner than my wife, and that's saying a lot. But she can't keep Billy out of the Jaguar Gentlemen's Club—that's Billy's happy place after payday on Friday nights."

He anticipated my next question: "Benjie?" he said. "No self-respecting prison would take that douchebag." He paused. "Well, some of the guys I met at Joliet might—they might appreciate his ample posterior."

Zeus took a sip of cold morning coffee and returned the Styrofoam cup to its perch on the cleanest dashboard in the Willard Sanitation fleet. "Surprised by the company you keep, Tippy Toes?" he said.

I kept my eyes focused on the approaching entrance to the county dump, and considered my response. I was surprised and more than a little sobered by the revelation that I was working with a jaw breaker, a serial car thief, an armed robber and druggie, and a murderer and wife-maimer. Until now, my imagination had almost always outstripped the mundane realities of people I encountered. But my fertile imagination had not prepared me for the hard-ass likes of Zeus, Grits, Billy Bart and Pickles.

"Nah," I lied. "About what I expected."

Chapter 8: "Poh-low"

After a few days of working with Zeus, I knew I'd found my garbage guru—and, I hoped, a friend. Since happening upon Brett and Lyla thrashing on the couch, I was in the market for a new friend, and Zeus was the most likely—and only—prospect on the horizon. He made me laugh so hard my ribs hurt, which felt as welcome as the first swallow of icy Stroh's beer that the beret-wearing, broken-armed customer gave us after we emptied his dumpster filled with horse shit.

From the corner of my eye, I saw a fit, middle-aged man wearing a black polo shirt, tight-fitting white riding pants, and an improbable—at least anywhere near Freedom—black beret. He approached us after Zeus and I rolled the green metal dumpster from its enclosure outside the stable to the back of the truck and slapped the compactor's large chains, both topped with big hooks, to handles welded on each side of the dumpster. We threw open the dumpster lids with a clanging flourish. Then Zeus punched the black button that turned on the truck's high-pitched hydraulic system that caused the compactor blade to retract and the dumpster to lift until the horse shit began sliding out of it into the trough with a slow sucking noise. I had been holding my breath since opening the dumpster but finally had to breathe before the chains lowered the dumpster to the ground. I was surprised that the smell was not nearly as bad as I feared, and that a hay-infused sweetness made it nearly pleasant.

"How 'bout a beer, fellas?" the customer said, holding two bottles by the neck with his right hand and extending them in our direction. He looked maybe 50 years old, and had a tan face and weather-creased eyes. He wore a black sling around a left arm that was encased in a plaster cast.

Zeus turned with arched eyebrows and sized up the man, whose approach from a huge three-story house located half a football field away, he hadn't noticed. I looked to Zeus for guidance—it was the first time anyone had offered me a beer while I was on the job. Zeus nodded and reached for the beers and handed one to me. "I never turn down a free beer—or a free anything else for that matter," Zeus said. He took a swig of the beer and stroked his beard. "So what did you do to your arm?" he asked

The man held the cast up for us to examine and, evidently, admire.

"Polo," was the one-word explanation, and he said the word "polo" with a faux British accent that elongated it into "poh-low." Then he shrugged as if no further explanation was needed. After a perfunctory smile, he turned around and returned to the big house, looking pleased with himself for having rubbed shoulders with the servant class.

Zeus looked after him, reversing the lever and shaking the final dregs of shit from the bottom of the dumpster with a jerking vengeance. When the dumpster reached the ground, we unhooked chains, and Zeus nodded for me to roll the empty dumpster back to the stable. He took a long swig of his beer and got into the cab. "Let's get the hell out of here," he said, ramming the truck into reverse. He was stone silent as we drove down the long, tree-lined driveway and turned onto the road. Then he took his beer and held it out the window, turning it upside down and draining what remained of its contents.

"What?" I said. "Don't like Stroh's?"

"Don't like rich assholes who think they can make me kiss their fruit-soaped asses for a bottle of beer."

"Fruit-soaped asses?" I said. There was no acknowledgment from Zeus, who was in a full muttering and beard-picking boil over what had seemed to me to be an innocent, well-intentioned encounter.

"You know who that was," Zeus said. "That was Andy LeFleur—the heir to the LaFleur stadium construction fortune. That asshole never picked up a hammer or lifted a sheet of drywall in his life, and he thinks a couple of working men like us will piss their undies if he hands them a beer with those soft lady hands of his."

"He just gave us a beer, Zeus," I said. "He was a little snooty, but he seemed like an OK guy to me."

"Did you hear the way he said 'poh-low?'" Zeus said, lifting his right arm as if it were in a sling to mimic our beer benefactor. "Gentlemen, will you please gaze upon my delicate limb, which has a booboo from playing 'poh-low' with my rich friends."

"So the LaFleurs are rich?" I said, eager to shift the topic and for the storm to pass.

"Rich ain't the word for it. That family bleeds money from their assholes. And you should see his wife—she's half his age and makes Bridget Bardot look like Delores down at the Wrench.

"When her husband's not here, she likes to come out of her mansion wearing little black dresses and heels, and asks me if I can come in and help her move a sofa in the living room."

"Do you help her?"

He cocked his head. "Help her what?" he said.

"Do you help her move the sofa?"

Zeus' anger faded and was replaced by a mischievous grin.

"We have moved the sofa on several occasions," he said. He looked at the still mostly full bottle of Stroh's I was holding. "You shouldn't have an open container in the cab," he said. I dutifully handed him the beer. He pulled to a stop and checked in the rearview mirror to make sure there was no one behind us. Then he drained the bottle and handed me the empty.

"All that bitchin' made me thirsty," he said.

It was midafternoon when I decided to ask a question that had been nagging me since the first day I met Zeus. It was, I knew, a personal and potentially intrusive question. But I was convinced that Zeus and I were becoming friends.

"So, Zeus, why are you humpin' garbage when you could be doing something else?" I asked.

Zeus gave me a hard look, and I knew I was on uncertain ground—and that if I were wise, which most certainly I was not, I should retreat. Then he shook his head and smiled, and I knew I had been granted safe passage. "Got a wife and kid," he said. He pointed to the dashboard where he'd taped a photo of a little girl with curly red hair sitting on the hood of his GTO. He handed it to me.

"She's beautiful," I said. "Look, all I'm saying is you could be doing something else. You could be selling things or running your own business. Hell, you could probably go back to school and still be a doctor or lawyer if you wanted."

Zeus snorted and adjusted his grip on the steering wheel, which had a laced leather grip like you'd find on a sports car. "You're a dumb-ass little shit, aren't you?" he said. "First off, when I say I have a family, that means I need to support that family. I got rent, car payments, food, doctor's bills—all that bullshit."

"You could find a way," I said. Zeus shook his head sharply, and I knew that I had gone too far and it was time to shut up.

"You think some college would take a 35-year-old with a felony record and not even a high school degree. Even if I got myself some education, who would hire an ex-con with nothing on his resume except forty-two months in Joliet and seven years of humpin' garbage?" he said.

We rode in silence. Zeus took a right turn, and we passed a strip mall with a Brown's Fried Chicken and a Jewel-Osco supermarket. A block later, we turned into a subdivision called North Haven filled with large, respectable homes surrounded by the manicured lawns of large, respectable people who had large, respectable jobs in the city.

Then the storm passed from Zeus' face, as if the finger of a funnel cloud had lifted from the horizon. "Besides," Zeus said, as if there had been no pause in our discussion. "If I became a rich man and bought one of these big-ass homes, I wouldn't be here to guide you on the path to sanitation enlightenment."

He motioned to a white brick home on our right, where a slender, middle-aged woman with long blond hair tied in a white scarf dragged a plastic bag to the curb. Her pink quilted robe was loosely tied at the waist, and a soft morning breeze blew it back to mid-thigh.

"Now, Tippy Toes," he said, "behold: a damsel in distress."

We climbed out of the cab, and the woman was waiting for us when we came to the back of the truck. Zeus pulled on a pair of tight leather work gloves. She stepped back, as if dazed by the sight of this knight in a glowing white T-shirt and sporting a godhead beard. Then she stepped forward, sliding off her reading glasses and slipping them into a pocket of her robe.

"May I be of assistance, madam," Zeus said, with a smile that somehow seemed more beguiling, more wicked, for its eruption in a flowing field of beard.

"I, well—I was hoping you might take some clippings from the back yard for me," she said. "They are too heavy for me to bring to the curb."

"Please," Zeus said. "Allow us."

"That would be lovely," she said.

"Then I shall dispatch my assistant," Zeus said, beckoning me with a kindly yet authoritative wave of his gloved hand.

I nodded, swung my carry can over my back and jogged up the driveway. I glanced back and Zeus was still talking to the woman, who removed the scarf that held up her disheveled morning hair, freeing it to cascade to her shoulders. Zeus was leaning against the back of the truck, and she had taken a step, perhaps two, closer, oblivious to the stench of the truck bed. I nearly laughed out loud, and I knew that Zeus was indeed a maestro. And I was an 18-year-old who had much to learn.

~ ~ ~

Benjamin Willard III's blue pickup appeared in the rearview mirror a little after 3 p.m. He followed us for several blocks, parking on the side of the road a hundred yards or so away, pulling his truck up each time we pulled up, his fat head silhouetted against the afternoon sun.

Zeus and I stood at the back of the truck, our carry cans perched on the edge of the trough ready to sling our barrels over our backs.

"How dumb does that moron think we are?" Zeus said. "Does he think he's invisible?"

I nodded but said nothing. It was my first day working with Zeus, and already I could see there was an anger simmering within that could boil over at any time. And the very sight of Benjamin Willard III infuriated him.

The Garbage Brothers

After several blocks, the big boss finally emerged from his spy den, tucked in his crisp khaki shirt over his ripe melon belly, straightened his cap and strode purposefully toward the garbage truck, carrying a clipboard.

He had timed it so that we all arrived at the back of the truck at the same time—Zeus and me with our carry cans full and heavy, Benjamin Willard III with complaint slips.

"Halloo boys," he nodded amiably.

Zeus dropped his can with extra force on the edge of the trough, making the boss wince at the injury to one of his carry cans, which he regularly reminded his crew cost $37 each at Midwest Sanitation Supply.

"Good afternoon, Mr. Willard," I said.

"How are you doing, young man?" he asked. His eyes looked blurry, as if he were gazing through a pair of kiddie goggles at the bottom of a pool. It was obvious that the boss had already spent a good portion of his day in a bar.

"What the hell is it now, Benjie?" Zeus asked. The boss swallowed hard and lifted the clipboard, as if he couldn't remember the half-dozen or so words that his wife had written on a blue complaint slip in big block letters with a series of exclamation points that looked like darning needles inserted into an eyeball.

"I have a complaint from a neighbor on Lord Nelson Way that you were, uh. . ." We watched as the big boss groped for words that might keep him from being attacked in broad daylight by an enraged Zeus. ". . .That you were socializing with one of our customers," he finally said.

I glanced at Zeus, expecting an eruption. But I was surprised to see him smiling with his head cocked. "Yes, Benjie, a female customer and I were indeed socializing. And the lady has asked us to tea of a 'morrow," he said. "Would you care to join us?"

"Tea? Of a 'morrow?" the boss said, looking nervously at Zeus and then at me, as if hoping for an explanation. Then he took off his cap and rubbed his fuzzy sweating head, turned and walked back to the truck.

"Dumb-ass moron," Zeus said. "That man—right there . . ." He gestured at the boss as he drove past us, avoiding eye contact and doing his best to look like a man with somewhere important to go. ". . .That man is drowning in a river filled with his own shit."

I looked at Zeus with appreciation. I'd never met anyone with such edgy brilliance. Even Brett, who was more than half crazy himself, was a faint ember next to Zeus' incandescence.

It was time to impress. Time for me say something to signify I wanted to follow in the steps of a Zen master. "I guess we're all drowning in rivers of our own shit," I said. It was the best I could come up with, and I waited anxiously for his response.

Paul Neville

"Well, you sure as hell are, Tippy Toes," Zeus said. He hitched his carry can over his shoulder, chuckling to himself as he strode past a "Keep Off the Lawn" sign and up a grassy slope toward two shiny aluminum trash cans in front of a three-car garage. I thought I saw someone peek through an upstairs curtain, but I wasn't sure.

Chapter 9: Pickles and the Snowmobile

Then came the week I had dreaded since beginning work at Willard Sanitation. There was no avoiding it: Benjamin Willard III required his summer helpers to work with each of his drivers and to learn their routes so the helpers could substitute for the drivers if they were sick or on vacation. That meant that I eventually would have to drive a truck and run all the routes on my own, a prospect that seemed unattainable after less than a month on the job. It also meant that I would have to work with the hulking convicted killer named William "Pickles" Peterman.

Although the past year had exposed me to some of the sharper vicissitudes of life, including my father's sudden passing, I firmly believed I was too young to die. After all, I was 18 and just beginning to find my way in the world. The list of important things I had yet to accomplish was long and daunting, but there was no question about my top priority. To my great and secret chagrin—and certainly not for lack of effort—I was still a virgin who had yet to climb the pinnacle of manhood, although I certainly had climbed my own pinnacle, sometimes several times a day. And here I was fearing that before shedding my virginity, I might be shot to death by Pickles, perhaps with the same gun he'd used to kill his wife's paramour at the Pink Flamingo.

The omens did not appear aligned in my favor. At breakfast, on the Monday marking the start of my fourth week at Willard Sanitation, Pickles seemed in a fouler mood than usual, if that was possible. I assumed that he was unhappy about having to take me on his route, and he refused to acknowledge my arrival as he clenched the handle of his coffee cup and stared at the Union Pacific calendar.

"Whathamatter, Pickleth?" Billy inquired. "Ith you a little bit hungover?"

Pickles ignored Billy's inquiry, and I did my best to avoid physical contact with my glowering bench mate's great mass.

Delores brought his regular order—one piece of toast smothered in a sea of white gravy with flecks of sausage swimming in the pockets of grease. "Here you go, Mr. Doom and Gloom," she said. "Shit on a shingle. Just the way you like it—heavy on the shit, light on the shingle."

Pickles stared up at Delores. His eyes were an intense gray and blue, and they had Delores fixed in their glare. I was struck by his middle-aged features—the receding hairline, the double chin, and jowls that were beginning to form on each side of his great face—and their similarities to those of my late father. Put this garbage man in a dark blue suit, with a pressed white shirt and silk tie with regimental stripes, and he might pass for a vice president of marketing—the title of which my father took so much pride and carried to his grave.

"Here I go what, Delores?" Pickles said.

Delores' eyes narrowed, and I could see she wasn't intimidated.

"Here you go. Slide this plate of toast and gravy in your boxers and have a party," she said.

Pickles reached up for the plate, gripped its edge, and I thought for a sickening moment he was going to hurl it at Delores. Instead, he smiled and slid it under my frozen face.

"Take it, Tippy Toes," he said. "You'll need it by the time we're done today."

"Thcrew Tippy Toeth—give me that thit on a thingle," Billy said, reaching over the table with a thick, grease-tattooed hand and pulling the plate into what Zeus referred to as "Billy's eating zone."

"I gueth you forgot to put in your teeth thith morning," Billy said, gesturing at Pickles with a spoon filled with gravy. While the rest of the crew ate with forks, Billy's weapon of choice for biscuits and gravy and every other meal was a large soup spoon.

Pickles adjusted his bulk and leaned forward on his elbows, emerging from his funk. "I got my goddamn teeth in, asshole," he said. He reached into the front of his mouth, gripped his two upper front teeth with his thumb and forefinger, and pulled out a full set of hinged false teeth that looked as if they had been made by a village blacksmith a century earlier. He held them with both hands several inches above the already half-empty plate of biscuits and gravy, and clacked the chompers together several times.

"Wanna borrow 'em, Billy?" he said.

Billy never blinked an eye and his gravy-laden spoon never stopped shoveling. Pickles popped his teeth back in his mouth, and returned his gaze to the Union Pacific calendar on the wall above Billy's head.

"Why don't you tell little Tippy Toes here how you got your lovely teeth," Zeus said. I leaned forward to glance at him on the other side of Mount Pickles, and his eyes gleamed with rank mischief.

"Don't wanna. And go screw yourself," Pickles said.

"Aw, Jesus Christ, that damn snowmobile story. I heard that about a hundred times too many," said Grits, who had just arrived and somehow floated like a wraith past Billy and into his window seat.

"I'll tell the thtory then," Billy said, wiping his mouth with a grease-stained shirtsleeve.

"Go fuck yourself," Pickles said.

"Thertainly, Pickleth. I will fuck mythelf," Billy said. "But firtht I will tell your new helper here about how you lotht your prethiouth chomperth."

Pickles offered no response, and Billy continued, savoring his narrator role. "It all began one dark and thtormy night in January."

"Just tell the story, Billy," Zeus said.

"Well," Billy teased. "where wath I?"

"At the goddamn beginning," Zeus said, clicking the ash of his cigarette into a black plastic ashtray next to a red ketchup squirt bottle that had the yellow outline of a waitress who looked a lot like Delores.

"Ah yeth, the beginning," Billy said. "Well, I think it wath about two yearth ago that Pickelth here bought himthelf a brand-new thnowmobile from Thearth thtore in Wilton."

"It wasn't goddamn Sears. He bought it from Jake's Farm Supply," Grits said. "If you're going to tell the story, get it right."

"All right, it wath Jake'th," Billy said. "And it wath the biggetht, fathteth mathine on the floor and Pickleth jutht walked up to Jake and thaid: 'I'll take that big mother right there and I'm drivin' it right off the floor.'"

Pickles emerged from his detached state to offer a grudging affirmation. "That's right," he said. "That's what I told Jake: 'I'll take that big mother right there and I'm drivin' it right off the floor.'"

"Well," Billy continued, "It wath thnowin' outthide like nothin' you've ever theen. There wath three feet of thnow on the ground, and Pickleth jutht fired up that monster and drove it out of the thtore and took off through the fieldth like a wild man. And thath when he thaw it."

Billy paused. The entire room paused. And I knew I had a part in this play and my cue had just been delivered.

"What did he see?" I asked.

"A thowy hill that Pickleth knew he and hith new thnowmobile could take off from like a goddamn eagle," Billy said.

Pickles adjusted his bulk in the seat, lit a cigarette and glanced at me out of the corner of his left eye to see if I was impressed. Billy had left Pickles suspended in the air like a great fat bird, and I had to know how the story ended. "Well," I said. "What happened next?"

Billy arched his bushy eyebrows and smiled. He wasn't about to prematurely produce the goods. This was too fine a story to be rushed.

"Well, firtht you have to underthand that thith wathn't really a hill," Billy said. "It wath a big berm."

"A berm?"

"The berm that thurroundth the munithipal thewage treatment pond."

"The pond was frozen, right?" I asked.

Billy pondered the question and the crew savored it like the first pull of cold beer on a hot July day. "Thewage lagoonth don't freethe tholid in the winter. It wath jutht half frothen," he said.

I sat back, picturing Pickles leaning forward against the wind and driving snow, the great, roaring snowmobile airborne beneath him and the snowy broken crest of the berm behind him. And below—a half-frozen sewage lagoon.

Billy closed his eyes and inhaled the tension in the room. Then he spoke.

"Well," he said. "I'm thorry to tell you thith thtory hath a thad ending. The thnowmobile landed in the middle of the pond and thunk like a rock."

"What about Pickles?"

"Well." Another pause. "Old Pickleth jutht plowed through the thit like an ithebreaker and thmacked headfirtht into the concrete rim of the pond. Broke hith jaw and knocked out almotht all hith teeth."

I turned and looked at Pickles, who reached into his mouth and with a thumb and forefinger pulled out his false teeth and waved them a couple of inches from my face.

"Oh my God," I said.

"No, just call me Pickles," he said, slipping his teeth back into his mouth. "But I am God this week as far as you're concerned. Now get off your ass—we got some goddamn garbage to hump."

Chapter 10: Et Spiritus Sancti

I learned on day one of my Pickles week that he began his workdays with a detour to the Snake Pit, where Ernie had his breakfast poured and waiting on the bar. Pickles had nothing to say to the motley assemblage of fellow morning drinkers, nearly all of whom at this end of the building were fellow drivers. He gave Ernie a nod, hoisted the shot of peppermint schnapps and then drained the short glass of Stroh's. Then he stood, cleared his throat, turned and headed for the door. Pickles was a morning drinker, but he was a morning drinker who knew he had a hard day's work ahead.

Ernie waved a bar rag in farewell and I trailed in pursuit of my mountainous driver. "Et spiritus sancti," the bar owner said in a voice as gravelly as the Snake Pit's parking lot. Behind him in the kitchen, a skinny young man wearing a Chicago Bears stocking cap and a sleeveless T-shirt crossed himself and never missed a beat chopping onions for the chili vat.

"Forgive me, Father, for I have sinned," Pickles said over his shoulder.

"Goddamn right you've sinned," Ernie said. "Ain't got no intention of quittin' neither, do you?"

"Not for some time, Ernesto," Pickles replied. "The bitter end will be bitin' at our asses before we know it."

Dust-flecked sunlight shafted down through scattered morning clouds as we walked to the truck without talking. During my first weeks on the job I learned that Pickles fluctuated, often suddenly, between three moods. He spent most of his time in silent, sullen solitude, eyes fixed on the road when he was on the route, on his drink when he was at the Snake Pit, or on the Union Pacific calendar at the Greasy Wrench. But in an unpredictable flash he could turn into as charming and funny, even witty, a man as any I'd ever met. The third mood—the one that everyone else within fist, knife or bullet reach of Pickles knew to avoid at all costs—was a bilious, brooding and boiling anger that Billy had warned me to flee upon first sighting. It was this formidable state of mind that Zeus had told me ensured that Benjamin Willard III would never fire Pickles for insubordination or any other workplace sin. "Let's just say our friend Pickles has a high degree of job security and it ain't because of the Teamsters," Zeus said.

So far I had only seen the first two moods exhibited by Pickles, and I had every intention of avoiding the lethal third. For that reason, I engaged him in light conversation now that he'd had his morning tonic at the Snake Pit. "Where we headed, Pickles?" I asked as we climbed into the cab.

Pickles stopped and stared, as if taken aback by my boldness. "The fuck's it to you?" he said. "It's all garbage, ain't it?"

"Just curious," I said.

"Hightown," Pickles said, punctuating his answer with a fart. "We're going to goddamn Hightown."

"Why does Willard Sanitation have routes in a town that's thirty miles away and near the Wisconsin border?"

"We go to Hightown because last year our idiot boss bid too low on a route without thinking how much time and gas it takes to get there and back—and without thinking about what a pain in the ass it is to work in that shithole."

"It's all garbage, ain't it?" I said, hoping Pickles might be amused. He lifted an eyebrow as if considering whether the best way to deal with my impertinence was to slap me unconscious or drag me behind the truck. Then he started the truck, eased it into first gear and pulled onto Highway 40 heading north.

"Going to goddamn Hightown. With a goddamn wise-ass for a helper," he said, gripping a steering wheel that looked like a chicken neck in his huge hands.

Like all the older vehicles in the Willard Sanitation fleet, the springs on Pickle's truck had long ago been pounded flat, and the cab jounced, clanged and creaked with every crack and bump in the road. I glanced at the dashboard for a radio, but it, like those on all of the company's trucks, had been yanked by the boss in his futile quest for increased efficiency.

Unlike the other drivers, Pickles had no replacement transistor perched on the dash. Instead the big man hummed softly to himself, now and then drifting into a low croon. I strained to listen to the words in the noisy cab. "And that's why," he half sung, half hummed, "that's why the lady is a tramp."

I looked out the passenger-side window of the cab, so Pickles wouldn't see my smile. My convicted-killer driver was a Sinatra fan just like my father had been. I considered asking Pickles about his musical preferences, but I knew that his appetite for queries from summer helpers was limited and that I had already exhausted my morning quota.

Most of Willard Sanitation Service's routes were in Chicago's newer and affluent northern suburbs, which had grown like skunk cabbage in the low-lying fields and prairies that surrounded the Big City or were built on top of old farm towns whose essential organs—feed stores, schools, churches and grange halls—had either been torn down or converted into boutiques and

The Garbage Brothers

restaurants. Hightown was different. It was a crooked industrial finger of tank farms, factories, warehouses, bars and strip joints that twisted north along Lake Michigan's western shore. Most of the people who lived in Hightown's sagging bungalows and grimy brick apartment buildings worked in the service of those who lived in the wealthier suburbs to the south, laboring in the factories that supplied them, cleaning their homes, cooking in their restaurants, stocking their groceries, filling their potholes, fighting their fires and patrolling their streets. Hightown was a blue-collar city, but its blue had long ago faded to gray.

Pickles drove up the main drag, past the bars, laundromats and tattoo parlors. He honked his horn with the butt of his right hand and waved at a short, bull-shouldered man with a big belly who was working his wheelchair over a curb to cross the street.

"There goes ol' man Jaroux," Pickles said, speaking more to himself than to me.

"Who?" I asked.

"Brownie Jaroux, nimrod. Owns the Eight-Ball Tavern at the corner," Pickles said. "He was a middleweight and a big name when you was still hangin' on your mama's titties," he said.

"Never heard of him."

"Goddamn kids don't know nothin' these days."

Pickles made a sharp right turn into a narrow alley and braked to a stop. "Get out of the truck," he said. "Let's see if the other drivers have taught you how to work," he said.

I grabbed my work gloves, a leather pair with holes in the fingers and thumb that Zeus had given me. I climbed out of the truck, which wasn't easy because it was only a couple of feet from the brick wall of an apartment building. I crabbed my way down the side of the idling, vibrating truck, and the smell of the exhaust and garbage from the vehicle and bum piss from the alley made me gag. When I got to the back of the truck, I could see an alcove that held a rusty 50-gallon drum filled with a stew of ashes and drooling wet garbage.

"What am I supposed to do?" I said.

"Empty the goddamn barrel," Pickles said.

I yanked on the gloves and bent down, straddling the barrel with my knees like I was riding a rocket and wrapping my arms around the middle of the can. I strained to lift and then strained again. Nothing. One more time, and the can lifted maybe an eighth of a grunting inch. Sweat poured off my forehead. I crouched for a third try, and I felt a large hand on my shoulder. Pickles. He pulled on a pair of gloves from his back pocket and brushed me aside. He grabbed the rim and with a powerful jerk tipped it forward on one edge. Then holding the top rim of the barrel with both hands like the steering wheel of a ship, he rolled it out of the alcove and across the gravel alley, and set it upright behind the trough.

"First you gotta move the barrel behind the truck," he said. Then he tilted the barrel forward toward the rear of the truck and crouched low by its right side. With his left hand he gripped the top rim, and with the right the bottom. Then with one swift, smooth motion he lifted it, his right knee hoisting the bulk of the weight, and the side of the barrel slammed onto the edge of the trough. He balanced it there, grunt-walked to the back of the can and rolled it back and forth, banging it against the sides of the trough. Then, just as the garbage started to pour out, he let the can drop to the ground.

"Now you do it, sonny boy," he said.

He stood, hands on his hips, watching me as I stood over the can. "Try rolling it first," he said. "Just tilt it on its edge and then roll it."

I planted my feet facing the can, bent my knees and pulled the can toward me. But nothing moved.

"Make it sudden—jerk it," Pickles said.

This time I gave a mighty pull, and the can broke loose from the ground and tilted toward me. I held the rim with both hands, balancing the can, and then twisted it, expecting nothing and feeling shock and a flush of satisfaction as it moved with surprising ease. Left. Right. Left again. Right. Then I let the barrel rest fully on the ground just a couple of feet behind the truck.

"Now, tilt it forward again, hold it at the top and bottom, then bend down, put your knee under it down low and kick up hard," Pickles said. I obeyed, keeping the can tilted at its precarious balance point and sliding myself around so my knee was braced underneath.

"Now—all at once—kick up with your knee, then push the can onto the edge and work your way behind it."

I looked at Pickles in disbelief. Then somehow I turned off my switch to my brain and did exactly what he said, and I could feel the can lift, inexplicably and magically, to the edge of the trough.

"It worked," I said to Pickles. I was so proud, so impressed by myself that I wanted to step away and take a bow in the alley.

"No shit it worked," Pickles said. "Now roll it side-to-side to shake the garbage loose, then tip it forward and empty it."

Once again, I did exactly as Pickles instructed, and everything worked exactly as he said it would. I let the barrel fall on the pavement and rolled it back to its alcove.

Pickles walked to the cab, stopped, turned and looked back. "Did you check the ashes before you dumped that barrel?"

"What do you mean check the ashes?" I said.

"Jesus. Didn't no one tell you yet about checkin' burn barrels for embers? Next time take off a glove, stick your arm in the barrel to see if there are hot ashes inside," he said. "You gotta go all the way up to your shoulder. If you don't, someday you'll be drivin' around with a fireball up your ass."

"I eat the chili at the Snake Pit," I joked. "Always got a fireball up my ass anyway."

He stared at me without expression, although I hoped I saw a faint glimmer of amusement in his eyes. "Just check the ashes next time, Tippy Toes," he sighed.

"Got it," I said.

He hitched himself into the driver's seat and slapped the door with his palm.

"Hop on the back," he shouted.

I stepped up on the small steel-grate platform at the back of the truck, gripped the metal grab bar with my right hand as if I'd been doing it for years, and let my left arm hang casually behind me. I did it like I'd seen Zeus do one day when he hitched a ride on the back of Billy's rig from the Greasy Wrench to the garage. Then I slapped the side of the truck and looked at Pickles in the driver's side rearview mirror.

"Ready—let's get humpin'," I yelled. Pickles slid the truck into first gear and accelerated as the truck hit a pothole that caused me to fly a couple of feet in the air and land with just the tip of one foot on the platform.

"Hold on with two hands like I told you, dumbshit," Pickles yelled.

I waved my right hand in acknowledgment and immediately reached for the grab bar as the truck swung hard on to Main Street.

Chapter 11: Meeting the Niece

It was Sunday, my only day of rest from garbage labors, and I sat in my Corvair in a weed-lined cul-de-sac that had one home on it—a disheveled ranch house with an overgrown front yard that served as a boneyard for rusting vehicles in various stages of dismemberment. I had come, despite misgivings and trepidation, to accept Grits' invitation to meet his niece at a family barbecue.

"She says she wants to meet you—I don't know why, but she does—and my wife told me to make it happen—so that don't give me any choice in the matter," Grits told me on Friday in the garage after work.

"Thank you, I'd be honored to come," I said, folding a pale green paycheck in half that the boss had just handed me and sliding it into the back pocket of my filthy jeans.

"I don't give a good goddamn whether you feel 'honored,' " Grits said. "Just show up, eat what's on your plate, keep your hands to yourself, and go home early." Then he walked away.

Zeus overheard our conversation and stood stroking his beard, arching his eyebrows, and rocking back on his heels—all indications, I'd learned, that he was amused. "If Grits' wife serves squirrel or possum, don't eat it," Zeus advised. "I saw him parked on the side of the highway the other day checkin' out roadkill."

Grits was right. My motivations for showing up at his house on Sunday had nothing to do with being "honored" by his invitation. Simple truth was I wanted, hoped, desired, needed, craved, and yearned with every ounce of my 18-year-old being to get—to use sanitation vernacular—my ashes hauled. I wanted the carnal knowledge that it seemed nearly every sentient male my age already possessed.

In middle school, I had examined in magnifying-glass detail the Playboy magazines that my father kept in his briefcase in the entryway of our home—the briefcase I used to crawl to on my hands and knees down the hallway from my bedroom, where I was supposed to be doing homework. I would open it, my shaking hand pressed up against the spring latches to keep them from alerting my father, who was watching TV and drinking his fourth martini on the white Naugahyde couch in the family room. The Playboys were a welcome upgrade over the slim volume that appeared in my bedroom when I was in grade school. "A Story About You" was a Presbyterian publication that I was dismayed to find had no photographs of the female form but that did have an interesting diagram of the female body, including a dotted overlay showing the location of the fallopian tubes and other biological whatnot. But it didn't take long before the drawings lost their allure and the sirens in my father's Playboys took their place. And now there was this driving, pulsating need to visit that place that the Presbyterians had solemnly and ineffectively warned must not be visited outside the sacred institution of marriage.

There were two kids in the cul-de-sac playing catch with a football—a boy who looked maybe 11 or 12, and a girl about half that age. The boy, a husky kid with a crew cut and ruddy complexion, was wearing jeans, a Chicago Bears T-shirt and high-top tennies. He grunted as he heaved the ball, and the small, thin girl with long, white-blond hair wearing a dirty yellow dress and pink rubber flip-flops leaped out of the way as the incoming missile approached, and then chased its bouncing, haphazard path.

"You the guy my dad said is coming to dinner?" the boy said. His sister watched with ravenous curiosity.

"Yeah, I'm the guy."

"Figured," he said. "I'm Henry and that's my sister Sadie chasing the ball." He turned toward the house. "Hey, Iris," he shouted. "Your future hooosband is here."

"OK," I said. "Thanks a lot."

"Welcome." He paused. "You play football?" he asked.

I played halfback for Sydney O. Roxbury High School my senior year."

"I wouldn't brag about it—they're the worst high school team in the state," he said. I nodded; the kid was right. The Roxbury Patriots, the team on which I had been fourth-string halfback, had recorded a perfect 0-12 record the previous year.

"Were you any good?" the boy asked.

"No," I said, deciding it was better to be honest with a kid who clearly had no qualms about telling the truth and who may have seen me play on the rare occasions the coach sent me on the field.

"My brother Henry's real good," interjected Sadie, who had returned with the football and handed it to her brother. "He's the best player at Carmichael Elementary. Gonna be a star for sure."

I looked at Henry, who handed me the football and then spun around and started sprinting up the street that led to the cul-de-sac. "Going long," he yelled. "Hit me." About 20 yards out he stopped, but I gestured for him to keep running. Then I threw the ball. It arched high and dropped about ten yards short of Henry.

"Almost got to me," he shouted.

"Slipped out of my hand," I said.

"Hate that when it happens," Henry said. He sprinted toward me, scooped up the ball and heaved it toward his little sister, whose attention was fixed on me and not on the incoming missile. The football hit her in the small of her tiny back. She went down like a rag doll, lay in stunned silence for several seconds, then unleashed a writhing scream that scoured from my mind every word of the artfully composed greeting I had prepared for Grits' niece.

"Goddamn it all to hell, you kids—what's goin' on out there?" The familiar, grating nasal voice came from inside the house. Grits appeared behind a screen door holding a half-quart can of Stroh's and looking even more gaunt than he did at work. He wore an old flannel shirt over a pair of baggy khaki work pants. A cigarette drooped from his lips and, as he opened the door, he signaled me with a nod of his head to come inside. I stepped into an entryway cluttered with coats, hats, hand tools, work boots, and baseball bats. I followed Grits into a warm, well-lighted kitchen filled with intoxicating smells. I saw a small, busy, dark-haired woman with large brown eyes framed by librarian glasses. She had a pale and prematurely wrinkled face, and hair that hung limp in the July heat to just above her shoulders. She was sliding a baking pan containing ham and sweet potatoes into the oven. She put down a red-and-white checked potholder and turned to meet me.

"This is my wife, Mary Rose," Grits said.

I reached out and shook a soft warm hand that made me feel safe and welcome, even in the presence of her menacing husband. "So pleased to meet you, Jesse," she said in a small but strong voice. "My husband has told Iris and me so much about you."

"Really?" I said, looking at Grits, whose head had disappeared into a vintage green GE refrigerator that looked as if it had been salvaged from the garbage and that I knew probably had. Grits was a scrounger of the first order, and he returned from his routes every day with the cab and sometimes the garbage hopper loaded with what the rest of the crew referred to as "Grits' souvenirs" that he loaded into his beat-up pickup to take home. Grits grabbed two cans of Stroh's from the fridge and gestured for me to follow. He walked through a family room, which had a couch covered with a ratty comforter the color of old underwear and a La-Z-Boy recliner with a duct-taped tear in the back cushion. He ducked through a tear in a screen door into a back yard that was more brown dirt than grass. A variety of mismatched lawn chairs were arranged in a semicircle, and in one of them sat a slender young woman with a head of short brown hair and the biggest, roundest, brownest eyes I had ever seen. At first glance, she looked as plain as prairie; unlike Lyla there was

The Garbage Brothers

nothing exotic or mysterious or Martinique about her.

Yet I couldn't stop looking at her eyes. And at her mesmerizingly short blue-jean cutoffs.

"This is my niece Iris," Grits said. "Iris, this is Tippy Toes."

"Jesse," I said. "Call me Jesse."

"He ain't nothin' but Tippy Toes to me." Grits said. "But you call him anything you want."

"I will, Uncle," she said. She reached up with a slender tanned arm that I thought may have been the most perfect limb I had ever seen in my life. "Pleased to meet you, Jesse."

I just stood there, silent and mesmerized. "Good God, ain't you got nothing to say? You run your mouth all the time at work," Grits said. A cigarette dangled out the left side of his mouth, and he looked at me with disdain and a touch of amusement at my discomfort

"Happy," I said. Then, realizing that didn't make much sense, I tried again. "Happy to meet you, Iris." I shook her hand, and as I did I noticed that my arm had thickened considerably from my garbage labors. There was even a manly scar—well, a scab, actually—where my arm had been scraped a couple of days earlier by the rusting edge of an upturned 50-gallon drum. This was the arm of a workin' man. Better yet, the arm of a workin' man reaching out to hold the hand of another workin' man's unexpectedly attractive niece.

"I'll take that beer," I said. Grits handed it to me and went back into the house. I pulled up a tattered lawn chair next to his niece. She closed a familiar-looking paperback that was open on her bare legs and smiled. My mind churned, burned, turned as I searched for something, anything, to say.

"So what are you reading?" I asked.

"Sci-fi," she said.

I could not believe my good fortune. Suddenly I was on familiar ground. I knew science fiction like Billy Bart knew nudie mags. Like Zeus knew how to make small talk with housewives. Like Pickles knew his way around a handgun. "Ray Bradbury," she said. "I'm re-reading *The Martian Chronicles*."

"My God," I said. "You like Bradbury?" I nearly stood in amazement. My mouth opened. My eyes grew big. My pupils dilated. If I were a puppy, I would have wet the floor.

"He's my favorite," she said.

"Me, too." I said. We sat in the lawn chairs, with broken nylon straps that dangled to the ground, and my awkwardness faded. We sprinted through our favorite Bradbury novels—she'd read all of them, some more than once. "The Martian Chronicles" was her favorite, as it was mine. She said one of her dreams had been to illustrate one of his books. She described a sketch she had done after reading one of his short stories, "Fire and Ice"—the one about stranded space explorers trying to return to the shelter of their ship in the narrow window between the deadly cold of the night and the killing heat of the day. She drew one of her legs under her on the chair, and I stared at her tan smooth thighs. Then I felt a cold, cylindrical object pressing hard against the back of my head.

It was a bottle of Stroh's. "Sight-seein', Tippy Toes?" Grits said. "Have another beer and keep your eyes on the damn horizon."

Iris looked at her uncle with a mix of amusement and irritation. "We're busy talking about books, Uncle," she said.

"You was talkin'," Grits said. "Tippy Toes was lookin'."

Grits considered the two of us, holding his cigarette with a drooping ash tip that looked like it could fall any moment. He reached through an open button on his shirt and scratched his concave belly, then hitched his pants, and left. Iris smiled. "My uncle can be difficult," she said.

I nodded and decided, being within earshot of the house, to say nothing.

"Let's go for a walk," Iris said.

She stood, motioned for me to follow, and we walked through a gap in the side yard bushes and down a dirt path that led to the Fox Breath River and the fields of corn and soybeans that lay beyond it. We talked; trickles of words turned into torrents. She told me she worked at a clothing store at the Wilton Mall and that she wanted to become a graphic artist and, if that didn't work out, a grade school librarian like her Aunt Mary Rose who had raised her since she was 6. I told her about my father's sudden death, my mother's plans to move and my need to find a place to live. And I shared about my failure to find a college that would accept me, my summer job at Willard Sanitation, and my introduction to Grits, Pickles, Zeus, Billy and Benjamin Willard III.

"Benjamin Willard III," Iris said. "My uncle says he wants to hang that man by his lips every time the boss hands him another complaint slip," Iris said.

"Sounds about right."

I glanced behind to see if Grits was following us with a machete, preparing to chop me into pieces and leave my parts for the crows. But there was no one behind us, and we were walking away from the back yard through a field of corn—the vibrant green stalks were just above knee level and looked as if they might be chest high by midnight. We reached the edge of the field where there was a berm covered with undergrowth. She pulled aside some branches, and there was a small, steep downhill path. She gestured for me to proceed. "This leads down to the river," she said.

Ten plunging steps, the last five of which I skidded on my rear end, and we were at the Fox Breath River, which in July looked more like a small creek than a river. The water barely flowed, and we climbed over a fallen cottonwood and sat on it. We were quiet, listening to the soft ruffling of the water and the chirping of crickets in the fields all around us.

I felt as if I needed to say something, and was searching for an opening, anything to say, when she leaned over without the slightest warning and gave me a quick gentle kiss on the lips. It was just a small kiss, but I felt as if someone had turned on a flashlight in the dark cellar of my being. I stared at her in amazement and with complete gratitude. My spine vibrated like the air conditioner unit on the back wall of the Greasy Wrench.

"We've got to get back to the house," she said. Her words were a relief, as I had emerged from my shock and was considering whether I should return her grazing kiss with a firmly planted one, and wondering where I should put my right hand, which was clinging to the mossy bark of the cottonwood. I considered her shoulder or maybe, God help me, somewhere else, and the choices, logistics and potential consequences made my circuits sizzle.

Then she was off the log, pausing for a mind-frying second to pull down the bottoms of her cutoffs from the wonderful point of near indecency. She scrambled up the berm and into the rabbit hole that led to the field of corn before I knew what was happening. I followed her back to the house, where slabs of baked ham, sweet potatoes and glops of coleslaw waited on white paper plates. The family was inside eating on TV trays and watching a "Lassie" rerun on a black-and-white television.

Iris and I took our food outside into the back yard and ate and talked—or, more accurately, I talked. I told her about my first weeks at Willard Sanitation Service, and my "baptism in the sea of garbage" and the men who hauled it. "Your uncle scares the living shit out of me," I confided.

"He scares the shit out of a lot of people—and for good reason," she said. I was disappointed; I had expected, hoped, that she would tell me that her uncle's gruff exterior was misleading and that he was a kind, loving man at home with his family. That his disemboweling demeanor was all bluff and bravado.

"My uncle doesn't understand me—I learned growing up to keep my distance from him," she said. "But my aunt and I have been close ever since I started living with them. She's like a mother to me."

We continued to talk until long after Henry and Sadie had come outside to say good night, and then Aunt Mary Rose came to do the same. We sat in the dark, fireflies flickering around us. We talked about books, plans, dreams, friends and foes. Anything and everything. Just after midnight, I said I needed to go, that I had to be at the Greasy Wrench in a few hours. I walked out into the summer night, breathing in the river of coolness that had drifted into the cul-de-sac. I had never met anyone like Iris. She was not only attractive but she was the easiest and most comfortable girl to talk to I'd ever met. And, to my great amazement, Iris seemed as interested in me as I was in her.

I noticed a faint red glow at the end of the driveway. It was Grits, smoking a cigarette and leaning against the driver's door of my car.

"Where'd you disappear to with that little niece of mine?" he said.

"We walked down to the river."

"We walked down to the river," he repeated with a mocking tone. He stared at me. Hard. I wanted to look away but I couldn't. "Understand this, shithead," he said. "You do anything to that little girl, and I will barbecue your balls for the next picnic."

I looked away and said nothing. Grits stood in front of my car door and didn't budge when I reached for the door handle. I was afraid, but I also was angry, and the anger was winning. "Look, Grits," I said, "you invited me to your house to meet your niece. I met her and we had a good time. And now I'm going home. That's all I've got to say to you."

Grits considered my words. He leaned forward, the tip of the cigarette clenched in his tight lips poised perilously close to my left eyeball. "Listen to me, you little pussy son of a bitch. You have been warned."

He stepped aside. I got into my car and drove up the gravel road that led to the highway, watching Grits and his glowing cigarette in my rearview mirror—and thinking about his lovely niece and the road ahead.

Chapter 12: A Family Reunion

Thanks to Billy, I was scheduled to work a second consecutive week with Zeus. As we lifted our carry cans from the back of the truck to begin work Monday morning, Zeus asked if I was free the next Sunday to come to his wife's family reunion at Flat Rock State Park, just across the Wisconsin border and a couple hours' drive from Freedom.

The invitation surprised me—after four weeks on the job, the other drivers made clear that they still regarded me as an aggravating and boss-imposed nuisance. When Zeus saw that I was taken aback, he grinned and shrugged, lifting the palms of his spotless leather work gloves toward the blue summer sky. "My wife says maybe I'll act like a better person if I have someone I like there," he said. "No way I could ask Pickles, Billy or, God help me, Grits," he added. "I need someone who doesn't look like he's on parole, and that's you."

I couldn't believe that Zeus had just bestowed "someone-I-like" status on me. Just when I was beginning to think I would never shed my pariah status, one of the drivers—by far the coolest, smartest and wittiest—had declared me a friend, and that gave me hope that the others might follow suit. I reveled in my good fortune as Zeus described his wife's family and embarked on what I recognized as a classic Zeusian rant that could easily last until lunch. "I can't stand a single asshole in Totina's entire asshole family," he said, fingers jitter-bugging through his beard as he stood behind the truck working the compactor blade. "Just an endless parade of assholes—daddy asshole, mommy asshole, sister asshole, sister's husband asshole." He paused from his asshole enumeration and added, "Oh, yeah—Totina said to tell you that you can bring someone with you to the reunion if you want," he said.

"Maybe I'll bring Grits' niece," I said.

"You serious?" Zeus said. "You want to go somewhere with someone who is actually related to that inbred goober?"

"Just thinking about it."

"Well, maybe you should think again," Zeus said, backing up the blade and reaching deep into the trough with a spotless leather work glove to pluck out a Penthouse magazine and flip open the centerfold, which showed a bare-assed woman paddling a canoe carrying another bare-assed woman sunbathing in the bow. "Think about how much of your life you want to spend stuck in Freedom humpin' garbage for Willard Sanitation."

"What's that got to do with Grits' niece?" I said, trying to catch a better look at the centerfold without being obvious.

"You look hard enough at that hillbilly niece of his and she'll start droppin' babies. Hey, don't look at me sideways because you know that's exactly what's gonna happen," he said. "And you'll keep workin' here until your balls sag to your ankles because you gotta support the little mama and those baby monkeys." He jacked the handle back and forth to compress the load and gain enough space to delay our dump run until noon. "I'm just telling you to think about it—think long and hard."

My deliberations lasted for maybe five seconds—my version of long and hard. Iris and I had spoken on the phone several times since the night we'd met at Grits' house, and Zeus' wife's family picnic seemed like an opportunity to take our relationship to the next step—and that next step hopefully would include the long overdue loss of my virginity.

After work I called Iris and asked if she wanted to drive with me to Wisconsin on Sunday and spend the day at Flat Rock Lake State Park with Zeus' wife's "asshole family."

"Sure, I'll come," she said.

"You think it will be OK with your uncle?" I asked.

"Would it matter if it wasn't?" she asked.

"No ," I said, knowing that she could tell that wasn't quite the truth.

"OK then," she said. "I'll see you Sunday. And I'll bring a blanket."

"To sit on?"

"Yes," she said with a soft laugh that made me want to run in small circles. "A blanket to sit on."

Chapter 13: Zeus' Lightning

Early Sunday morning I stopped at the Greasy Wrench to gas up the Corvair for the two-hour drive to Zeus' wife's family reunion at Flat Rock Lake. I strolled into the cafe like a regular to get a cup of coffee loaded with cream and sugar to go. The place looked empty except for a pair of long, thick legs sticking out of the far booth where the Willard Sanitation crew gathered on weekdays for breakfast.

Delores was behind the counter cleaning and filling salt and pepper shakers. She glanced up and smiled at me. "What are you doing here, sweetheart? Forget it's Sunday?"

"Going with Zeus to his wife's family reunion at Flat Rock Lake," I said, trying to sound cool and indifferent about it—as if my hanging with Zeus on an off day was a regular occurrence. "Taking Grits' niece along."

Delores set a Mason jar of pepper and a yellow funnel on the counter and cocked her head, looking at me with curiosity and concern. "You're taking Grits' niece to a family reunion?" she said. "How did this happen?"

I was torn between being irritated by Delores' concern and flattered by her maternal attention. "I met her a couple weeks ago at Grits' house. Do you think there's something wrong with me taking her to the reunion?"

"Well, honey. . . ," Delores said.

"Jesus, Mary and Joe." The groaning exclamation came from the booth with the legs extending, and it was Pickles. "He's just taking her to a goddamn family reunion, Delores. He's not marrying her," Pickles said. "Not yet anyway."

"I'm not planning to marry anyone," I said.

"Well." It was Pickles again, and there was a chuckle that got detoured by a coughing jag. "Tippy Toes," Pickles said, lifting his great head and torso on his elbows and looking at me with red-faced wonder. "Why do you think Grits wanted you to meet his niece? You think he wants you two to be tea-sippin' companions. That ain't the way they do things down in Hicksville where he's from."

"I think he just wanted me to meet his niece," I said.

"God save us, Delores—the kid's an idiot," Pickles said.

Delores handed me a white paper cup filled with coffee and thick with cream and sugar. "Here you go, sweetie," she said. "You're no idiot, and you just never mind us. Go and have a good day with that sweet girl."

I nodded goodbye. "See you both on Monday," I said.

"Go with God. . .if you can find him at that family reunion," Pickles said as he eased back into his prone position in the booth.

Delores patted my arm. "Go," she said, giving me a gentle nudge toward the door. "Have fun with that sweet girl, you hear me?"

"I hear you," I said.

Iris was waiting at the end of the driveway when I drove into the cul-de-sac. She was wearing a pair of short blue jean cutoffs and a plain white T-shirt that she filled in all the right places. And she smiled in a way that made it seem as if we'd known each other for years instead of days.

Mercifully, there was no sign of Grits, although I saw Mary Rose through the kitchen window—she was at the kitchen table having her morning coffee and no doubt waiting to see her niece off for the day. Iris opened the passenger-side door, sat lightly and leaned over and kissed me on the cheek, and I felt a surge of warmth that had nothing to do with the coffee I'd bought at the Greasy Wrench.

It was a long drive to Flat Rock Lake, and the talk flowed freely as the farms and small towns blurred past. We talked about Iris' hope to go to college to study clothing design, and Henry and Sadie, who had already started teasing her about having a new boyfriend. "And my aunt thinks you're wonderful and that we've got a great future."

I glanced at her, wondering when I'd been elevated to serious suitor status, a classification that had intriguing consummation possibilities but which still seemed a bit startling and premature. After all, we'd known each other less than two weeks, but the sight of her long tan legs and the frayed jean shorts that just covered their confluence eased my concern. "How old were you when you started living with your aunt and uncle?" I asked.

She paused, as if considering where to begin. "When I was a little, my family lived in Nashville, and my mama worked downtown at a department store—it was called Harvey's, and she sold makeup and fragrances," Iris said. "She used to bring home samples, and my little sister and I would put on so much you couldn't hardly breathe in the house."

"What about your father?"

"His name was Ray, and he was a truck mechanic," she said. "He could work on anything with four wheels, but his specialty was the big rigs. He died when I was 4, so I don't remember much. I remember he took me once to the garage where he worked, and there was a big engine hanging by chains from the rafters. My daddy pushed it and made it swing, and I thought it was going to fall and crush us."

The Garbage Brothers

"Is that how your father died?"

"No, he died driving home late one night from a bar," she said. "Most nights he went out drinking after work, and came home after my sister and I were in bed. My mama always said he'd die driving drunk, and she was right. One night his pickup went off the road and hit a big oak tree. I don't remember much else, but my aunt has an old home movie that shows the two of us at a family reunion. We were doing silly walks that made us look like drunken sailors," she said. "Most of my memories of him are like those movies—just flickers and blurs."

She paused and I reached over and took her hand, noticing how thin, soft and warm it felt in my hand. "I'm sorry," I said, trying to think of something more helpful to say but coming up with nothing.

"Right after that the store where my mama worked went out of business and she couldn't find a job," she continued. "The three of us moved in with her sister Mary Rose's family in a trailer home just outside Gatlinburg," she said. "Things went pretty well for a couple of years, and then my uncle was arrested for stealing cars and got sent to the penitentiary."

Iris said Mary Rose, fed up with the family's poverty and bleak prospects, landed a scholarship to attend a community college where she studied to become a school librarian. Meanwhile, Iris' mother cleaned houses and started hanging out after work in the local bars, and eventually moved out to live with a millwright in Knoxville, taking Iris' little sister with her and leaving Iris with her aunt. Not long after her uncle got out of prison, Mary Rose graduated and applied for a job as an assistant librarian at a grade school in faraway Freedom, Ill., When she was hired she shocked the family by moving north, and later sweet-talked Grits' parole officer into allowing her husband to transfer jurisdictions to Illinois so he could be with his family.

"Do you still see your mother and sister?"

"We met them at a highway rest stop on our way out of Nashville," Iris said. "She handed me a Snickers bar and said, 'So long, kid.' That's the last time I saw them. My mother got sent to prison a few years later for writing bad checks, and my sister went into foster care. I don't ever hear from either of them."

"I'm sorry," I said again.

"Don't be," she said, drawing her beautiful legs under her and looking out the passenger window at the prairie horizon. "That was all a long time ago."

We pulled into the Flat Rock Lake State Park at midmorning. I parked the car in a half-filled lot and from the back seat grabbed a couple of old lawn chairs that I'd found at the dump. We followed hand-scrawled signs and red balloons that marked the way to the Rutkowski family's lakefront reunion.

As we walked, I imagined that we were a trendy couple pictured in an article on "The Proper Outdoor Picnic" in one of my mother's Sunset magazines. Never mind that I was working as a temporary sanitation worker without plans for his future, not even a place to live for the remainder of the summer. Never mind that Iris lived with her aunt's family, and had a minimum-wage job selling clothes at the mall. And never mind that we were heading to the reunion of a family I didn't know except for a garbage truck driver named Zeus who happened to be married to Vernon and Irene Rutkowski's youngest and notoriously well-endowed daughter Totina. Despite all that, I thought we were the very soul of cool.

We descended a grassy slope to a broad and brilliantly blue lake dotted with red-and-blue rental rowboats and picnic sites beginning to fill for the day. The Rutkowski family reunion was in full swing, with more than a half-dozen couples in shorts—stocky Midwesterners with thick, pale limbs that protruded like bratwursts from polyester garments—exchanging polite Sunday conversation, beers in hand, as two barbecue grills spewed intoxicating clouds of smoke from sizzling sausages. Two adjoining picnic tables were filled with elderly women wearing pants suits and calf-length dresses, straw hats with ribbons, and big sunglasses.

Despite the alluring picnic smells, this was not a group I was eager to mingle with, especially when I wanted to make a good impression on Iris during our first outing. I spotted Zeus about 50 yards away sitting on the grass near the edge of the lake, wearing a pair of freshly laundered blue jeans that were rolled up to mid-calf and a radiant white T-shirt. Practicing somersaults in the grass nearby was a willowy red-haired girl, whom I recognized as Zeus' 4-year-old daughter Lily from the photograph he kept on the dash of his truck. It was an idyllic scene except for one thing: Standing directly in front of Zeus was the readily recognizable Totina, who was delivering a finger-jabbing lecture to her husband. Zeus sat in silence, fingers burrowing in his resplendent, uncombed beard. Standing behind Totina—and clearly in full and head-nodding agreement with his daughter's tirade—was a stocky older man wearing a blue polo shirt, Bermuda shorts, white crew socks with red-and-blue stripes pulled high on gleaming white legs, and a pair of shiny black dress shoes. I recognized him from Zeus' detailed workday tirades as Vern Rutkowski, Totina's father, owner of the largest insurance agency in Toledo, Ohio, and the man whom Zeus routinely referred to as a "walking hemorrhoid."

I walked slowly with Iris toward Zeus, hoping that Totina would suspend her rant to acknowledge the arrival of her husband's guests and welcome Iris. But Totina's verbal lava flow only intensified with the arrival of new spectators, and I caught snippets as we approached.

The Garbage Brothers

". . . you and your goddamn drugs," and ". . .sick of you asking my father for money" and, evidently her favorite expression based on its frequent repetition, "And further fuckin' more. . ."

As we approached, Zeus nodded briefly and then turned back to face Hurricane Totina. I watched Zeus and his wife with pity, surprise, and interest. Pity that any human being should be subjected to such a ruthless public flaying. Surprise that Zeus, who I knew had a low boiling point, would submit to such a bruising assault, and interest in the bouncing of Totina's epic breasts in her low-cut blouse as she shook her head and jabbed a forefinger at her husband.

"Maybe we should just leave," Iris whispered. I was about to agree when Lily popped up in front of us and took Iris' hand without introduction. "Want to play with me in the water?" she asked, widening a pair of blue eyes that could not be refused.

Iris and I kicked off our shoes and walked barefoot in the moist grass, Totina's voice fading in the distance. Lily walked between us, holding our hands and talking a thousand miles an hour about why crows were her favorite bird because they were always talking to her but she didn't know what they were saying—did we know? Did we know her mother was going to have a baby sister or brother? (She hoped it was a sister.) Did we like yellow Jello with marshmallows and mayonnaise because that's what her mother brought to the picnic. And, oh yes, did we know that her father told her she could dance more beautifully than any child in the "whole fucking universe?"

"Whole fucking universe?" Iris asked.

"That's what my daddy says."

"What do you think is going on back there?" Iris asked after Lily had run ahead far enough not to overhear.

"Zeus is probably catching shit for using drugs and borrowing money from Totina's father, and who knows what else," I said. "Zeus says his wife and father-in-law have dedicated their lives—and probably their afterlives, too—to making him crazy."

"Sometimes people catch shit for good reason," Iris said. "My father did. My uncle does every day from my aunt. Maybe Zeus is getting what he deserves."

I said nothing, unwilling to join Totina, her father and now Iris in piling on the only member of Willard Sanitation who had treated me with respect. We walked along the water's edge and watched as Lily pranced and jumped and did cartwheels, and all the while she continued to chatter. As she talked, I sneaked a look at Iris as she and Lily waded knee deep in the warm lake water, each step leaving pillowy clouds of silt. Lily bent over to pick up a rock, the bend became a kneel, and the bottom of her brown dress dipped into the water, wicking the water up in the direction of her pencil arms. Iris walked beside her with a big sister—or was it a maternal—ease.

"We should head back," Iris said. "They'll think we stole Lily and went home."

"Hey, I'm not leaving before eating some of Totina's yellow Jello," I said.

We turned around, retracing our steps as Lily meandered and prattled alongside. We returned to Camp Gloom, where it seemed matters had gotten worse. Zeus had evidently erupted—Benjamin Rutkowski was storming off, his big butt waggling, to the parking lot, probably to sulk in his shiny black Buick LeSabre; Totina was sobbing, head in her hands. Zeus stood by the water heaving pebbles as far as he could.

I took in this fractured diorama, breathed in the hot lakefront air, and I knew with a sudden clarity that this was the time for me to do what any true friend in my position would do. I needed to engage Zeus in a firm, manly and insightful talk with a confidant who was wise far beyond his years—yours truly, Tippy Toes.

Zeus stood facing the lake, hands now jammed in the front pockets of his jeans and his great beard jutting into the morning breeze. I lifted my right arm to put it on his shoulder, glancing back toward Iris to let her know that I was now going to the rescue of my friend. Zeus needed me. And I was here for him. Zeus' arm, hard as a steel bar, blocked mine just as it was about to land on his shoulder. "Get the fuck away from me, Jesse," he growled.

"Zeus," I said knowing that, despite this unexpectedly harsh response, Zeus needed a comrade who would firmly and patiently overcome his resistance and stand with him in his misery. I reached out with my arm again and put it on his shoulder.

"I'm here for you, man," I said.

I didn't see the punch coming. But I heard it—a whistling, astonishingly swift and hammering blow that came from down low and piled into the left side of my face with a dull, sickening thud. I saw a flashing red light like the ones I used to see in the Looney Tunes cartoons when Daffy Duck got hit in the head with a mallet. Then an orange-red mist descended over me without a sound.

I woke up staring at a ridiculously blue Wisconsin sky and a raggedy circle of faces that included the entire cast of the Rutkowski family reunion. Zeus' wife was there, leaning over me with an understanding look on her face and her glorious cleavage in full display. So was Zeus' father-in-law, who looked more confused than concerned and who was pushing on the bridge of his tortoise-shell eyeglasses with a thick forefinger to keep them from falling into my face. Lily was there, gazing at me with wide-eyed concern. Zeus knelt by my side, looking oddly messianic. He was talking, but I didn't understand what he was saying.

Someone was missing. I wasn't sure who at first. Then I knew. "Where ith Irith?" I said, my tongue so swollen and painful that I could barely talk.

"She's gone to get your car to take you home," Zeus' wife said.

"Thath nithe," I said.

Zeus smiled, and so did the rest of the assembled family, as if their Rutkowski demons had been cast out by the sacrifice of a lamb named Tippy Toes. He leaned over me, and for a moment, with his face framed by the sun behind his long hair, Zeus looked like Jesus.

"Zeuth, what the hell?" I said. "Thought you wath my friend."

"I'm sorry," Zeus said. "You didn't deserve it. But I don't let anyone touch me when I'm pissed—at least anyone who isn't swingin' tit."

The "T" word dispersed Rutkowskis like a murder of crows after a firecracker.

Zeus stood straight, and looked down and grinned. "Oh man," he said. "Can't wait to hear you and Billy talkin' tomorrow at the Wrench. Gonna sound like a lithperth' convention."

Chapter 14: Billy's Big Dream

Chewing my breakfast was painful the next morning at the Greasy Wrench. And dealing with the smirking amusement of Grits, who had heard from his niece about what happened at Zeus' family picnic and had briefed Billy and Pickles before I arrived, was even harder.

Zeus was already sitting in the booth when I arrived, and he acted as if nothing happened—as if coldcocking the summer help was routine business. Maybe it was, I thought. Maybe the rest of them were waiting for their turns to knock Tippy Toes unconscious and knock some sense into any outsider foolish enough to think a Willard Sanitation driver might be his friend.

I cocked my head, looking sideways in an attempt to hide the bruise and black eye on the left side of my face. Two teeth were wobbly and my jaw felt like a busted screen door. Pickles scooched an extra half inch into the booth when I arrived. He sipped his coffee and spoke with his eyes mercifully fixed on the Union Pacific calendar. "You and Zeus have a little lovers' quarrel?" he asked.

"Tippy Toes must have told Zeus he don't like hippie hair. Wants him to get one of those Pat Boone haircuts," Grits said.

"Jeethuth Chritht," Billy said. "You two love birdth thould kith and make up before Benjie getth here."

Zeus put down his jellied toast—he preferred a thin glaze of Smucker's strawberry, impeccably applied with a clean knife. He made a show of dabbing his mouth with his napkin, then he pursed his lips, swung his head in my direction just over Pickles' medicine-ball belly, and let loose a loud airborne smooch.

Showtime. I knew by now my survival at Willard Sanitation hinged on my responses to such moments. Despite the jagged pain, I pursed my lips and let loose an even louder smacker and lifted my arms in a mock embrace, the middle finger extended on each hand.

The table erupted. Pickles dipped his huge head into his chest and tried unsuccessfully to stifle a guffaw. Billy clapped his hands and pushed back on the back of his booth so hard I expected the cinderblock wall behind it to give way. Even Grits lifted a bone-thin arm and saluted. Zeus shook his head, smiled, and took a precise bite of jelly toast.

The Garbage Brothers

"What the Sam Hill is goin' on over here?" Delores said, leaning over me with a protective hand on my shoulder. "Leave you boys alone for a moment and you start slobberin' over each other."

"Come over here and thit on my lap, Deloreth, and I'll thow you thum thlobberin'," Billy said.

"I see enough slobberin' in this restaurant every day," she said.

Pickles cleared his throat, and it sounded like a walrus warning off a competing suitor.

"Gentlemen—and I'm being kind to you, Billy—let us remember that there is a lady in our midst."

"You talkin' about Deloreth or Tippy Toeth?" Billy asked, head cocked, studying Pickles and puzzling on his defense of Delores. The waitress usually was fair conversational game and, as every crew member could attest, could give as good as she got.

"Talkin' about you mindin' your goddamn mouth in front of the goddamn lady," Pickles said.

Delores reached between them with a full pot of steaming coffee. "Well," she said, "this goddamn lady's pourin' coffee. Anyone want a refill?"

Each member of the crew, starting with Billy, held out their cups. Once they were filled, Zeus leaned forward, smiling, and extended his cup in my direction. "A toast to my friend Tippy Toeth," he said.

"White or whole wheat?" Delores said.

~ ~ ~

My morning with Billy began with monthly commercial stops—businesses that had huge dumpsters that had to be wrestled from their tight enclosures into place behind the truck. I'd throw open the lids with a clanging flourish, hook the compactor blade's thick, greased, clattering chains to handles on each side of the dumpster, pull the magic lever on the side of the truck and let the swooping, scooping blade, powered by the truck's mysterious and powerful hydraulic system, do the rest. As I emptied the dumpsters, Billy sat in the cab reading a nudist camp magazine that the dump's backhoe operator had given him in exchange for an unopened Sara Lee pound cake Billy had salvaged the previous day. Parting with such a gastronomic treasure was difficult for Billy, but he loved to study the black-and-white photos of naked, smiling campers playing volleyball and competing in archery, especially if they had, as Billy liked to say, "thtupendouth boothumth."

After each dumpster was lifted, Billy reminded me to stand underneath it and rock it up and down until every balled-up lunch bag, tissue and orange peel was dislodged, and I had risked my future mobility under the dangling steel containers that weighed well over 1,000 pounds. Then I yanked the lever to lower the dumpster, unhooked the chains, and dropped the lids with a stupendous clash that I knew with smug happiness would aggravate all office workers within earshot. After the containers were dumped at each stop, I slapped the side of the truck with an open palm to signal Billy to pull forward, and then hopped on the helper's platform as it passed, a location that was my favorite place to ride. Even with an aching jaw, there was something so damned cool about jumping on a moving garbage truck, hanging on with one gloved hand and letting the other dangle free while I watched the people around me stuck in their miserable little cars and lives looking at me with what I was certain was envy of my freedom and my workin'-man, garbage-slingin' ways.

By noon, we had been to the dump once, without stopping at the Snake Pit for lunch, and Billy worked his way through the grocery sack lunch that his budget-minded wife packed for him every day—mostly peanut butter and honey sandwiches. He reached in the bag and pulled out one for me, wrapped in wax paper that was held in place with a rubber band that squeezed the Wonder Bread in the middle like a belt squeezing a fat man's stomach.

"Try one of thethe, Tippy Toeth," he said. "You will never be the thame. The honey ith nectar from the godth."

I climbed into the cab, put my feet on the dash, and unwrapped the sandwich, which I knew would hurt to chew but didn't care because I was starving. The truck was parked next to an empty lot in the shade of an old willow tree, and an afternoon wind blew through a nearby wheat field.

"Billy—what do you do when you're not humpin' garbage?" I asked.

"I work on truckth—Benjie'th truckth, my pickup—any truck that needth fithing," he said.

"Yeah, and what else?"

"I go to the Jaguar for happy hour every Friday after work. If you weren't thuch a child you could come with me and Pickleth and buy uth beerth."

"What else?" I wasn't really curious but was enjoying the break from work and wanted to extend it as long as possible.

He paused and gave a sly grin, as if he'd known the question was coming. As if he'd planned it all along and had lured me to this point in the conversation.

"Politicth," he said.

"Politics?"

"Thath what I thaid: politicth. You might be interethted to know that I have dethided to run for townthip thupervithor."

Billy waited eagerly for a response, but I had none. I just looked at him, trying to figure out what the hell to say. "You theem a bit thurprithed," he said.

"Didn't know you were interested in politics."

The Garbage Brothers

"Becauthe I'm a filthy, dirty garbage man and a Polak with a lithp?" he asked, enjoying my discomfort at the question.

"No, not at all," I lied.

"Well," he said, "Really I'm interethted in truckth, bulldothers, road graderth, all that thtuff," he said. And I think Thuthie, Thandy, Therry and Thally—and the other kidth in thith town detherve a real park with a thwimming pool, and I would build one for them if I wath thupervithor."

"But isn't Eldon Kersnocki—the old fart who owns the Greasy Wrench—the current township supervisor?" I asked. Old was a kind description for Eldon, the octogenarian owner of the Greasy Wrench Truck Stop who, rumor had it, owned all of Freedom's business establishments with the exceptions of the Jaguar Gentlemen's Club and Gary's Grab and Go. Eldon lived in a tiny apartment in the back of the truck stop, and wandered into the Greasy Wrench every morning at 6:05 a.m. sharp for his daily constitutional. His appearance meant anyone who had to use the truck stop's only working bathroom was flat out of luck for at least 20 minutes. That was Eldon's personal record for brevity, according to Zeus who kept tabs on such details.

"Isn't Eldon doing a good job?"

"Eldon doeth a good job of milkin' townthip tathpayerth by havin' his truckthtop do all the maintenanthe on townthip truckth and equipment," Billy said. "But his mechanicth do a thitty job and Eldon chargeth the townthip like the Greathy Wrench wath a Rollth Roythe dealerthip. And if he took better care of the truckth, they'd latht ten yearth longer. Pluth,"—Billy held out a greasy finger that had a chunk of peanut butter clinging to the knuckle—"And Mr. Eldon Kerthnocki wouldn't know a park if one bit him in the butt. Not that he hath any butt left to bite."

"But a township supervisor does a lot of other stuff—runs the township home, oversees road crews, prepares budgets," I said. "You want to do all that?"

"It'th not exthactly brain thurgery," Billy said. "If Eldon can do it, anyone can."

Billy took another bite of his sandwich and paused. I could tell there was something else—something I was pretty sure I didn't want to hear.

"Tho I've been thinkin'," he said. "I want you to be my campaign manager."

"You want what?"

"I want you to help get me elected," he said. He reached into the paper bag on the seat between us and pulled out two small cans of Del Monte fruit cocktails. His greasy hand dug into the bag and returned with two plastic spoons. He handed me one of the cans after peeling off the lid, lifting his eyebrows as if he were handing me a plate of escargot en brioche.

"I don't know anything about political campaigns," I said.

Billy popped the lid on his fruit cocktail and the syrup leaked onto his hand, which he licked with a tongue that was the first part of him I'd ever seen that wasn't coated with grease. "You're a college kid," he said. "You'll know what to do."

"I'm not a college kid, remember? And I don't know how to get you elected."

"What exthactly ith my job at Willard Thanitation, Tippy Toeth?" he said.

"You're the foreman."

"Do you really want to thay no to the guy who doeth all the work thcheduleth and who runth thith company becauthe Benji doethn't know hith ath from hith elbow?"

Billy had a point. I didn't want to end up being scheduled to work every day with Grits, who I was still convinced was torn between seeing me as his future son-in-law or slicing and dicing me with his knife. "All right," I said. "I'll give it a try, even though I don't have any idea what I'm doing."

"Exthellent," Billy said. "Good choithe, Tippy Toeth."

I took a bite of the sandwich and a lightning bolt of pain shot through my jaw, a reminder of Zeus' right hand and my place at the bottom of the food chain that was Willard Sanitation. I thought about taking another shot at talking Billy out of running for supervisor. But I knew it wouldn't work. The foreman had made up his mind.

I looked up and Billy was staring at me, his plastic spoon extended.

"What?" I said.

"Give me the cherry," he said. "I get all the cherrieth in the fruit cocktailth," he said.

I stirred the can until the bright red maraschino cherry rose from the bottom, and picked it out with my thumb and forefinger and dropped it on Billy's spoon.

"There you go, Mr. Supervisor," I said.

Chapter 15: Jesus and the Handcart

One of the positive things about working with Pickles was that the man rarely missed a lunch break. It wasn't that he was hungry. Mostly he drank his lunch—a couple of beers and shots of schnapps and now and then, if the big man's gut was cooperating, a ham and cheese sandwich—heavy on the mustard and hold the lettuce, tomato and mayo.

Pickles' lunch stop of choice in Highpoint was The Eight Ball, a tavern in a windowless former mortuary at the north end of Main Street. The proprietor was Brownie Jaroux, the former middleweight who Pickles had pointed out to me on my first garbage expedition to this gritty, gray city. Highpoint had more alleys than driveways, more bars than restaurants, and more mouths than teeth to fill them. Brownie was 56 years old, and his long-gone glory days were chronicled in yellowed newspaper clippings that hung in the bar. They showed a young man with a chiseled physique that powered his trademark "Death Ray"—a pile-driving punch that had earned him a shot at the middleweight title against Thaddeus Potowski three-and-a-half decades earlier.

But these days Brownie looked to me like an 80-year-old nursing-home candidate. He was wheelchair-bound with a bent back and a gut that extended under drooping shoulders like a gas-station toilet bowl. If Brownie was a car, his odometer would have left 200,000 miles—city miles, not highway—in the rearview mirror long ago

Pickles surprised me with a formal introduction to Brownie on my first visit to The Eight Ball, and Brownie responded with a bone-crushing handshake that lasted for an excruciating minute—a greeting that I was pretty sure would be followed by an amputation at Highpoint General Hospital two blocks down the street. The introduction was Brownie's standard initiation for Pickles' summer helpers, and my anguish and subsequent inability to close my hand for several days was cause for considerable mirth by Brownie and Pickles—and speculation on how long it would take before I could properly jack off again. "Betcha two beers it'll be late spring," Brownie said.

Pickles told me that Brownie had stayed in the ring for a decade past his short-lived prime—a long, humiliating slide of exhibition bouts and matches against younger club fighters. They were looking to fight a "name," and Brownie was an available and increasingly affordable name. He'd taken terrible poundings for ever-smaller amounts of money, and the end of his career came when no medical doctor, not even the most unconscionable member of the Illinois Boxing Commission, was willing to sign the forms required to let Brownie crawl back into the ring for one more fight. In the end, he was left with just enough money to buy The Eight Ball and settle in for what he told Pickles was "the long count." That meant until Brownie either passed on to his heavenly reward or eternal damnation—and he said his four ex-wives unanimously agreed it would be the latter.

A Mexican former featherweight named Jesus—Brownie insisted on the King James pronunciation—did most of the cooking and grunt work at The Eight Ball. Jesus crafted epic sandwiches with sheaves of meat carved fine with a knife that Brownie said had once been inserted between the ribs of a pistol-wielding drunk who made the mistake of demanding the contents of the tavern's till while his back was turned to the kitchen and its lethal cook.

Jesus posted the daily specials on a black chalkboard that hung over the bar above a cloudy gallon Mason jar of pickled eggs that looked like it had been sitting on the bar since the Korean War. On this particular day as Pickles and I surveyed the menu, the house special was Bloody Mary, grilled cheese with sliced tomatoes, and tomato soup.

"Jesus must have a lot of tomatoes back in the kitchen," Brownie confided to Pickles.

"Either that or you're going to run out sooner than you think," Pickles said as Brownie wheeled back into the kitchen with our order.

Shortly after that a man in his mid-20s bounded into the bar, looking like the first line of a bad joke. He had a short, aggravatingly precise flattop and was all pepper, bounce and attitude. He sat on a stool to the left of Pickles, leaned over the bar with a pointy right elbow that extended perilously close to Pickles' face as he eyeballed the framed newspaper clippings from Brownie's pugilistic past.

"So that's the old man who runs this place?" Mr. Bouncy Shorthair said. "Looks like he did some real fighting back in the day."

The man's presence seemed to aggravate Pickles, who preferred to do his drinking and eating without unnecessary conversation with strangers. "I can read, too," Pickles said. "Let my helper here know if you need help with the words."

Pickles' insult didn't diminish the newcomer's enthusiasm. "I'm a fighter myself," the man said. "Somebody told me about this Brownie Jaroux and I drove up from the city to check him out. Thought he might give me a tip or two, even though I hear the poor son of a bitch is a cripple now."

"So you came to see Brownie like he's on display at some museum?"

The Garbage Brothers

Pickles said without turning his head. "I think his advice would be for you to get the hell out of the ring 'cause it's clear you ain't got no business bein' there in the first place." Pickles took a drag on his cigarette and then exhaled a medicine-ball-sized cloud of smoke out the left side of his mouth in the direction of the pugilism enthusiast next to him.

Mr. Shorthair stood and stared at Pickles. "I don't like rudeness, especially in a fat man," he said. "Now what does a man have to do to get a drink in this bar?" He lifted his head and shouted, "Hey Mr. Death Ray, bring me a beer." Brownie stuck his head through the thick black curtain that kept any light from the kitchen from intruding on the barroom gloom. Brownie looked at his new customer and evidently decided he wasn't worth bothering with in person. "Jesus," he called over his shoulder. "Some guy out front wants a beer." But there was no answer from Jesus, who must have been off sucking on a cigarette in the back alley or maybe checking out the Playboys that Brownie kept in a rusty mop bucket next to the toilet in the men's restroom.

Pickles took a bite of his sandwich. "If you want a beer, you might try showin' a little respect," he said.

"I want my goddamn beer," Mr. Shorthair called out again to no reaction from the kitchen. "Never mind, I'll just get it myself." He walked around the bar, entering the sacred portal through which every regular at The Eight-Ball knew only Brownie and Jesus could pass.

"Sit down if you know what's best for you, sonny boy," Pickles said.

"Stay out of this."

Pickles shrugged his huge shoulders and smiled. "OK," he said. "Whatever you say. But if I was you, I'd turn around right now and walk out of this bar."

Brownie wheeled his chair in from the kitchen unnoticed by Mr. Shorthair. He watched the customer pick up a glass and put it under the tap. But the young man didn't know his way around a beer tap, and didn't know to tilt the glass to keep it from filling with foam. "Goddamn, this is a bullshit bar," he said.

Brownie called out from the far end of the bar. "Jeeeesusss, will you pour this trespassing ignorant little twat a beer." No answer. "Never mind," Brownie said. "Just fetch a clean diaper—he's gonna need it."

Then it happened. In a couple of blinks of the eye, Brownie and his wheelchair were rolling at full tilt toward the beer tap, where Mr. Shorthair was still trying to pour something other than foam into his glass. Without stopping, Brownie slammed the wheelchair footrest into the man's left shin, causing him to shriek and grab his leg. That's when Brownie's left hand shot out and hit Mr. Shorthair's chin, causing his head to cock sideways. That set up a whooshing blur of a roundhouse right that landed with a sound like a wet sandbag landing on a concrete floor. Mr. Shorthair lay motionless behind the bar.

"Death-ray knockout in the first round!" Pickles said. "Think that was worth the price of admission, Tippy Toes?"

I was speechless. I'd just witnessed a complete mismatch: a beat-up old fart in a wheelchair taking on a far younger man in his prime. And the old man had destroyed his opponent without breaking a sweat. "What the holy hell?" I said.

Brownie shrugged his broad shoulders. "He came in here looking for a fight and he found one—he's not the first," he said. We watched Mr. Shorthair for a sign of life; so far there had been nothing but a leg twitch.

"Jeeeesus," Brownie called out again. "Never mind that diaper. Bring the hand cart."

This time Jesus heard and heeded. The door to the kitchen swung open, and there was Jesus pushing a carry cart festooned with thick web straps. He wheeled it next to Mr. Shorthair.

"Jesus, be careful not to hit the glasses under the bar, will you please," Brownie said. "You break something, and you'll pay for it."

Jesus muttered a reply in Spanish that seemed to amuse Pickles and irritate Brownie, who took it out on Mr. Shorthair by pulling the straps extra tight after Jesus stood the still-unconscious man on the hand cart and prepared him for the short ride to the back alley.

"Hand me that five spot he put on the bar," Brownie said.

Brownie took the money from Pickles and stuffed it in the front pocket of the man's chinos. "First drink's always on the house," Brownie said. Then he picked up the glass that Mr. Shorthair had poured and which had settled to an inch of beer, and hoisted a toast.

"To the vanquished," he said. "Fuck 'em all."

Pickles lifted his beer glass. "Fuck 'em all."

I didn't have a drink to lift. But I had a bowl of tomato soup, and I lifted it off the plate and touched Brownie's glass and then Pickles'.

"Fuck 'em all," I said.

"God help us, Tippy Toes is beginning to think he's one of us," Pickles said.

Chapter 16: Summer Drift

The summer days meandered like the shallow, muddy Fox Breath River, which ran through Freedom on its way to the Des Plaines River and then on to the Kankakee, the Illinois and, finally, to the Mighty Mississippi.

By August, Billy's campaign for township supervisor had gotten off to a creeping start. His campaign manager was clueless on how to get the filthy, foul-mouthed, dirty-minded but well-intentioned foreman of a garbage-collection outfit elected to the pinnacle of political power in Liberty Township. Feeling guilty about my inattention, I drove one day after work to the Wilton Public Library and checked out the only book I could find that explained how to conduct a candidate's first political campaign: "So You are Seeking Office—a Guide for Women With a Vision." I flipped through the first and last chapter, figuring that I could pretend to know what I was talking about. I figured that pretense was all that was required, since it was clear Billy Bart didn't have a lisping prayer of defeating the firmly entrenched incumbent, Eldon Kersnocki.

The first chapter of the book was called "Goal Setting—Think Big, Ladies!" I endeavored to do this with Billy and accompanied him one day on his route. We'd decided against doing any political strategizing at the Greasy Wrench Cafe, since Eldon might catch wind of it and do something to increase the already prohibitive odds against Billy's electoral success. Eldon had taken to having a pre-bowel movement bowl of Raisin Bran at the cafe's counter near the table where the Willard Sanitation crew met for breakfast. Billy was certain he was eavesdropping on our conversations, trying to learn if Billy was serious about running for township supervisor or whether it was all a big haw-haw joke like the time, a few weeks earlier, when Billy had pulled out a Kodak Instamatic and taken a picture of Eldon shuffling out of the john with his pants half unbuttoned and his horn-rimmed eyeglasses hanging off one ear.

Our on-the-job goal-setting session did not go well. I followed the outline in the first chapter, asking Billy to identify three things that he "passionately desired" to accomplish as a duly elected township supervisor. "The book says you're supposed to dream big—challenge yourself," I said.

"Well, I'm not townthip thupervithor yet tho how can I challenge mythelf," Billy said.

"OK, let's say you are elected, what three things do you want to get done?"

"Thath thtupid," Billy said. "I'm not the thupervithor. When I'm thupervithor, I'll know what to do."

"Three things," I pleaded.

"OK," Billy said. "I want to get elected, and then I want to make thure Eldon doethn't tell the cook to poithon my pancaketh the next morning. Then I want to make Eldon hand over the keyth to the townthip garage in January when I take office. And after that I want to tell my campaign manager to go thtick hith little book up hith rear end."

"That's four things," I said.

"Hereth one more," Billy said, flipping me the finger before grabbing his carry can and loping off toward the next house.

I stuck the campaign book on Billy's dashboard in the hopes that he might read it. And that was where Billy's campaign rested for the time being, and I was happy to set aside my responsibilities as campaign manager and tend to other matters. Such as wooing Grits' niece.

Freshly showered after work each day, I drove to Grits' house, where Mary Rose made me glorious ham and egg sandwiches on white bread slathered with mayonnaise, poured me endless cups of coffee thickened with milk and tablespoons of sugar, and talked with me until Iris came home from her job. Despite my transparently impure motives regarding her niece, Mary Rose liked me; she made no secret of it, and I liked her. I had never met anyone quite like Mary Rose, a chronically tired but still somehow vivacious woman who, unlike my prim, reserved mother, spoke her mind and heart, laughed so hard she snorted coffee and then dabbed her nose with a wrinkled green lace hanky that she kept tucked in her bra. She seemed to regard whatever I said as the most fascinating thing she'd heard that day. She lived in her warm, chaotic, paperback-book filled kitchen when she wasn't working at Carmichael Elementary a couple of blocks away, shelving books and breaking the silence of the school library with old-timey gospel songs that she sang with the soft ease of a baby breathing. She told me her Savior had told her to go to school at Western Tennessee University while Grits was serving his grand-theft time at the state penitentiary, and she said that "he," meaning the Lord and not her wrongdoing husband, had scooped her up in the palm of his hand and lifted her right out of Tennessee. Then he set Mary Rose and her brood down in Freedom, Ill., where Carmichael Elementary had hired her as an assistant librarian. They were later joined by Grits who, despite his many flaws, had the sense to know that his car-stealing ways had worn out his welcome in Tennessee and that his only hope for staying on the straight and more-or-less narrow was Mary Rose.

"The Lord might have a place in mind for you, too—and a hand to lift you up and take you there, Jesse," she told me one afternoon. "He might even have someone to go with you."

I put down my sandwich and considered. "Maybe I'm already in that place," I said.

She smiled and patted my mayonnaise-smeared hand. "All shall be revealed in perfect time," she said.

~ ~ ~

Iris and I talked, too, when we weren't making out like bandits rooting through a rich man's house. I rejoiced that I had finally found, after years of fruitless searching and fantasizing, a girlfriend who seemed as enthusiastic as I was about sex, or at least in exploring the paths that led up to it. But the final path to the summit remained untraveled. "It's not right," she'd say, and "not yet" when I dizzily suggested we complete "The Deed"—and that was a matter of considerable concern to me. Our kissing and hugging seemed only to lead to more kissing and hugging, and I yearned for the perfect time when, as Mary Rose had nicely put it, "All shall be revealed."

Chapter 17: Pickles in Love

Benjamin Willard III was the first to notice something curious was happening. He stood at the head of the table at the Greasy Wrench and was midway through his daily sins and omissions soliloquy when he saw Delores hovering over the back of the booth to refill Pickles' coffee cup. Her long white fingers, lavender nail polish and all, were gently caressing the sun-creased nape of Pickles' thick neck. I followed Mr. Willard's gaze, and then it was my turn to be dumbfounded as the boss regained his composure and continued droning on about the female customer in Wilton whose hibiscus clippings had been scattered at the curb.

Pickles melted under the touch of Delores' fingers, and he looked up at her with St. Bernard eyes. "Thank you, Delores," he whispered. "The coffee is simply superb this morning."

Delores smiled and gently patted Pickles' shoulder before leaving to wait on another table. Billy, Grits and Zeus also must have witnessed this astonishing display of mutual affection, because we were all exchanging "what-the-hell" looks as the boss proceeded to the next complaint, this one about a surly response from a driver who the customer said looked as if he had just walked off a prison work farm. "That must be for you, Grits," Mr. Willard said, handing him the complaint slip with an admonition to remember that "customer relations is our most important service."

"And here I thought it was picking up their goddamn garbage," Grits said.

But no one cared about disgruntled customers this morning. Pickles had said and grunted many things over the breakfast table at the Greasy Wrench— most of them laced with profanities. But none of us had ever heard him say anything was "simply superb," much less the Greasy Wrench's coffee, which Billy regularly accused Delores of brewing in axle grease. Pickles seemed to welcome the looks of amazement and revel in the attention, aping the boss's stern countenance and silently mouthing his words. When the boss, miffed by the muffled sniggering, raised his eyes from his clipboard, Pickles' face assumed a reverentially attentive look as if every one of the boss's words were toasted manna from heaven served with a pat of butter and Smuckers grape jelly.

The Garbage Brothers

Billy finally interrupted and said what we were all thinking. He leaned forward on his greasy splayed elbows, chin an inch above the scrambled eggs he was shoveling into his mouth. He cocked his head and glanced at Grits, who took a long drag on a freshly lit cigarette and gave Billy an "I-ain't-got-a-clue either" shrug with his bony shoulders. "Tho what ith going on with you and Deloreth, Pickleth?" Billy asked.

We all stared at Pickles, who reached out and picked up Grits' pack of Camels. Grits gave a grudging nod of assent, and Pickles shook out a cigarette and lit it with remarkable dexterity for a man whose fingers seemed half the size of my wrist. He took a deep drag, held the smoke inside and exhaled. "Well, I appreciate your inquiry, Billy. I am most pleased to announce to all you limp-dicked losers that Delores and I are now a twosome," he said.

Pickles watched for the reaction and savored the surprise, even shock, on everyone's face. "Holy thit, Pickleth," Billy said. "You thly dog."

Grits looked faintly amused, as if Dave the backhoe operator had just delivered his dirty joke of the day at the dump. Zeus glanced at me and then at Pickles. He lifted his coffee cup in a toast. "Here's to the lovely couple," he said. Cups were dutifully raised, and Benjamin Willard III, lacking coffee, lifted his clipboard, beaming at the opportunity to be one of the boys.

I felt Pickles' elbow jam into my ribs. "Let me out, Tippy Toes," he whispered. "Before I drown in all this bullshit."

Chapter 18: Cherry Pie

One scorchingly hot Wednesday after work, I raced home, showered and put on a pair of clean jeans and a Zeus-inspired gleaming white T-shirt, and drove to Grits' house. Iris' black VW bug, so battered that it looked like something her uncle might have salvaged from one of his garbage pickups, was parked in the driveway when I pulled into the cul-de-sac. She'd invited me to come for dinner, saying her aunt and uncle and their kids planned to pile into Grits' Ford pickup and go to a drive-in movie in Wilton. That welcome development portended romantic possibilities, and I thought, hoped and fervently prayed that this might be the Night of Nights when lightning would flash and cathedral bells would ring.

The reason this had not yet happened was not a lack of eagerness or willingness on my part; it was a maddening, torturous and relentless absence of opportunity. I would have much preferred that Iris and I be the ones going to the drive-in, but Iris said her aunt told her she wanted to get to know me better before the two of us started dating.

"You're 18 and have a full-time job—I think you should be able to go out on a date if you want," I said.

"She's old fashioned and very religious," Iris said, adding that her aunt faithfully attended the Tabernacle of the Holy Winds Church whose sacred portal, she noted, her uncle refused to cross.

So for the time being we met at Grits' house, where Mary Rose was an ever-present fixture in the kitchen, and Henry and Sadie raced through the house or watched cartoons in the living room.

When he was home, Grits sat on the back patio drinking beer and whittling with his hunting knife—the same grim blade he said he would use to neuter me if I violated his niece—the thing I now, on the occasion of Iris' family's absence, fervently hoped to accomplish.

Iris met me at the front door. She was wearing loose plaid flannel pajama bottoms and a tight white T-shirt that looked immeasurably sexy. "Hey," she said, stepping outside the house and giving me a long, wet, warm welcome kiss as she stood on top of my sneakers with her small bare feet.

"Hey," I said. "What's up? Did you have a good day at work? I did—but I had to put up with a lot of BS from your uncle."

She ignored my babbling, took my hand and led me through her aunt's warm, cluttered kitchen and into the family room where the old sleeper sofa was opened into a bed on which there was a jumble of sheets, blankets and quilts.

This was it. My dream sequence. Well, not exactly. I never envisioned the duct tape on the Naugahyde cushions. Or the black-and-white TV that was playing a Huckleberry Hound cartoon, the one in which Snagglepuss tricks Huckleberry into believing his doghouse is a race car.

"When are your aunt and uncle getting back?" I asked.

"Not for a few hours—they're at a double-feature, so we have plenty of time to relax."

She leaned toward me and gave me a kiss. Just like in the movies. Long and slow and wet. She plopped down on the sleeper bed, took my arm and pulled me down next to her. Iris was in control, and I was delighted and relieved to have her at the helm. I put my arms around her, and the room began to blur, and I hugged her harder because that seemed like the right thing to do. One of my hands, probably the right because that was the way I'd always pictured it, slipped under her shirt, onto her back, and with her eager guidance moved to the front where there was no pretense, no familiar murmurs of "Don't." Just free sailing and—Lord almighty—no bra with devil snap hooks to impede.

I pulled up her shirt and managed a quick glance. Everything seemed to be there in its assigned and proper place. She made a soft humming noise, and the T-shirt was now covering her face. She pulled it off and then gave me a hard hug. Just as I was beginning to consider the weighty matter of her pajama bottoms, she reached down with both hands, and whoosh, they were gone and there was nothing underneath but Iris. I was struck nearly dumb by the difference between a real, breathing and very present naked woman and Playboy magazine centerfolds who folded in the middle and often had staples in their vital places.

"Take off your clothes," she said, and then, not waiting, she leaned forward to help. She started with my jeans, which she yanked off, leaving me in my gleaming white Munsingwear that I was suddenly and painfully aware had my last name written inside the waistband with a Magic Marker—something my mother continued to do years after I was done going to Presbyterian church camp for reasons that I did not understand and now had reason to regret. I was working on a strategy for furtive underwear removal when I heard the sullen thump of a car door in the cul-de-sac. Then there were two or three more thumps, which meant only one thing: Grits and his family were home early from the drive-in. And I was about to lose a precious appendage that remained at full salute and unaware of its bloody fate.

No time for ruminations or regrets. I bolted upright and groped for my clothes. Iris was already half dressed by the time I found my jeans under the sofa bed. I stepped into them only to find out they were facing the wrong way. Gasping with fear and urgency, I pulled them off, put them on the right way, struggling to yank the zipper over my still cluelessly protuberant organ. I lurched for my shirt. I could hear the front door opening and see the kitchen light streaming yellow, angular and unwelcome into the family room where I was just pulling on my shirt. Forward or backward? Didn't matter. Survival—and penile and scrotal retention—were all that were important.

Both of us were dressed now—more or less. My socks were on the floor, as were, God save us, Iris' underwear. Iris saw them the same time I did and kicked them under the sofa bed. We heard footsteps—cautious, inquisitive footsteps. The sound of Mary Rose hushing Henry and Sadie and telling them to stay in the kitchen. I remembered that my car was parked in the driveway, so Grits already knew I was here. Iris reached over and flipped on a small lamp. No time to put away the sofa bed. I reached over to retrieve my socks.

"Sit up," Iris said.

Grits was the first to step into the room. He looked bone thin like the blade of a skinning knife. He stared at me, knowing—knowing everything. Then Mary Rose appeared behind him, her glasses catching the light of the lamp.

"Well, hello, you two," she said, mercifully ignoring the obvious. "Watching TV?"

Iris smiled and nodded. "And cuddling a little," she said.

I smiled and nodded and said nothing. Iris reached down and held my hand and the warmth of her hand at that moment was perhaps the most reassuring thing I had ever felt in my soon-to-end life.

"Cuhhh-dddlin'?" Grits said, his slow drawl turning the word into a slow profanity. "You was cuddlin' with my damn niece on my damn sofa bed in my damn living room in my damn house?"

"Uncle, I'm 18 years old," Iris said.

"That's right," Grits said. "And that ain't legal cuddlin' age as long as you're livin' in my house."

"Good God, you were 15 when you and Aunty Mary Rose got married," Iris said. She was sitting straight up, which I wished she wouldn't do, since it revealed that her T-shirt wasn't pulled down in the back and that there was nothing but Iris underneath.

"Perhaps I should go home now," I offered, wanting with every ounce of my fearful, trembling soul to be walking out that front door with its busted screen. Just 10 steps, maybe twelve, and I could be in the safety of my baby

The Garbage Brothers

blue Corvair and speeding down Highway 20 to the safety of my home.

Mary Rose appeared in the uncomfortably tight space between Grits and me. Somehow, she had gone to the kitchen and pulled a half-eaten pie from the fridge and was holding it up for all to see.

"Cherry pie with ice cream in the kitchen in five minutes," she announced, and as she left, she took Grits' hand and pulled him into the kitchen.

Iris' fingers interlocked tightly with mine.

"C'mon," she said. "Time for cherry pie."

Chapter 19: Pickles Takes Flight

When I began at Willard Sanitation, the prospect of working with Pickles filled me with dread. That was in no small part because Zeus told me about Pickles' past convictions for murder and felony assault, and also because of the roiling black funks into which he regularly descended, often for days at a time. But my fears had begun to fade because I had survived so far without being shot, stabbed or beaten to death. Pickles and I now had actual conversations. Not just about where to find the garbage cans behind the red brick house at 2515 Mule Creek Lane or about what Pickles memorably insisted were the "perfectly perfect" breasts of the woman at 1363 Meridian Ave. But rivulets of genuine communication.

"So Pickles—what's going on with you and Delores?" I asked him one morning as we were driving from the garage to begin our route. He gave me a sideways glance to see if I was making light of him, which I certainly wasn't. Even at the tender and foolish age of 18, I knew not to mock a man who had shot his wife's lover in the gut and then fired another shot that shattered her hip and landed her in the township home.

Pickles reflected as if giving himself permission to confide in a kid several decades younger than him. "I've seen Delores every workday morning for years, and never thought much of it. Then we started talking—not just the stuff that she and Billy throw at each other every day, but really talking. At first it was about things that happened on my routes and that happened to her at the cafe every day. Then we started talking about her two boys and about our backs—we both have lower lumbar issues, you know."

He shook his head and palmed his forehead, as if confiding in me was painful. "Here's the thing, Tippy Toes, I never met such a kind and beautiful woman my entire life. And for some strange reason, Delores actually seems to like me."

His face flushed, and I nodded, searching for something safe and true to say. "Well, it seems clear you two are crazy about each other," I said.

Pickles didn't reply, and we were both taken aback by the sudden, unexpected plunge into conversational intimacy and vulnerability. After a while, I asked, partly to fill the void in conversation, "How long have you two been serious?"

The Garbage Brothers

"If you must know, I asked her out for the first time a couple weeks ago. She took Sunday off from work and we went out to brunch at Alfredo's in Wilton and then drove to the Big City and went to the Lincoln Park Zoo."

"Wait, you took Delores out to brunch and then to the zoo?" The thought of Pickles engaging in these social activities was astounding. Brunch was something my family used to eat after going to church on Easter, and the word "brunch" appeared nowhere on the Greasy Wrench Cafe's menu. As for a stroll at the zoo, to be honest Pickles' felonious history and fearsome demeanor made him more of a candidate for residency in the zoo's gorilla house than for a leisurely Sunday date.

Pickles looked amused by my surprise. "You think I only eat at the Greasy Wrench?" he said. "I am a regular at Alfredo's. And Delores asked to go to the zoo because she likes the peacocks."

"I like the chimps," I said, not knowing what else to say.

"Everyone likes the chimps," Pickles said. "Delores likes peacocks. That's called taste, Tippy Toes."

~ ~ ~

The morning ended at the Willy Wilkerson Airport, where we emptied the huge green dumpsters from the terminal, which consisted of a single cinder-block building, the adjacent JoyStick Bar & Grill and a service hangar. Unlike other stops, there was no interesting garbage—no Polaroid negatives of naked women like the ones the drivers mined in the Holiday Inn's dumpsters—Pickles stayed in the cab, tapping his fingers on the steering wheel and alternately singing and humming his beloved Sinatra songs.

At the JoyStick, one of the busboys, a goofy looking kid with a bad complexion and buck teeth the size of floor tiles, wheeled out a metal trash can filled to the brim with the kind of wet red-and-yellow grease that only a true greasy spoon exudes. I saw Pickles in the large rectangular rearview mirror that extends from the driver's door beckoning me with a crooked finger. I walked up the side of the truck, and he said, "Manager here called Benjie last week to complain that I left a mess after my pickup. So you tell the kid he has to dump that can himself, and let's see the manager complain about that when his loading dock gets coated with grease."

I shrugged. "The kid could get hurt—that barrel's heavy," I said.

"Just do what I say, nimrod. Then sit back and enjoy the show."

I walked to the back of the truck and nodded to the busboy who looked as if he had just come on duty, wearing clean black-and-white checked pants and a gleaming white kitchen shirt. I nodded toward the front of the truck, giving him an apologetic shrug. "Driver says you have to dump this can by yourself." The busboy looked confused, then gripped the can with two hands by the rim and lifted, straining until the can was maybe two feet above the ground and tantalizingly close to the rim of the truck's trough. Then the busboy, gasping from the weight of the viscous, shifting sea of fat, gave one last heave. The can slammed against the bottom lip of the trough but was still upright and filled with sloshing grease. He looked at me, eyes pleading for help as grease began to drizzle down the sides of the barrel and on to his clothes.

I stepped behind the barrel, checking to make sure we weren't visible in the driver's side mirror, reached down with both hands and helped tilt the barrel and empty the grease into the trough. He started to thank me, and I held a finger to my mouth and gestured in Pickles' direction. The busboy nodded, carried the empty barrel back inside the kitchen and returned with a bag filled with maple bars. "Thanks," he said. "You saved my ass."

I gave him a thumbs up and walked over to Pickles' side window and handed him the bag. "The kid dumped the barrel all by himself—he must be pumpin' iron," I said.

"You're lyin' through your teeth, Tippy Toes," Pickles said. "That kid couldn't lift his own dick to take a piss." He gave me a hard look and crammed an entire maple bar into his mouth. "I'm gonna let it go this time because it's a nice day and I'm in a good mood. But don't ever do that again. You hear me?" His mouth was full, but I understood every word he was saying and nodded my agreement. "I hear you," I said. I stepped up to the running board under the driver's door and Pickles began to pull away from the JoyStick Bar & Grill. "So how'd you know I helped lift the barrel?" I asked.

"Did you ever stop to think that trucks might come with two rearview mirrors?" he said.

I looked over and saw the big mirror on the passenger side. "Oh yeah," I said. "Hey, hand me a maple bar."

"No maple bars for you today, Tippy Toes," he said. "You have to pay your 'stupid tax'."

We headed for the last stop in the airport complex—the dumpsters behind the hangars that lined the airstrip. It was midafternoon, and the sun radiated off the pavement. I took off my sweat drenched T-shirt and tossed it into the cab past Pickles, who wrinkled his nose in feigned disgust. When he turned onto the service road next to the runway, I climbed over the hood of the truck and sat with my feet resting on the front bumper and my hands gripping the hood ornament. I looked back and Pickles gave me a thumbs up.

"Cleared for takeoff," he yelled, and then swerved over the long yellow warning line on the tarmac and onto the airport runway and floored the accelerator. I glanced back; Pickles had his full left arm extended out the window, flapping it up and down like a great, thick-winged hawk—a hawk holding a half-eaten maple bar. "Hey Pickles, we're on the runway," I shouted.

The Garbage Brothers

"We're flyin', Tippy Toes," he howled. "Flyin' like a couple freakin' birds." He shifted into high gear, and even over the straining of the engine I could hear him singing one of his Sinatra favorites: "Come fly with me, let's fly, let's fly away."

I frantically looked ahead and behind for incoming aircraft or planes taking off on the runway. "Pickles, you're insane," I howled into the wind. "You're goddamn crazy." And then, in one of those magical moments not uncommon to 18-year-olds and, apparently, 50-year-old garbage truck drivers, I felt myself caught up in Pickles' beautiful madness. I stuck both my arms out flat and straight like an oversized hood ornament. And on we flew, down the runway, past the hangar, past the parked planes, the cinder-block radio tower with its red blinking light and the head of a man inside who was standing, watching us with binoculars. Past the blue pickup with a plump man in sharp, pressed khakis standing in front of it. Clutching a clipboard and wondering why in blue shitstorm blazes one of his garbage trucks was hurtling down the runway at the Wilton Airport.

I looked back at Pickles and saw that he also had seen the boss, and he eased off the gas pedal for the inevitable return to Earth and Willard Sanitation reality. He pulled in his left wing, put both hands on the wheel, middle fingers extended, and grudgingly pulled off the runway and turned back in the direction of the hangar.

There would be no more flying away and floating down in the blue. Not on this day.

Chapter 20: The Sunbather

On Monday morning, Billy informed me over breakfast that he had scheduled me to be his "bobo" for the week. That was fine with me. I was more comfortable working with Billy, who could have an exuberant conversation with a dumpster, than I was with Grits, whose malevolent death-stare I avoided at the Greasy Wrench as I scarfed my breakfast.

Our route for the day was Rivergreen—a wealthy and ostentatiously unassuming community of low-slung houses designed by Frank Lloyd Wright wannabes and scattered in the woods and bottomlands along the Fox Breath River. After breakfast, Billy pulled his truck, usually the cleanest and best maintained in the fleet, out of the garage, while I waited, hands in my jeans pockets against the morning chill and the first slants of sunlight warming my back. Billy ape-leaped out of the cab, motioning for me to follow him to the rear of the truck where he pointed at a perfectly new, unsullied and unscuffed gray carry can resting in the trough next to his custom-made, double-sized orange can.

"Well?" he said.

"Well what?"

"Well, waddaya think about your brand-new carry can? Look here." Billy plucked the new can out of the trough, and there it was on the side, stenciled in large black uppercase letters: "TIPPY TOES."

"Jutht don't let it go to your pointy head," he said.

"I'll try not to," I said. But as Billy and I drove past the other drivers straggling out of the cafe, I sat up a little straighter and returned Grits' glare with the confident look of a proud owner of a personalized carry can.

The morning was perfect. The shade from the massive oak and elm trees provided respite from the mid-August sun, as did moisture from the river bottoms that a savvy developer a few years earlier had snapped up for next to nothing and then subdivided into pricey, low-slung brick and river-rock custom homes.

We picked up the garbage at all two dozen homes on winding Baxter Loop and then turned left on Highway 20. A slow, vibrating anticipation built as we neared Lyla Packington's house. Despite my ardent pursuit of Iris and her miraculous, thanks-be-to-Jesus interest in me, I still clung to the misguided hope that Lyla would come to her senses and realize that I, not Brett, belonged on the basement couch of her affections. As I emptied her neighbors' garbage cans, I imagined the joy of informing Lyla that it was too late—that I had succumbed to the charms of another woman—but that I might be willing to consider a quick dalliance to ease her conscience.

My anticipation was stoked by my recollection of the story Billy had told the crew at breakfast on my first day of work at Willard Sanitation. He had described a previous summer helper's—Little Pete was his name—encounter with a naked female sunbather, who had continued to provide "vithual thtimulathion" for Billy and others for several memorable summers. I harbored the secret and unspoken hope that the house in question might be the Packington residence, a secluded house that lay at the end of a winding gravel and tree-lined driveway matching the description in Billy's story. Yes, there were lots of similar homes in Rivergreen, but wasn't it just possible, even likely, that this shameless beauty was Lyla—the same girl who had once tormented me by recounting how she had provoked the nuns at her parish school by wandering the white sand beaches of Martinique in a state of beauteous and nubile toplessness? If Lyla had rambled half-naked in Martinique, then why wouldn't she have upped the stakes and gone totally and gloriously naked in her Rivergreen back yard?

It all made perfect sense to me. And when we finally arrived at the Packington's narrow driveway, I jumped off the back of the slow-moving truck with my new pristine carry can and started jogging down the driveway. Billy stopped the truck "Where exthactly do you think you're going?" he asked.

"Just getting the garbage at this house, Billy," I said, trying to look as innocent as I could about what I fervently hoped might be waiting behind the house at the end of the driveway; the maddening prospect of seeing Lyla in her glorious, tawny altogether.

A wicked satori smile erupted on Billy's stubbled face. "Tho Tippy Toeth thinkth he might thee himthelf thum bare boobieth, doeth he? He rememberth the thtory old Uncle Billy told him about the naked lady thunbathin' in her back yard."

I stopped and turned to face my accuser. There was no arguing. I was undone.

"How did you know thith wath where Mith Nudey-Pie lives?" Billy asked. As I struggled to come up with an answer, Billy dismissed me with a flick of his right hand. "Aw, get out of here and go thee if there ith anything to thee today," he said. "Jutht you keep your handth on your carry can and out of your panth," he said. I turned and sprinted down the gravel driveway before Billy changed his mind.

I ran with the carry can draped over my back, holding the wire handle with my leather-gloved right hand. After two months on the job, I was stronger than I'd ever been in my life. My shoulders felt broad and powerful and my arms had ridges where muscles had never existed. Gone was the child who had not long ago visited Lyla P.'s house. And here was the new working man whose transformed presence would make Lyla rethink her misguided decision to choose Brett over me. And if she happened to be out sunbathing in her altogether on this glorious morning, she would lift her head, ever so slightly, and see before her the new Jesse – tanned, muscled, capable and desirable—standing before her. And all would be changed in the blink of a wide-open eye.

Then there I was standing in front of the Packington house, which was quiet with no sign of activity. So much the better, I thought. Perhaps Lyla's mother was lunching with her artist friends in the Big City, as she often did. I walked around the left side of the house and took a first tentative step into the back yard. I glanced to my right—and there, lo and behold and God Almighty, on the patio were two bare feet topped with pearly toenails resting at the end of a yellow banana lounger. And those feet were attached to ankles and those ankles were attached to sturdy legs that were attached to ample hips and, above that a pair of Jayne Mansfield-sized breasts that draped to their respective sides as if keeping watch for voyeur sanitation workers.

Her eyes were covered with a precisely folded white towel, and she was either asleep or hadn't heard my approach.

I stared, astonished and uncertain, having had little—well, none, actually—experience on how to proceed in such circumstances. Detailed and fervent fantasies aside, I expected to find nothing but garbage cans in the back yard to claim my attention. But here I was in the presence of real—wonderfully real—nakedness, and I didn't know how to proceed. Should I cough or scuff my feet to announce my presence? Should I remain silent and frozen in place, and just give quiet thanks to God for his glories—rather Lyla's—revealed?

But something wasn't quite right. Lyla had many memorable physical attributes but sturdiness, ampleness, and Jayne Mansfieldness were not among them. These were not the ankles, legs, hips or breasts of the slender Lyla I remembered. Nor was the double chin that extended from the towel covering her face. And it was at that chilling moment that I realized I was gazing upon the naked body of, not Lyla, but of her mother, Mrs. Anita Packington, who clearly was not "lunching" with her artist friends in the Big City. And it was highly doubtful that Mrs. Packington would be pleased to find out that one of her daughter's high school friends was ogling her considerable wares.

A hasty retreat was in order. For some reason, one that would have pleased my high school English teachers, I recalled a passage in James Fennimore Cooper's "The Deerslayer" in which Natty Bumpo avoided detection by hostile natives by sliding his toes down ever so carefully to avoid snapping twigs. Slowly, slowly, twig-free step by twig-free step, I backed away until I reached the corner of the garage.

I turned and ran down the long driveway, trees around me blurring and my Converse sneakers barely touching the gravel. I arrived at the truck where Billy was dumping garbage from a nearby house into the truck and eagerly awaiting my report.

"Well," he said. "Wath Mith Nudey-Pie out lounging in her yard with her daithieth on dithplay?"

"No," I lied. "No Miss Nudey-Pie. No daisies. Nothing."

Billy considered me with suspicion. "Tho where ith the garbage then?"

I stared at him in silence. I couldn't tell Billy what I had seen. And I was torn between being aroused by my Technicolor memories of Mrs. Anita Packington in the buff—and heeding the distant but still audible Sunday school voices from my childhood that warned against the "lust of the flesh" and "unnatural acts" that surely included seeing Lyla's mother bone-naked and worse, savoring the sight.

"Thweet Jeethuth," Billy said. "Tippy Toeth, you're a lyin' thack of thit, aren't you?" He picked up his carry can and headed down the Packington's driveway. "I'm goin' down to thay hello to my Mitith Nudey-Pie—that ith if you didn't frighten her away," he said over his left shoulder. "You jutht keep humpin' down the road. And, oh yeah, you might try jumpin' up and down to thee if you can get thothe tiny tethticleth of yourth to drop."

Chapter 21: The Special Job

Several weeks had passed since Zeus' sucker-punch at Flat Rock, and we resumed bantering when we worked together. But something was missing in the relationship, and that something was not hard to identify: It was the step back I'd taken after my attempt at friendship had been rejected with a hard right I could still feel in my jaw when I chewed my hash browns at the Greasy Wrench. I left it to Zeus to pick the topics for discussion on anything concerning his family or future. On this Friday afternoon, he talked about his brother Darnell, who lived in Las Vegas, and was obsessed with a showgirl with the intriguing name of Chastity. Zeus said Chastity actually was a stripper who had two children who Darnell tucked into bed at night while Chastity pursued a show biz career—a career that Zeus said was heavy on the "show" and was really about giving Darnell the business.

Zeus recounted a recent phone conversation with his "idiot brother" as we stood at the back of the truck and watched the great blade scoop the trash we had gathered from the houses around us. It was something we saw countless times every day but never lost its ability to mesmerize. Something about the way the blade took what seconds before had been loose and free and then swept it up and compressed it with mysterious might into a massive block of orange rinds, broken furniture, tuna cans, newspapers, grass clippings and coffee grounds demanded to be studied, respected and perhaps even worshiped.

Zeus sensed the boss's presence before I did. He emptied his carry can, and then straightened as if he'd been jolted with electricity. His beard bristled like that of Charlton Heston's Moses on the mountaintop in the fiery presence of The Almighty. Except that Benjamin Willard III was neither welcome nor divine, and he always brought bad news.

"Halloo there, boys," he said. "How's it going today?"

"As you can clearly see, we've got another block to go and we're done for the day," Zeus said.

The boss glanced at the Timex on his fat, freckled left wrist.

"It's 2:45 p.m.," he said. Then he paused, as if to emphasize the obvious. "You still have got an hour and 15 minutes left on your shift," he added.

"Very good, Benjie. What do you want us to do? Drive around the block and check to see if anyone has thrown anything new away? Have tea with the ladies in the neighborhood?"

The boss smiled, as if he were doing us a favor by overlooking the loss of what would probably be 10 or 15 minutes of work by the time we finished the route and got back to the garage.

"I was stopping by to give the two of you a chance to earn some extra money Saturday. There's a home out by the old cannery near Wilton that needs to be cleared out tomorrow. The owner died—an old lady—and her kids want to put it on the market."

"How much are you paying?" Zeus said.

"Two-hundred bucks cash," the boss said. "You divide it with Tippy Toes however you want."

"How much do you keep, Benjie?"

Benjamin Willard III's fingers tightened on the clipboard and his face pinked. "That," he said through tight lips, "is proprietary information."

"That's bullshit," Zeus said. "You don't even know what proprietary means. You've screwed over every driver on this crew by payin' 'em dogshit money for extra jobs that make you buckets of money. Then you try to keep it secret, but we find out. We always find out."

The boss squirmed, and the pink in his face ran down his neck and began turning red. Zeus glared, but it was clear that Benjie's offer was tempting. "All right," Zeus said, shaking his head back and forth. "We'll do the job."

The boss beamed and extended a moist right hand, which Zeus ignored. "Benjie," Zeus said, turning to pick up his carry can, "You better not be screwing us over."

But Benjamin Willard III was already gone. We saw the back of his big fat head and his blue pickup turning the corner.

"Asshole," Zeus said.

Zeus and I met early Saturday morning at the Greasy Wrench for breakfast and to meet the boss, who would take us to the special job. Despite his misgivings about the house cleanup, Zeus was in a bristling fine mood. Delores was in splendid form as well. She kept our coffee cups filled and teased me about making Pickles look bad by working on a Saturday. "Seems like you never take a day off, either," I said.

"I take all the time off I need in my head," she said. "Right now I'm in Jamaica sitting in a bikini on a balcony overlooking a big blue swimmin' pool."

"Where's Pickles in that picture?" Zeus asked.

"He's the pool boy and he's cleaning the pool with a net on a big ol' pole."

"Delores," Zeus said, leaning forward and working his fingers through the morning snarls in his beard, "would you please tell me exactly what it is you see in Pickles?"

"I just told you if you were paying attention," she said. Then she glanced at me. "I forgot there was a youngster present," she said.

"I'm 18 and ready to hear anything," I said.

"No you ain't, honey," Delores said, patting me on the shoulder. "No, you ain't."

~ ~ ~

A half-hour later Zeus and I pulled up to the house we'd been hired to clean, a run-down home with a fake-brick facade on the front. The door was unlocked, and we walked inside through a busted screen door, and saw in the living room a stained brown couch and a faded green velvet easy chair. Zeus eyeballed the sparsely furnished place with relief and surprise, and drew his fingers through his beard.

The boss pulled in behind the garbage truck, got out of his blue pickup, and walked to the front door.

"Gotta admit this doesn't look too bad," Zeus said. "We should be able to get all this stuff outta here in a couple hours."

"Well, it might take you a little longer," the boss answered. He took out a fat black wallet, removed four $50 bills, and handed them to Zeus who passed two of them to me. "Want to make sure you men get the pay you deserve," Then he glanced at his watch. "Gotta get moving, fellas," he said. At the front door, his plump right hand pushed through one of the gaping holes in the screen. He crashed into the frame, which came partially off its hinges and blocked his path. He disentangled himself, adjusting his cap and ignoring Zeus' guffaws, and strode to his pickup as if nothing had happened.

"Just put that screen door in the garbage with everything else," he called out before leaving.

"Maybe we should put the whole house in the truck," Zeus said. The boss was already in his pickup and pulling away. He gave us a military salute, touching the brim of his hat, and was gone. Zeus surveyed the ratty neighborhood of dilapidated homes that looked a wind gust away from collapse. "This is such a shithole neighborhood it doesn't even have a name," Zeus said.

"Maybe it's called Shithole, and maybe this was the mayor's house," I said.

Zeus ignored me. "You want to know what I hate about places like this?" he said. "They're where people like me end up living the rest of their fucking lives." He looked at me hard and raised a forefinger in my direction, then spoke like an Old Testament prophet. "Listen to me, Jesse," he said. "You get the hell out of Freedom first chance you get."

I started to protest and then shut up, remembering his hard-fisted response to me at the family reunion. If fear of Zeus wasn't the beginning of wisdom, it was an essential ingredient.

Zeus paused from his rant, took a deep breath and gazed at the tree line that marked the distant interstate highway. Then he sighed. "Damn it to hell," he said. "I'm going inside to check the rest of this place out. You bring in the carry cans and shovels from the truck. We'll start with the small shit."

"Hey, Zeus," I said before he turned to enter the house. "Thanks for splitting the money with me."

"Well," he said with a smile. "I figured I owned you one after Flat Rock," he said.

I walked to the truck and put two big flat shovels inside the six stacked carry cans, picked them up, and headed for the house. When I stepped through the broken screen door and went inside, I didn't see Zeus. "Yo, Zeus," I called. "Where do you want me to start?"

No answer.

I set down the barrels and shovels and walked through the kitchen, the soles of my work boots grinding on the gritty linoleum floor, and then into the living room with its ancient, torn green shag carpet. At the end of the room an open door looked as if it led to the cellar, and I figured that was where Zeus must have gone. I walked to the door, peered down the stairs, and inhaled an unexpected breath of warm, sweet, decaying air that reminded me of the landfill. Then I saw Zeus' white T-shirt. He stood part way down the stairs, his back facing me. He was motionless.

My eyes adjusted to the darkness. He wasn't moving for a reason. He couldn't go further. The cellar was filled two-thirds of the way toward the ceiling with great heaping mounds of garbage. The smell was deep and dark and moist and strangely sweet for garbage that had been sitting, molding and compiling for years.

"Holy shit, Zeus," I said. "Holy, holy shit. This is just amazing." I ran out of words.

Zeus turned, eyes rimmed with red fury. "You dumbshit," he said. "We have to haul all this out."

I shook my head. "Gotta be a mistake. Mr. Willard couldn't have known about this—he never would have agreed to do the job."

"He knew. Why do you think he gave us our money in advance? He's probably getting a thousand bucks from the person who hired him for this job. And why do you think he hauled ass out of here before we saw this? In a half-hour he'll be sitting at a bar and laughing about it."

I walked down the stairs and stood next to Zeus. There was just enough light coming through a window well on the far wall that I could see yellowed newspapers, crushed milk cartons, Twinkies' and Mrs. Wagner's Pies' wrappers, grocery bags filled with empty pop cans, and crumpled potato chip bags.

"So where do we start?" I asked.

"You can start anywhere you want," Zeus said. "I'm walking off this job." He turned and stomped up the rickety old stairs with such clomping force I was afraid he might fall through into the garbage pit below. But he made it to the top and I could hear him walk through the house and out the front door, kicking the broken screen as he left and yelling when apparently it sprung back on its one intact hinge to kick him back. Then there was silence.

I took another look at the sea of garbage, then went up the stairs and to the front door. Zeus sat looking disheveled, an unusual sight, in the driver's seat of his garbage truck. The window on the passenger's side was open and I climbed onto the sideboard, emboldened by the realization that the steering wheel and side-view mirror left no clear path for Zeus to visit his wicked right-hand wrath on me.

"So what do you wanna do, Zeus, give the money back?"

"I can't—Totina would kill me." Zeus looked weary and resigned.

I had none of Zeus' beard-curling fury and indignation at our predicament. I was still filled with amazement that someone would fill the basement of their home with garbage. I had never seen or heard of anything like this. Never even considered the possibility that someone might turn their house into a landfill.

"I guess we'll both start in the basement. . .unless you want to do it all yourself," Zeus said. "Screw Benjamin Willard III and his wobbly white ass. If he comes back here we'll bury him in this shit."

Having surrendered to his fate, it took surprisingly little time for the storm clouds to clear from Zeus' head. He devised a system in which we filled the six carry cans we'd brought with us and then dragged them up the rickety stairs and out to the truck, singing, "Heigh ho, heigh ho, it's off to work we go"—the song was my contribution and a fine one—and then flushed the garbage into the truck. By noon, we'd emptied Zeus' truck at the dump—that was 10 tons of garbage, enough to fill a swimming pool. Zeus and I settled into a fine, sweaty rhythm, shoveling and hauling and shoveling and hauling followed by more shoveling and hauling. We talked about anything and everything that came to mind, starting, as garbage men often do, with the female anatomy—a subject on which Zeus held forth at length with professorial expertise and detail.

"Totina is the real thing," he said. "None of that silicone bullshit in those big mamas."

"Iris' are real, too," I said.

"I doubt you'd know the difference," Zeus said.

"Yeah," I admitted with a grin. "To tell you the truth, my experience is severely limited."

Zeus looked up and smiled. "A garbage man with integrity. Now that's a rare thing."

We speculated about the old lady who had owned the house, and we stopped now and then to pull items out of the garbage for clues—empty wine bottles, prescription vials and peach cans—she loved the melbas with heavy corn syrup. There were pizza boxes, most with leftover pieces that the years had turned into what Zeus called "pizza jerky." There were empty cans of tuna fish and dog food. And there were newspapers—great piles of newspapers—along with enough romance novels to fill a library wing.

"I'm thinkin' we might finish before dark," Zeus said midafternoon. "If not, then we're done anyway."

That was when my shovel hit something solid and buried a foot or so beneath the surface.

"There's something down there," I said.

"Yeah, more garbage," Zeus said.

"No, I mean there's really something down there."

I pushed down on the shovel, pulled back the handle and felt something rising through the newspapers, milk cartons, plastic bags and other debris. Then there it was—the furry, desiccated remains of a dog leg that was attached to, God help me, a matted, medium-sized gray dog whose gaping jaws and jagged brown teeth were bared.

"Holy shit," I howled. "What the hell—oh, my God—it's a dead dog."

I threw my shovel down and turned to escape up the stairs. But my pivot foot slipped in the shifting debris, and I fell into the garbage and could feel the dog carcass against my side. "Shit, shit, shit, shit," I screamed. I scrambled to my feet and looked for Zeus, who was standing midway up the stairs, hands on his knees, leaning over so far his long hair covered his face, and laughing so hard he could hardly speak. "Oh, my God," he said. "Oh, my God." That was the best thing I've ever seen. You should have seen your face."

"Screw you, Zeus," I said, struggling to my feet.

"Oh, my God, oh my God," Zeus howled, eyes closed with the pain of laughing.

"Well, I see you were the first one to run up the goddamn stairs," I said.

"Only because you slipped and fell."

It was then that we heard Benjie's truck pull into the gravel driveway. We heard his slow, cautious steps on the linoleum of the entryway above. "Halloo, boys," he called. "Where are you at?" As if he didn't know we were hauling crap from the cellar.

Zeus held a forefinger to his mouth and tiptoed down the cellar stairs.

He took his shovel and slid it under the dead dog's torso, and lifted it with surprising ease. "Spot here is as dry as a bone—hardly weighs anything," he whispered. He ascended the stairs, holding Spot the mummy dog, stiff legs extended, in front of him. We're down here in the basement, Benjie, cleaning up the little mess we found."

The boss was silent, no doubt considering what kind of reception he would get in the cellar from the workers he had deceived. Doing this to "Tippy Toes" was no problem—the entire crew believed that God made summer helpers to exploit. But everyone at Willard Sanitation, including Benjie, understood that Zeus' fury was a rabid genie best left in the bottle.

"We're just coming up for a break, Benjie," Zeus called. "No need to come down here and get your nice uniform dirty." Zeus climbed up the stairs, the mummy dog lifted high for Benjie to see. I walked behind Zeus, recovering from the shock of my archaeological find and eager to find out what mischief percolated in Zeus' brain.

The story of Benjamin Willard III's encounter with Spot the mummy dog was one for the ages—a story told for years and embellished and refined by the crew of Willard Sanitation. It would become an epic tale—with the mummy mutt transforming into a Great Dane and an ambulance summoned to revive a boss who had suffered a heart attack. In one version, Zeus successfully demanded that the boss give us an extra $1,000 for the "pain and suffering" caused by the exhumation of the mummy dog.

None of those things happened. I was there. But the real story was, as is usually the case, better than the invented ones.

Zeus paused at the top of the stairs, hidden by the cellar darkness but able to see that that the boss was standing in front of the cellar door. Then Zeus sprang up the last step, yelling "Hahhhh!" like an attacking samurai and holding Spot the mummy dog in front of him.

Zeus came to a full stop, but his momentum caused the carcass to fly off the end of the shovel—Zeus later insisted that he yelled "Sic him, Spot!" although I don't recall it. All I heard was a low, bewildered moan from Benjamin Willard III as the mummy dog collided chompers-first into the boss's chest. Benjie tumbled backward, moaning, on the kitchen floor, his big soft rump cushioning his fall. His cap flew off as Spot skidded up his chest and came to a rest with his snarling snout and bared teeth resting inches away from the boss's face.

"Oh my God, Benjie," Zeus said, feigning profound concern. "I had no idea you were standing there."

"What the holy hell, Zeus?" the boss howled, wriggling out from under the carcass and rolling to his knees with surprising agility for a fat man. He brushed himself off and looked, eyes squinting, at Zeus.

The Garbage Brothers

Zeus kept a straight face, which clearly was not easy. "Benjie," he said, "I can't tell you how sorry I am." He gestured to me, standing at the top cellar stair. "Tippy Toes here is sorry, too."

"Tippy Toes?" he repeated. "Why would he be sorry?"

Zeus glanced my way, with a "Don't worry—it's-gonna-be-OK" look in his eyes. "He tripped me," he said.

"Tripped you?"

"On my way up the stairs. It was an accident. Either he wasn't looking or couldn't wait to get away from the cellar of trash down there that you didn't tell us about when you got us to agree to do this bullshit job." Zeus paused and then added. "A bullshit job for which you now owe us an extra hundred dollars."

Benjamin Willard III was an incompetent boss but he was no fool. He clearly understood the unspoken deal he had just been offered: In exchange for parting with another $100 from his plump wallet, he would be safe from further retaliation from Zeus—whose legendary wrath could manifest itself in ways ranging from a beating to robbing his boss at gunpoint—for tricking us into emptying a basement filled with garbage.

"You'll finish the job?" the boss asked.

"Yeah—if you give us the extra money and promise you won't fire either of us for turning you into a landing strip for a flying mummy dog," Zeus answered.

The boss winced at "landing strip" and "flying mummy dog"—descriptions that virtually ensured that the story would be circulated and embellished for years to come. "Any chance you'll agree not to tell anyone about this?" he asked.

"Nah," Zeus answered truthfully, shaking his head with a truly evil grin. "Not a goddamn chance of that, Benjie."

The boss shrugged and pulled out his billfold, which was attached by a small silver chain to his Sam Brown belt. He handed Zeus two $50 bills, and Zeus passed one to me. Then Benjie cocked his head and gave me a fatherly smile. "Let's try to be more careful on the stairs next time, son."

I picked up an empty carry can and headed down the stairs to the cellar. "Welcome back to hell, my friend," Zeus said. "We may be doomed but we squeezed another hundred bucks out of that old fart."

"Welcome back to hell, yourself," I said, relishing that Zeus had just called me his friend. I shuffled through the garbage to where I'd unearthed the mummy dog and picked up the shovel that I had thrown down in horror. "You know," I said, "It's just possible that ol' lady might have buried a husband here."

"Dibs on the wedding ring," Zeus said.

Chapter 22: A Poem for Pickles

Pickles and Delores were now an official item at the Greasy Wrench, although Delores kept up the flirtatious banter with the customers, which was good for tips and the closest thing the cafe had to a floor show.

But all was not well at the moment on the Pickles-Delores front. There were, as he confided while driving to a route one rainy August afternoon, "serious complications." They started with his wife, Milicent, whom Pickles had shot in the hip a decade earlier. He did it after finding her in the sack with an insurance salesman at the Pink Flamingo Motor Inn in Freedom right across from the Greasy Wrench Truck Stop. Norman Phillips was the salesman whom Pickles dispatched to the next actuarial world with a couple of blasts from a gun that Milicent had bought for her husband as an anniversary present to protect himself from rabid dogs on the route. "I did kill a dog—just not the kind she expected," Pickles told me. He'd told the jury that he hadn't meant to shoot Milicent, that the bullet that shattered her hip was intended for Mr. Phillips. The jurors believed him, although Milicent understandably remained unconvinced.

Pickles said he still visited his wife on the first Sunday of each month at the Liberty Township Home for the Indigent, where the supervisor had years ago learned that Pickles could not be relied upon for financial support. Milicent had been assigned a second-floor room that looked out over a grove of trees that surrounded a potter's field where Milicent informed Pickles on his visits that she was bound "any day now."

"I guess 'any day' means 'any decade' to Milicent," Pickles said.

"Delores knows about Milicent," Pickles said. But Milicent had not known about Delores until she caught a whiff of what his bedridden wife identified as "a woman's scent" when Pickles gave her a perfunctory peck on the top of her small, unhappy head at the end of his most recent bedside visit. She confronted him on the spot, and Pickles confessed that he'd fallen for another woman and wanted a divorce.

"William, I will sign the papers on the same day you bring me a gun so I can shoot you in the hip," Milicent replied. "And you can tell your little girlfriend she should bring me flowers for saving her from marrying the godawful likes of you." Pickles said Delores didn't take the news of Milicent's refusal well.

As we drove to the dump around noon to empty our first load of the day and then stopped at the Snake Pit, Pickles said that Delores was so angry she threatened to bring Milicent an embroidered pillow as a gift and then smother her with it.

"Why does Delores want to get married?" I asked. "She told me she's already done it once, and it didn't end well."

"Actually she's been married three times, and they all ended bad," Pickles said. "Now that Delores is sober, she wants to get hitched again to convince a judge out in Colorado to give her custody of her boys. I mean she and I are crazy about each other and want to get married, but she really wants to get her boys back."

I considered pointing out that marrying a convicted killer was probably not the best way to convince a judge to grant her custody. But I wasn't sure how Pickles would react. Plus, there was a more immediate problem that needed to be addressed. Pickles said Delores was furious, accusing him of secretly wanting to stay married to Milicent, and she had refused to talk or look at him for the past three days. As a result, Pickles moped in the cab while I picked up all the garbage on his routes.

Pickles was miserable and I was exhausted. It was time for an intervention, and I remembered my attempt to sway the ever-elusive Lyla P. midway through our senior year by reciting a poem I had memorized for Mr. Schmidt's English class. It had gotten me nowhere with Lyla, who broke out laughing before I reached the third stanza, but I thought it might help Pickles win back Delores. Plus, it was the only idea I had.

"A poem," I told him as we pulled away from the Snake Pit. You need a poem to show Delores you love her and make her forget about Milicent and marriage."

Pickles was incredulous. "A poem?" he said. "You think I need a goddamn poem?"

"Trust me," I said. "Women love poetry. Makes them forget their troubles. Delores needs to remember how much you love her—and how much she loves you."

"Well, give me the damn poem then," Pickles said. "I'll try anything."

I had memorized two poems in my life. One was Robert Frost's "Birches," which I always thought was a fine poem. I particularly liked the lines:

"I'd like to get away from earth awhile
And then come back to it and begin over.
May no fate willfully misunderstand me
and half grant what I wish and snatch me away
 Not to return. Earth's the right place for love;

I don't know where it's likely to go better."

But that poem wouldn't work for Pickles, and it certainly wouldn't work for Delores, who might not be sure who Pickles thought might be snatched up not to be put down again. A risky poem for a man who had been convicted of second-degree murder by the state of Illinois.

The second poem, I thought, might actually work on Delores—"work" meaning it would convey the thought that Pickles loved her no matter what. Even if Milicent wouldn't give Pickles the divorce that would allow him to marry Delores.

"Got it," I said.

"Got what?" said Pickles, whose mind had evidently moved on during the time I was weighing poetry options.

"The right poem." We were near the intersection with the highway that led to the dump, and Pickles pulled the truck onto a broad, dusty shoulder under a shade tree.

He put his hands on the steering wheel, and pushed himself back into the driver's seat. The truck idled and Pickles' face looked drained. I realized that this was not an idle game being played out for my amusement. Pickles Peterman was distressed. He really did care about Delores and her desire to be reunited with her twins. If ever a man needed the sweet salve of verse it was Pickles. And here I was a practitioner—young and inexperienced, yes, but willing to be of assistance to my fellow man.

"It's by Robert Burns," I said.

"Don't care who wrote it—just tell me the poem."

"It begins, 'Oh my Luve's like a red, red rose.'"

"Luve?" Pickles said.

"Old Scottish for love. Robert Burns was a Scot. Don't worry, Delores will get it."

"I'm not saying 'luve' to Delores," Pickles said. "Might say 'love' on a good day but never 'luve'."

"OK, just say 'love' instead when you recite it to Delores. Just let me finish the damn poem. It's short."

Pickles lifted a giant's eyebrow at my impertinence and then let it go. He closed both eyes.

"Better be short if I gotta memorize it," he said.

I closed my eyes. And there we were, two garbage men in the middle of the Great Midwest, sitting under a scraggly oak on the side of the road with our eyes closed, waiting for the poem that was in my head, the one I'd memorized from the poetry anthology that I'd despised until I actually opened it one day and read the Robert Burns poem on page 262.

"Oh my luve is like a red, red, rose

That's newly sprung in June:
Oh my luve is like the melodie
That's sweetly played in tune."

I opened my eyes to check on my audience. Pickles cocked his head, as if listening to the summer breeze that wafted through the tree branches hanging over the truck. He nodded his head, lower lip extended in appreciation.

"Not too bad," he said. "Is that it?"

"Nope," I said. "There's more. Here goes—'As fair art thou, my bonnie lass.'"

"Boney?" Pickles interrupted.

"Bonnie. It means beautiful."

Pickles smiled. "Got it," he said.

"As fair art thou my bonnie lass, So deep in luve am I;
And I will luve thee still, my dear
Till a' the seas gang dry."

"Gang means gone," Pickles volunteered.

"Yep."

"Keep goin'," he said. "But it better end soon."

"Till a' the seas gang dry, my dear,
And the rocks melt wi' the sun;
And I will luve thee still my dear
While the sands of life still run.
And fare thee weel, my only luve!
And fare thee weel awhile!
And I will come again my luve,
Tho' it were ten thousand mile."

I could hear that summer breeze still rustling through the oak. After a few seconds, Pickles opened his eyes, and I thought I could see a touch of moisture at the crinkled edge of his right eye. He cleared his throat like an ailing walrus, leaned forward and started the truck. He shifted into first, gassed the engine and the truck jounced onto the highway. He reached over to the glove compartment, took out a battered green notebook and a pencil stub, and handed them to me.

"Write that fucker down," he said.

Chapter 23: The Oven

When I got home from work that afternoon my mother was sitting at the kitchen table with a cup of Lipton tea and a Kleenex box. Always impeccably dressed and styled with a short, tight bouffant that required weekly visits to the hairdresser, my mother was wearing a black pants suit with a jacket that was buttoned despite the summer evening heat. She looked a decade older than her 45 years. They say mothers know their sons, but sons also know their mothers. And I knew mine had something to tell me.

"How was work, Jesse?" she asked in a slow, purposeful voice—the one she used to lay the groundwork for something difficult to come.

"Work was fine, Mother." My friends had all called their mothers "Mom" growing up, but mine insisted on "Mother" because she thought it was more dignified. But my mother didn't look dignified at this moment. Just sad and resolved.

I thought about trying to cheer her up by telling her that I had just taught a love poem to one of the drivers who was in love with a waitress, but I knew she wouldn't appreciate or understand the story, which involved a universe as foreign to her as financial distress had been before my father's death. And I'd never done much confiding in my mother who, like my father, thought parenting was something best done from a proper distance, and was even more distant after my father's passing.

She fixed her eyes on the half-empty tea cup. "I received a full-price offer for the house today, and I have decided to accept."

"OK," I said, absorbing her words and curious to see if the news would set off any emotional depth charges inside me. But there were none. I had already absorbed the blow of my father's death, and my mother had mourned in private, leaving me to grapple alone with the uncertainties ahead. I looked forward to moving on from the tedium of waiting. My mother and I had lived in the home the past two years, and I felt no ties to it. Everything that was meaningful to me—my job, my new friends, Iris—existed outside the house and outside what remained of my sad, disintegrating family. My mental bags were packed. I was ready to leave.

"That's good," I said. "Now you can move to Indianapolis near your sister. That's still your plan, right?"

The Garbage Brothers

"Yes, it's still my plan," she said. "But I want to check to see if you've changed your mind about staying and want to come with me."

I looked at her, and she already knew my answer. We both knew that she didn't want me to go to Indianapolis with her and was asking only because she thought that's what a responsible mother should do. My mother needed to save her life by starting a new one and leaving the old behind. And I was part of the old life that needed—and wanted—to be left behind. It was a right and necessary match, but she needed to be reassured.

"I'm staying here. I'll find a place. I can afford it—the job pays enough."

"It's just a summer job. What will you do when it's done?"

"Either find another job or go to college—or maybe the owner will want me to stay on." The suggestion that I was still hoping to get into college was a lie, and we both knew it. Respectable colleges did not accept high school graduates whose grade-point averages were mired in the "bottom quartile." But my mother and I needed to maintain the lie so that we could move on to whatever awaited us in our respective lives.

"I can help out some when you find a college, but you'll have to apply for scholarships," my mother said. "Have you checked to see if your employer has a scholarship fund for its workers?"

Her suggestion was ludicrous—and her understanding of her son, where he worked, the motley crew of felons and discontents with whom he spent his days—was so naive and clueless that I wanted to laugh. Like the drivers at the Greasy Wrench laughed—so hard I would wheeze and choke and howl artful profanities. But I knew my mother needed to believe she was leaving behind an enterprising son who was going to find a way to succeed in life despite his 18-year failure to provide any indication he was capable of doing so. She couldn't, wouldn't, see me as I was—a summer helper at a sanitation company who didn't have a clue what he was going to be doing in six months—and who was beginning to think a career in sanitation looked pretty good considering the lack of alternatives.

"Don't worry, Mom," I said. "It's all going to work out."

It took two days for me to find a tiny studio apartment near Freedom, a couple of miles from the Greasy Wrench. The room was in a dilapidated two-story house on the shore of Diamond Lake, a decent-sized body of water loved by blue-collar boaters and fishermen. I was disappointed that the apartment's only window looked out on a frontage road and a trailer park on the other side of the street. But at least the thought of the lake was there, along with the sound of outboard motors and the curiously appealing smell of gasoline and dead fish from a dock next door. Despite its flaws, the place met my basic needs, starting with the increasingly urgent need to have a place with a door that locked and curtains that closed where Iris and I could finally be alone.

I borrowed Billy's pickup, and I moved some odds and ends from the house that my mother wasn't taking with her to Indianapolis: a picnic table, a double bed from the guest room, a box of plates and pots and pans, and an old Motorola portable TV, whose red-and-white metal cabinet delivered unnerving shocks when it was turned on and off. Aside from clothes, the only thing I took from my room was a box filled with my favorite books and my father's dagger.

Iris visited on my first night in the new apartment. I invited her to dinner and cooked a hot dog and baked bean casserole, which I embellished with ketchup, chopped onions and thick slices of Velveeta and then baked for an hour in the smallest oven I'd ever seen. When it was hot and bubbling ready, I served it on paper plates, set it out on the picnic table, and poured some Annie Greensprings green apple wine in two Styrofoam cups filled with ice.

"This is a nice place," she said, looking as if she might actually mean it. As we stood by the stove, she took my right hand and then my left, pulled herself to me, and kissed me long and hard. I felt disoriented, unnerved and unsettlingly, deliriously happy. My artful game plan, one that drew heavily from an Esquire magazine article titled "How to Make Sure Your Romantic Evening Ends With Fireworks," was to engage Iris in casual conversation over dinner and then retreat to the couch for deeper, extended and artfully planned foreplay. It went out the window.

Iris walked to the couch—I came with her—whether she drew me along or I floated, I can't remember, and then she pulled off her T-shirt and stepped out of her shorts. "My God, you're not wearing underwear," I said. Then because I didn't know what to say next, I added, "You know the casserole is going to get cold."

She unbuttoned my jeans. "Then we'll just have to put it in the oven," she said.

Chapter 24: Settling In

I walked into the Greasy Wrench the next morning a changed man. But no one noticed. Billy was arguing with Pickles who insisted on taking his vacation the same week as Zeus and now refused to yield to his boothmate. With a mouthful of hash browns, Billy explained to Pickles how seniority worked—employees with the most years on the job got first dibs on vacation time.

Pickles took finger-wagging issue, insisting that "seniority" should be based on the age of employees and pointing out that he was 23 years older than Zeus. Pickles also noted that he worked more years at Willard Sanitation if Billy counted the two years he'd worked there before serving a sentence for what Pickles euphemistically referred to as the "Pink Flamingo incident."

"Those two yearth don't count on your theniority," Billy said. "You had to thtart all over again when Benjie hired you again after you got out of prithon."

"That's jutht bullthit, and you know it," Pickles said. A chill descended. Few topics were off limits at the Willard Sanitation booth, but Billy's lisp was one of them. Company legend was that the drivers had to carry out a former driver who was foolish enough to question the foreman's "thceduling thtupidity" and got knocked cold by Billy, who climbed onto the table where he delivered a kneeling haymaker and was back in his seat and mopping egg yolk off his plate with a piece of toast before the offending party hit the ground.

"Look, I gotta have that week off. I told Delores I'd drive her to Colorado so we can get married and she can ask a judge to give her the boys back," Pickles said.

The bells rang on the door, and we all looked to see if it was Benjie. But it was Grits, who usually was slumped and morosely smoking in his booth seat by this time and whose absence had gone unnoticed. He walked to our booth and stopped in front of me and looked down, the knife on his belt at precisely my eye level. "You wanna tell me why my niece did not get home until 3:30 a.m. last night?"

I looked at the Union Pacific calendar and considered my options— telling the truth about my loss of virginity to his niece not being one of them.

"We just got to talking and lost track of the time, sir," I said. I regretted saying "sir" as soon as the word left my mouth. Zeus sniggered, and Billy and Pickles put their seniority dispute on pause to watch Grits eviscerate Tippy Toes for violating his niece.

"I'm thinkin' it wasn't no talkin' what kept your eyes off the clock," Grits said. "I'm thinkin' it was that somethin' I told you was off limits. Somethin' I warned you to stay away from."

The bells jangled again on the cafe door, and this time it was Benjie, who after one step toward our booth could see the look on Grits' face and paused as if considering a hasty U-turn. "Hey, Benjie," Billy called out, much to my relief. "Would you explain to Pickleth here how the theniority thystem workth? He won't lithen to me."

Delighted to be hailed as a figure of authority for once, Benjie strode with purpose toward our booth. Billy stood and Grits slid into the booth with a glare that made it clear he and I were not done. As Benjie launched into a stultifying discourse on seniority in the workplace, I reflected on the monumental event that had occurred less than 12 hours earlier in my $150-a-month studio apartment on the less-than-pristine shores of Diamond Lake. After 18 years and against all odds, I had finally conquered that most elusive of summits, and I could still feel the lava sloshing up and down my spine. I was indeed a changed man, one who was willing, if necessary, to endure the wrath of Grits.

Eventually peace was restored to the Willard Sanitation booth. Weary of Pickles' pouting and even more weary of Benjie's discourse, Zeus yelled "screw it all anyway" and yielded his scheduled vacation week to Pickles. After a few final sips of coffee, the drivers straggled out of the cafe and headed to the garage.

Billy assigned me to work with him again, insisting that he needed time to prepare me to be a replacement driver in August and September, when most of the drivers took their vacations. His real motive was to get some time with his useless campaign manager. His campaign had gotten off to a slow start, and so far had yet to gain any momentum. The only things I'd done on Billy's behalf were checking out the library book for female political candidates that Billy thought was useless and lacked graphic photos, and tacking a hand-lettered cardboard sign on the "Community Happenings" bulletin board at the Grab and Go Market that read: "Billy B: Hauling Liberty Township to Glory." The store manager promptly removed the sign, explaining that Eldon Kersnocki, who bought the supplies for the cafe at the store, had demanded its removal.

I suggested that Billy consider challenging the incumbent supervisor to debate at the upcoming League of Women's Voters' candidate night at the

The Garbage Brothers

Sydney O. Roxbury High School gym. Billy didn't think much of the idea. "Jutht in cathe you haven't notithed, I have a thlight thpeech impediment," he said. Then there was the additional problem that Billy didn't have much of substance to say about Eldon except that he was "a thutupid thon of a bitch who doethn't know hith thkinny ath from a hole in the ground." The prospect for informative exchanges between the candidates was not promising.

Iris had begun spending evenings at my new apartment and even though two weeks had passed since Grits confronted me at the Greasy Wrench, he hadn't made good on his lip-curling vow to finish our conversation. She'd lie in bed sketching dress designs in a small black notebook that she told me she hoped would make her rich and famous some day and take her to Paris and Rome. I told her I was certain they would and that I would go with her and write novels in the cafes just like Hemingway. "We'll be the new lost generation," I said.

"Well," she responded, the eraser of her pencil poised at the side of her soft sweet lips, "Truth is we're already pretty lost here in Freedom. We don't have to go to Paris to do that."

Neither of us knew how to cook, and our attempts fell short of French cuisine. My specialties were mostly variations on the hot-dog casserole—lately I had been adding red wine and chopped onions and we agreed that it added a certain zest. In a bold culinary experiment, Iris bought a whole raw chicken at Gary's Grab and Go and dropped it in a pot of boiling water, one of its legs extending out of the water as if it were trying to hitchhike out of town.

We were two kids happily playing house—so happy that we were only momentarily distracted by Grits' muffler-challenged pickup, which rumbled past the apartment at least once each evening. Iris' VW bug was parked outside my apartment—there was nowhere to hide it. And always, there was fear that Grits would stop and that we would hear his footsteps, and then the whack of his Louisville Slugger breaking down my flimsy front door. But so far he hadn't stopped, and the danger only served to fuel our passion. Afterwards we'd go for walks by the lake, often stopping by the Lakeside Lounge, where we would drink Dr. Peppers in the smoky darkness and listen to pool balls clack and Merle Haggard on the jukebox. Then we would go back home and disappear into each other.

My next-door neighbor, beyond two layers of the thinnest, cheapest wall anyone could build, was a woman named Elsie Mondenhoofer. Elsie was 70 going on 95 with a tiny bun of thinning metallic gray hair and an endless supply of house-dresses and plush pink slippers that she wore when she shuffled daily at 4 p.m. to the Lakeside Lounge for two full-to-the-brim shots of apricot brandy and two packs of Kools.

When Elsie wasn't at the Lakeside Lounge or at the market next to it that stocked the vanilla pudding and bacon on which she subsisted, she was at home ensconced in a reclining chair with numerous burn holes on the cushions from the ashes of her cigarettes. I knew about the burns because one night I heard her screaming that her recliner was on fire. I yanked on my jeans and ran shirtless into her apartment—she always left the front door cracked open to air out the smoke—and by the time I arrived she had already put out the recliner fire by smothering it with the bottom of the same frying pan in which she cooked her bacon and which she rarely washed. That, in turn, set the grease on fire inside the pan, which I grabbed from her hand and threw into the apartment complex's gravel parking lot.

"You didn't have to run over here half naked—I had matters under control," she scolded, and instructed me to fetch the frying pan and put it in her kitchen sink once the flames subsided. Then she went back to watching her favorite TV program, "The Andy Griffith Show," which she liked to watch with her feet up and cigarette smoke whispering like incense from a glass ashtray on her lap. She regarded all the show's characters as family and talked about Andy, Barney, Floyd and Aunt Bee as if they were blood kin.

Every couple of days Elsie brought us two Dixie cups filled with vanilla pudding. "When you two are done in there, why don't you come over with your pudding and watch some TV with me," she told me one night when I answered the door. Iris was in bed hiding under a blanket. But Elsie knew she was there—the paper-thin walls meant she was as familiar with our activities as we were with her TV schedule—and she talked to both of us as if Iris were standing with me at the door. "Bring your little notebook, too, Iris, sweetie," she said. "I want to see those fancy dress designs Jesse told me about."

"OK, Elsie," Iris said from underneath the blanket. "How's the swelling in your ankles today?" Elsie suffered from swelling of the joints, and her ankles were the most afflicted. "Well," Elsie answered, "I think I feel well enough to beat you in a footrace to the Lakeside."

Iris peeked from under the blanket and grinned at Elsie. "We gonna run barefoot or in pink slippers?" she asked.

"Pink slippers, honey," Elsie said. "A lady doesn't go anywhere without proper footwear."

Chapter 25: The Secret Weapon

The Liberty Township election was three weeks away when Billy informed me that he would soon unveil a "thuper-thecret thurprithe weapon," one he was certain would propel him to victory over the incumbent Eldon Kersnocki and ensure Billy's righteous accession to the pinnacle of political power in Liberty Township.

As his marginally engaged campaign manager, I pointed out that I should know his plan, but Billy would have nothing of it. He dismissed my inquiries with a wave of his hand and a demonic grin of reassurance. "Don't you be worrying about thingth beyond your limited underthanding, Tippy Toeth," he said.

I wasn't really worried, just curious. I suspected that the surprise had something to do with a locked storage area at the back of a second, smaller Willard Sanitation Quonset hut, in which Billy worked on the trucks after the other drivers had finished their routes and gone home.

Pickles, Grits and Zeus avoided the place unless their truck needed repair or they wanted to check out a nudie mag from Billy's library. I also avoided Billy's lair, and entered only when the boss caught me trying to leave work before the end of my shift and sent me to see if Billy needed help. But there was little I could do to help, since I was mechanically impaired and Billy knew it. Every time I touched anything—looked into a tool box or reached for a rag—Billy told me to "run along like a good boy and find thome other plathe to play."

On one afternoon when Benjie sent me over to help Billy, he was nowhere to be seen. I figured he had walked up to the Greasy Wrench for a slice of apple pie and to gaze at Delores' hindquarters. Then I saw that the sliding door to a storage area that was usually padlocked was partially open. I could glimpse Billy inside moving around carrying what looked like two large flood lamps, one in each hand, electrical cords dangling from each.

"Hey Billy—what's going on?" I called out.

He froze in place, put down the lights and stepped out of the storage area. "Tippy Toeth," he said. "You thpying on your old Billy?"

"The boss sent me to see if you needed help greasing trucks," I said. "What were you carrying?"

"Nothin'," he said. "You jutht mind your own buthineth."

"Was it the secret election surprise you were telling me about?" I asked.

"Lookth can dethieve," he said, and he closed the door to the storage area and padlocked it. He turned and faced me, and there was an unsettling gleam in his eyes.

"I can take care of greathing the truckth," he said. "Jutht you go on home and thee about greathin' your thweety."

Chapter 26: The Box

At the beginning of each month, Willard Sanitation Service picked up a single, neatly sealed bag of trash at an oak- and elm-shadowed ranch house near the end of Old Sloan Road. There were few signs of activity at the house, and it seemed as if the people who lived in it were either away or hiding inside. The house was built of red brick that retained the day's warmth against the evening chill. The dark green shutters on the windows were always closed. The big yard of bluegrass, the kind that grows thick and strong even in the shade, looked as if a neighbor kid mowed it and didn't give it the attention it once received.

The house was on one of Pickles' routes. There were few neighbors, and most had weekly pickups. When I asked why this house had garbage service just once a month, Pickles said he didn't know. "They're old folks—I've seen 'em once or twice. Maybe they're gone a lot visiting family. And some people just don't make much garbage," he told me as we backed down the driveway on a warm late summer morning. "Why do you even think about such things?" he said. "All you need to worry about is emptying that can next to the garage so we can keep it moving and not spend the whole day yappin' about 'Why this?' or 'Why that?' "

The truck slowed, I opened the door, swung out onto the running board and stepped onto the asphalt driveway, my newly washed Converse sneakers gripping the surface. Iris had washed them the day before at a laundromat in a bout of domesticity that felt as good as the warmth of the concrete I felt beneath the thin rubber soles of my shoes.

A few loping steps and I was behind the truck, gesturing to Pickles to keep coming, turn his wheels a little more to the right and then go slower and now, my right hand emphatically extended, to come to a full stop. Pickles ignored my directions, and for good reason. Even after three months on the job, my ability to guide a driver wasn't great and my false confidence and the compensatory command with which I attempted to direct drivers didn't help. Pickles, Grits, Billy and Zeus—they all knew this about me, and my directions were, depending on the moment and the particular risks to life and property involved, a source of both amusement and aggravation.

But on this day, midway through my unheeded gesturing, I was distracted by a long black footlocker standing on its end next to the trash barrel. And taped on it was an index card with four words written in a precise hand: "Please take. Thank you."

Pickles saw the footlocker in the rearview mirror, and he was out of the truck and walking stiffly to the back of the truck seconds after pulling on the emergency brake. It was the siren call of the picker, the mystery load that no garbage man, even the most veteran, could resist. "OK, sonny boy," Pickles said. "Let's have a look-see."

I dragged the heavy footlocker to the rear of the truck, picked it up by the leather handle on each end, and put it on the flat ridge of the trough. The brass clasp was locked and there was an additional strip of duct tape wrapped around the box, a pathetic attempt at ensuring privacy that neither Pickles nor I dignified with a comment. I balanced the box on the edge of the trough as he lowered the blade just enough to apply the pressure needed to spring the clasp.

"Well, open the box," Pickles said.

I glanced at the house and there was no sign of movement. Still I felt uneasy, even though my months of working as a garbage man taught me that drivers uniformly viewed the flagrant disregard of social norms as a sacred perk of the trade. Everything that entered the garbage flow was fair game for viewing, fondling and confiscation—from Polaroid nudie shots in a Holiday Inn dumpster to half-empty vials of prescription meds to—and especially—discarded purses, which got a thorough searching and shaking for hidden cash or jewelry.

"Maybe we should do this somewhere else," I said. "This doesn't feel right."

"No one can see us, and there's probably no one at home. So open the goddamn box or get out of my way."

I lifted the lid, and inside were several rows of impeccably folded and packed clothing—blue pressed dress shirts, a half-dozen dark ties, a canvas belt, an Air Force garrison hat neatly folded in half, and a pair of promisingly large black Oxford shoes that Pickles grabbed and leaned against one of the truck's rear tires to try on. There was a manila envelope filled with official looking papers, all with a military precision. I pulled out a handful, and there was a gray-and-blue certificate recognizing the graduation of Lt. James B. Andrews from flight school in Galveston, Texas. Underneath it were commendations for marksmanship, fitness and navigation, and under that a letter assigning Lt. James B. Andrews to a flight squadron at Da Nang Air Base in August, 1964.

"This is military stuff," I said. "Air Force."

"Do ya' think, numbnuts?" Pickles said, and he reached into the box and pulled out the light blue hat, which he comically perched on his giant head and took a couple of preening, saluting strides as if he were on parade. He looked into the bottom of the box and his eyes lit up. He pulled out a leather flight jacket lined with lamb's wool, and on the chest the name Flight Lt. James Andrews.

"Jesus," Pickles said. "It's a fuckin' gold mine," and he put the medium-sized jacket over his massive upper body. It was a tight fit that scrunched his shoulders together and caused his big belly to stick out even more than usual. "Waddya think?" he said.

"You look like a St. Bernard in a little poodle coat," I said.

Pickles feigned a wounded look, stood tall, the bottom of the coat falling down his stomach, and did a surprisingly nimble jig that ended with one hand crooked over his head and the other cradling the bottom of his belly. Then he wriggled out of the flight jacket and carried it back to the truck cab. "Just dump the rest of this and no more pickin'," he said. "We need to get moving." I grabbed three of the blue shirts and the belt, and tossed them in the passenger window of the cab. Then I opened the trash can, grabbed the single black plastic bag, tossed it next to the open footlocker and pulled the lever that sent the great compactor blade into action. I watched as it sliced the box in half, making a sound like the crushing of dry bones.

It was a 10-minute drive on a winding rural road to the next neighborhood. I climbed up on the left front fender, straddling a mounted turn signal and resting my feet on the bumper. Pickles extended a long arm holding the flight jacket out the window. "Here," he said, "you take it. It don't fit my fat body."

"Thanks," I said, reaching back to take the gift. Pickles had never given me anything before, and he was known for jealously guarding his driver's hoard. His work locker was crammed with his pickings, and so, his fellow drivers said, was his room at the Pink Flamingo where he resided when he wasn't spending the night at Delores' apartment in Wilton.

"You sure about the jacket?" I said. "Put it on, Eddie Rickenbacker," he said. "Wait a minute," he added, and he handed me a pair of swimming goggles that he had fished from the stash he kept in the truck.

I put on the jacket, which felt comfortable despite the summer warmth. Then I put on the goggles and turned and saluted Pickles, who stared at me, shook his head no and for some reason didn't salute back.

"C'mon," I yelled. "Ready for takeoff."

Pickles pointed with his index finger at the front of the truck. I turned around and there was a Ford station wagon, tan with brown trim, parked on the street. And getting out of the car was a tall, thin woman with gray hair and a look on her face that seemed a million miles away. She looked neither amused nor angry. She was barely present at all, and she held out her right arm, palm up.

"My son's flight jacket, please," she said.

I slid off the front of the truck, walked 20 yards to the car and handed it to her. I took off Pickles' swim goggles and they dropped to the ground.

"Thank you," she said. Her eyes focused on me, sharpened and then focused again. "That footlocker belonged to my son. I set it out to be disposed of, not to have its contents taken."

"I am sorry," I said, and it was the gospel truth. So sorry and so ashamed that I wanted to stare at my feet and nothing else. But I could not avert my eyes from her gaze.

"I took three shirts—they're in the truck," I said. "Do you want them back?"

She shook her head. And there was, maybe, just the hint of a smile. "No," she said. "You may keep them. You seem like a nice young man."

She folded the flight jacket in half, and then in half again, almost as if folding a flag. I returned to the truck and got into the cab with Pickles, who pulled slowly out of the driveway and on to Old Sloan Road.

I looked at Pickles and started to speak but stopped. He was staring up through the windshield at the treetops that extended over the roadway. There was just a hint of color in the leaves. Fall was coming.

Chapter 27: Encounter at the Snake Pit

I didn't know exactly why Zeus disappeared into a black funk. But I knew better now than to try to come to his rescue. Besides, I'd seen all the drivers descend into the abyss, although Zeus and Pickles did so with greater frequency and longevity. Even Benjamin Willard III suffered occasional bouts of lasting malaise, which Billy diagnosed as marital in origin—"Lookth like Benjie hath a thevere cathe of blue ballth again," he would say. Billy was the only crew member who seemed immune to the dark visitor, and his irrepressible cheerfulness only made things worse for suffering colleagues. Sometimes it was hard to tell whether he was trying to help or mock the afflicted. "You are my thunthine, my only thunthine, you make me happeeee when thkies are gray," he serenaded the sullen and silent Zeus one morning at breakfast. Zeus responded by flicking a half-eaten piece of bacon at Billy, which the foreman devoured without hesitation.

It took two weeks before Zeus finally started speaking again, and I learned that his malaise was preceded by the departure of his wife and daughter. Zeus confided the development to me as we stopped for lunch at the Snake Pit after a late-morning dump run. Totina had taken Lily with her to live with her parents in Carbondale a few hours' drive to the south, where the "flat-topped old fuck," as Zeus called his wife's father Vern, ran a thriving insurance business. According to Zeus, Vern spent his days scheming how to make Zeus' miserable life even more miserable. "That man doesn't sleep in a bed at night. He hangs by his little claws from the ceiling of a cave while he dreams up new ways to mess with my life," Zeus said.

"Why does he want to mess with your life?" I asked. In the background, I could hear the clack of pool balls at the opposite end of the Snake Pit. We sat at the far end of the bar, keeping our distance from the other drivers who were eating—and drinking—their lunch.

"He says I have a dead-end job and that's because I'm a dead-end felon," Zeus said. "It's not like the self-righteous asshole never ripped anyone off by selling them bogus insurance policies they don't need."

Even though the departure of his family was bad news, I was relieved Zeus had opened up to me. I listened, watching his fingers burrow into that great beard. Waiting for him to tell me more.

"The man squeezes my balls hard and never misses a chance to ask about the money I owe him. Always asks when I'm going to pay him back. And to say he knows I never will, so he says, 'Never mind, just let me know the next time you're going to come begging for more money so I can make sure I'm out of town and put a sign in the window that says go to hell you good-for-nothing loser.'"

"You owe Totina's father money?"

"Yeah, I owe the asshole a lot of money, but most of it went to pay for clothes for his daughter and a couple of business opportunities that went bad."

"Business opportunities?"

"The old man loaned me a thousand to set up my brother and me in a body shop in my garage, and Darnell drove the business into the ground and went to Vegas with the money that was left, which wasn't much. And then goddamn Vern wants his money back like nothing happened and my brother wasn't the big jerk-off that he's always been."

"What was the other?"

"The other what?"

"Other business opportunity. You said he backed you on two business opportunities."

"Yeah, there was another. But we ain't gonna talk about that," Zeus said. He dug into his jeans and pulled out a wrinkled wad of one-dollar bills and put it on the bar top. "I got lunch," he said.

Ernie shuffled over and picked up the plates. "Keep the change," Zeus said, as he stood and stretched, and I noticed, for the first time since I had started working with him, that there was a grease stain on the front of his T-shirt.

Ernie counted the bills and put them in the pocket of his white apron. "Gee, you want me to keep all 30 extra cents?" he said. "You sure you can afford that?"

Zeus picked at his beard and, for the first time since the onset of his black funk, looked mildly amused. "Yeah," he said. "I should have left you a silver dollar to see if it would fit up your puckered ass where you keep the rest of your Florida stash, Ernie."

Ernie gave Zeus a gnarled, arthritic finger, and Zeus returned it. We headed through the dimly lit bar for the front door, and passed a half-dozen leather-wearing Renegades standing around a pool table. One of them I recognized as the man who Grits had warned me was a drug dealer and a bad ass of the first order—Largo was his name. They watched us leaving. Zeus paused just before we reached the door. "Wait in the truck. I'll be out in a minute," he said.

I opened the entrance to the Snake Pit, and the noon light streaked into the room. I stepped squinting into the heat, the highway traffic noise and the rattle and clank of garbage trucks pulling in out of the dump across the street and on to the highway. Putting a hand over my eyes to shield the light, I saw a blue Ford truck winding along the dirt road that led from the dump where the bulldozers created fragrant moonscapes. It looked like Pickles' truck, but I wasn't sure.

The Snake Pit's front door was solid and thick—Ernie apparently experienced more than his share of break-ins over the years. It was solid oak, and was an impressive barrier. Yet I heard, despite being several steps into the parking lot, the sounds of a sudden ruckus inside—a yell, and then a cracking, rumbling sound as if a heavy chair had been dropped on the floor.

I turned and went back, opening the heavy door slowly, cautiously peering inside. At first, I couldn't see anything as my eyes adjusted again to the dimness. Zeus was crumpled on the floor. Several drivers stood from their bar stools. Zeus, with his long hair and beard, was a frequent object of speculation and derision by his fellow drivers. But, by God, he was their object of speculation and derision. Yet none of the drivers was eager to start a fight with the Renegades, and the two groups—garbage men and gang members—had maintained an uneasy peace for years.

Largo stood over Zeus, holding up a pool cue. Then he knelt next to him and leaned down to talk softly into his ear, as if comforting a fallen sibling, as other gang members and drivers looked on.

Largo's eyes lifted to me and the light streaming in the open door. "You want something, kid?" he said. I shook my head no, and I let the door close behind me. Zeus reached up and grabbed the side of the pool table and tried to pull himself to his feet, but Largo put the butt of his pool cue on Zeus' chest, pushed him down and raised his forefinger in warning. Then the door opened behind me and the light cut into the room like a knife, and there was a shift in the air. The person who entered cleared his throat; the sound broke my stupor. A huge hand was on my shoulder, and a familiar, booming voice said, "What the hell's going on here?" Every head in the room turned to see who was speaking.

"Will you please get out of my way, Tippy Toes?" Pickles said. "You are blocking the darkness."

I moved to one side—actually I wasn't sure whether I moved or was picked up and set off to one side by Pickles, who strode without the slightest hesitation toward Zeus. Like John Wayne wading ashore at Normandy on D-Day.

Everyone in the bar froze, including Largo who lifted the pool cue off Zeus' chest and took two quick steps back along with the rest of his crew.

Pickles approached Zeus and helped him to his feet. As Zeus stood there wobbling and trying to find his balance, I saw a large—and startlingly purple—raised welt on his forehead where he had been struck by the pool cue. A trickle of blood ran down from a cut above his right eye. Zeus' assailant looked dispassionately at Pickles who was twice as big as him and who now took in the scene with amusement.

"Why Zeus," Pickles said, "can't you play pool with your business associates without falling down and giving yourself a boo boo?"

There was a rustling in the kitchen, and Ernie emerged. He was holding a baseball bat with both hands and he stood at the bar, lifted the bat and brought it down with a moderate thwack meant to be more impressive than it was.

"KNOCK IT...," he roared, pausing to clear a great wad of phlegm from his throat, "... OFF."

"Thank you so much, Ernie. Blessed are the peacemakers," Pickles said. "I'll have a grilled cheese with onions and a bowl of chili. Hold the thumb, please."

Zeus straightened himself out and nodded at Pickles. Then he walked past me, without acknowledging my presence, and out the front door. The door closed behind Zeus, and I stood in exactly the same place where I'd been standing for the last five minutes—or it might have been five seconds.

Pickles walked toward the bar where Ernie was delivering his chili, thumb inserted to the first knuckle. Then Pickles cocked his head, looked at me and pointed at the entrance. "Tippy Toes," he said. "Ain't never polite to keep your date waiting."

I nodded and walked out the front door. The sound of it closing penetrated my nightmare haze, and I was seized by guilt and remorse that I had not run to the rescue of my driver and friend Zeus. Instead, I'd stood there frozen with the fear of being beaten, stabbed, and crucified. There was nothing, absolutely nothing, I could do to make my feet or even my mouth move as I watched Zeus lying on the floor with his assailant standing over him. And I was gripped by a sad, growing reminder that I was a stranger in a strange and wild land, one in which I knew I did not belong.

When I got to the truck, Zeus was already in the driver's seat, running his finger along the seam of the tape that held his daughter's picture to the dash. He reached over and turned the driver's side rearview so he could see his face. He studied the huge pipe-shaped mound on his forehead. "Motherfucker!" he said to himself. Then he pulled up the neck of his T-shirt to wipe off the blood that ran from his eye down the side of his face.

"Zeus," I said. I paused, resolved to make a full confession. "I'm sorry I didn't help. I just stood there. I couldn't move. I'm so sorry."

"Shut the fuck up, Tippy Toes," he said, still studying his face. "I sent you out to the truck, didn't I? So shut up and don't talk about it any more."

"Zeus, tell me what the hell that was about," I persisted.

Zeus pulled off his T-shirt, used it to dab the cut on his eye, then reached underneath his seat and pulled out one of the clean shirts that he kept tightly rolled in a shoe box. He shrugged it on, turned on the truck ignition, and stuck an unlit cigarette in the side of his mouth. He reached into the ashtray for a lighter and as he held the flame to the tip, I saw his hand shake.

He took a deep inhale and slowly let it out, considering my question. I could see that his lip was also cut but there was no blood. Just a graying pink that showed above the profusion of gold beard into which his fingers had started to burrow.

"Oh," he said with that faraway half smile that was vintage Zeus. "Oh, we were just havin' us a lively debate about the origins of life on planet Earth."

Then he turned the truck onto Highway 40.

Chapter 28: Burnt Velveeta

Iris hadn't fully moved into my apartment, but sometimes it seemed as if she had. She came by most nights after work and, after some flailing passion, we would settle in with our books, bad food and the red-and-white portable Motorola TV that delivered moderate shocks when you turned it on or adjusted the volume—shocks that ran curling up your spine and got you thinking again about more passion. Truth be told, it was the tenderness of it all that I loved the best: the way she fell asleep while sketching fashion designs, her head on my shoulder and her breaths so soft you thought she was a baby.

Iris cooked dinner—she was a horrifyingly bad cook, nearly as bad as her Aunt Mary Rose was good. Iris' favorite was Wonder Bread with burned Velveeta and a dollop of canned chili spooned on top for accent. On special nights, she made tuna casserole, which consisted of a box of mac and cheese with a can of tuna dumped in it along with a can of peas and some potato chips that she mashed using the bottom of a Welch's grape jelly jar.

Thing was, I loved the meals and watching her cook them, moving in the tiny studio kitchen with grace inside her flannel bathrobe that kept me riveted, marveling and conspiring our next encounter, one that sometimes had Elsie Mondenhoofer next door coughing in a none-too-subtle plea for decorum. Then we'd talk into the night: about her sketches of clothing designs and the lecherous manager at the store where she worked; about the books I hadn't written yet but knew I someday would; about traveling to Spain, France, Greece, China—any place we wanted to go. One night I told her that I wanted to climb Mount Kilimanjaro. I made it up as I was talking, but she listened intently as if she believed I might someday actually do it and that I knew more about "Killy," as I called it, than I could half remember from a Hemingway short story.

Now and then reality intruded, and it usually came from Iris' childhood memories. One night she showed me a drawing of a young girl, maybe 12 or 13, riding bareback on a horse. Iris told me she thought it was what her little sister Patsy looked like now. After their mother went to prison for check fraud, Patsy had disappeared into the state of Tennessee's foster care system and Aunt Mary Rose said she'd heard the girl eventually had been adopted by

The Garbage Brothers

an Adventist family in Gatlinburg. Iris didn't know her sister's new last name, but finding it, and someday finding Patsy, were at the top of the list of things Iris intended to do someday. It was her Kilimanjaro.

Often Iris stayed the night, and when she did sleep was a long time coming. We'd lie in bed long past the time Elsie had turned off her TV next door—our neighbor liked to watch Johnny Carson although she had a hard time staying awake past what she called the "moneylogue" and she thought the band leader had the look of a "hardened homosexual." Somewhere, somehow I would fall asleep in the middle of a soft conversation. Then, usually around 2 a.m., I would hear a truck pulling out of the Lakeside Tap and coming toward the apartment, and hope it wasn't Grits' pickup, which had a hole in the muffler and sounded like a ball-peen hammer on an oil drum. The kind of oil drum in which the body of a young man could be stuffed if the limbs had been severed.

Chapter 29: "Where's Zeus?"

Zeus was never the first driver to show up at the Greasy Wrench. That honor belonged to Billy, who arrived almost without exception at 4:30 a.m., just a couple of minutes after Delores opened the joint. Pickles arrived next, although he was, as Delores often noted, present in body only.

Any flicker of spirit or animation did not appear for another half-hour until he had smoked several cigarettes and downed four cups of coffee laced with cream and sugar while staring at the Union Pacific calendar. The next crew member to arrive usually was Grits, although his spectral presence barely stirred the air, and he too preferred silence to engaging with either the beaming Billy or the catatonic Pickles. Zeus was always the last to slide into the booth, usually in just enough time to order breakfast and chat up the crew before the boss arrived for the morning briefing.

But on this morning, just one day after the Snake Pit incident, Zeus had not appeared by the time Benjamin Willard III showed up with his clutch of complaint slips.

"Anyone know where Zeus is?" the boss asked.

"Probably got his head caught between his wife's big titties," Grits said, then mumbled something inaudible across the table to Pickles, who blew a soft wall of smoke and said nothing. None of the other drivers seemed to know that Zeus' wife and daughter had left town, and Pickles' silence cued me to say nothing about the previous day's incident at the Snake Pit. That was fine with me; I did not want to explain why I hadn't done anything to help Zeus. How I'd been too frightened even to run away.

The boss gazed across the highway at Gary's Grab and Go parking lot, where Zeus usually parked his beat-up GTO. "Don't see his car," he said.

"Very good, Benjie," Grits said. "That would probably explain why he's not sitting here waiting for you to hand out all your little blue slips and drive us all crazy."

Benjie proceeded to hand out all his little blue slips. Billy had a rare no-blue-slip day, and he beamed as Grits and Pickles gave him middle-finger salutes. Pickles had his usual half-dozen customer complaints, including one from a Mrs. Hoover who said he had refused to take the washing machine that her husband had trundled to the curb despite his neuralgia and doctor's orders to restrain from such arduous activities. Mrs. Hoover added that Pickles made matters worse by taking the hand truck that her husband used to take the washer to the curb while leaving the washing machine behind.

"You are supposed to take anything that the customer leaves at the curb," Benjie said.

"What if somebody leaves a bomb at the curb—or a body? Am I supposed to take those, too?" Pickles inquired.

Benjie ignored the question and pocketed the remaining blue slips. "Well, I think it's time to get to work, gentlemen," he said. Billy stayed seated, palms upturned. "Tho what we gonna do about Theuth'th route?" he said. "If he don't thow up, who'th going to do it?"

"Can you pick it up today?" the boss asked Billy, who shook his head an emphatic, dramatic no. "Got downtown Wilton today," he said. "Thath a killer. No way I can pick up a thecond route."

The boss's beady eyes shifted to Pickles. No, he couldn't do it either. "Really would love to help you out Benjie, but I've got an appointment with my podiatrist at 3:30 p.m. for an inflamed bunion," he said. Benjie turned to Grits. "Hell, no," the thin man said. "Not with my hemorrhoids acting up the way they've been."

Billy shook his head, grinning at Grits. "Your hemmorhoidth?" he said. "You are a fuckin' hemmorhoid."

"You know, Benjie," Pickles observed. "You could get your nice little uniform dirty for a change." The boss nervously grinned, as if he'd just heard a risque joke. Then his eyes landed on me.

"Tippy Toes," he said. "You should know the Rivergreen route by now."

I nodded, more to be agreeable than out of any conviction. I'd done the Rivergreen route with both Billy and Zeus maybe a dozen times. But the route—the turns, the houses that were twice-a-week pickups and the ones that were once-a-week—were a blur. And I had yet to drive a truck more than half a block on any of the routes.

"Sure," I said. "No problem."

Chapter 30: Fire in the Hole

I pulled Zeus' green Chevy, the oldest and smallest truck in the Willard Sanitation fleet, out of the garage, the engine coughing and the dumpster chains slapping against the empty truck body as the front wheels cleared the potholed entrance. I extended my right arm, as I had watched Zeus do, to wedge his transistor radio between the dashboard and the windshield. And as I did so I saw the photo of Zeus' daughter taped to the dashboard, and I wondered if Zeus had left town to find his family. Then I remembered the massive purple welt on his forehead, and hoped that Zeus had not suffered a brain hemorrhage and that he wasn't lying helpless, or worse, on the floor of his lonely house. And I hoped, most of all, that he hadn't gone back to the Snake Pit.

I checked the rear views on both sides and was relieved to see the garage's front entrance still intact. Then I gave the "Green Goddess," as Zeus called his truck, a punch of gas and pulled onto the gravel drive that led to the Greasy Wrench. I was hoping to see Zeus' GTO pulling into Gary's Grab and Go parking lot where he left it on workdays. But another part of me hoped he wouldn't show and deprive me of the chance to experience the glories of being a driver. I shifted into second, double-clutching as I'd watched Zeus do hundreds of times. I hadn't picked up the garbage at a single home or business as a solo driver, but it felt as if I was no longer a summer flunky and was now becoming a goddamn knight in the service of goddamn Willard Sanitation Service.

Sure, it was my first time soloing, but I was pretty sure I could figure everything out. After work I often sat in the trucks parked in the garage and practiced running through the gears. I'd worked with Zeus and the other drivers on all of the routes. I knew how to empty a truck at the dump, and had even done it once for Billy while he visited with Bruce the backhoe guy and checked out the first-ever full-color edition of Australian Women's Nude Volleyball. And Zeus had shown me how to look good for the ladies, pressing the meat of my upper arm against the outside of the driver's door so it looked even more muscular and manly than it already was.

My driver reverie was shattered by a thudding on the passenger door. I looked to my right and saw a khaki cap bobbing up and down, and under

The Garbage Brothers

it a couple of inches of pink forehead. I stopped the truck and a sweating Benjamin Willard III pulled himself up on the running board and peered inside the cab with a look of consternation.

"Jesus Christ," he said. "Didn't you hear me yelling at you to stop back there?"

"No, sir, I didn't hear anything," I said. The boss looked like he might say more but instead he handed me a half-dozen blue customer-complaint slips intended for Zeus and a pink special order—I was supposed to empty a half dozen burn barrels at the shooting range and Ryerson Family Hunt club off Raccoon Lane. Did I know where that was and could I take my head out of my ass long enough to make sure that I picked up the extra stop?

Yes, I assured him with measured, professional calm. I could manage everything and anything. The boss stepped off the running board, and I pulled out on Highway 40 in front of an oncoming car that swerved into the next lane to miss me as the driver laid on the horn. I gave the driver a finger—a mandatory garbage-truck driver response for all motorist grievances—and then I realized that I had missed the Highway 20 turnoff for Zeus' route. I flipped on the turn signal, checked the rearview mirror and turned into the Jaguar Gentlemen's Club parking lot to turn around. I glanced across the street, and I saw the boss standing in front of the Greasy Wrench, hands on his hips, staring at me and wondering where the freaking blue blazes I was going. I cut through the Gary's Grab and Go parking lot and turned onto Highway 20, grinding the gears as I shifted.

Despite my rough start, the morning went surprisingly well. Billy and Zeus, who worked the Rivergreen route on alternating days, had taught me well. I remembered the streets, the turns, the stops, and where the cans and dumpsters were located. I worked both sides of the street, loping between houses, draping the carry can casually over my shoulder just like Zeus. I wore the new leather kid gloves that he kept tucked under the driver's seat, and I kept my T-shirt clean, more or less, although I knew it was filthy by Zeus' standards. I waited for the boss to show up with Zeus, looking sheepish and hungover in the passenger seat of the boss's blue pickup, his gray carry can in the back. But it didn't happen; I was on my own.

Midmorning, I drove into the back gate of the Ryerson Family Hunt Club, where I found, just as the pink ticket Benjie had given me indicated, six 50-gallon barrels filled to the brim with ashes. Before I dumped them, I put my palms on top of each to make sure they weren't hot. Billy, Pickles, and the other drivers insisted that I stick my arm in the barrel all the way down to the shoulder, a miserable task that I regarded as more of a hazing ritual for summer helpers than a safety requirement. A thorough gloves-off patting on the top of each barrel would do just fine, I decided. I was, after all, a driver today. A sovereign. And best of all, I was nobody's damned "bobo."

After the stop at the hunt club, I returned to the Rivergreen route, which included Lyla Packington's house. I had not returned to her house to pick up garbage since the day I had happened upon Lyla's mother sunbathing in her memorable all-together, and I didn't think she had seen me before I had fled the scene. But I wasn't certain about that, and I was unsure about how to handle a repeat performance if it occurred.

But on this day, Anita Packington was tending tomatoes in her backyard garden, fully dressed in a denim shirt and tight, bright yellow pants. She was holding a small, sharp spade in her right hand.

"Why, hello, Jesse," she said, and I was relieved that she looked puzzled at my appearance, a carry can casually draped over my right shoulder, in her backyard sanctum. "Is this your summer job?" she asked.

"Yes, it's my summer job," I said, noticing that her shirt was buttoned at the neck despite the late morning heat.

She palmed a medium-sized, radiant red tomato and twisted it off the vine. "And how is your summer going, Jesse?" she asked. "Are you getting ready to head off to school?" She paused. "And where is it that you will be going—I have forgotten."

I thought about telling her that I was still waiting to hear from several schools and undecided which to attend. That was the lie I usually told, but it was also a lie that I was getting tired of telling. "I didn't get accepted into any of the schools I applied to, Mrs. Packington," I said.

"Oh my," she said. "I'm surprised to hear that."

Well, I thought, there's probably any number of things you might be surprised to hear, Mrs. Packington. She studied a plump September-ripe tomato in her hand and then set it in a wicker basket at her feet. "Is this your first time picking up garbage at our house?"

"No," I said. "Not the first time."

She smiled, and there seemed to be a question forming that she left unspoken. "Well," she said, "it was so lovely seeing you again, Jesse."

"It's been lovely seeing you, too, Mrs. Packington," I said.

I took several steps before I heard her voice. "You can call me Anita now," she said. "You're a young man who has graduated from high school."

"Yes, Anita." Speaking her first name felt awkward, but it also left me with a slight jolt of electricity up my spine.

"Would you like some tomatoes to take home with you? They're ripe off the vine."

"No, thank you, Anita," I said. "Please give my best to Lyla."

"She's off to school for early orientation. I will tell her hello for you, Jesse."

The Garbage Brothers

I emptied the Packington's underground trash can, taking care to scrape a wet clump of avocado-colored tissue stuck to the bottom. Then I let the galvanized steel cylinder clank with finality back into its silo, and pushed the foot lever that triggered the heavy lid to shut. I jogged with the half-empty barrel around the side of the house and down to the winding tree-lined driveway. There was a familiar blue pickup waiting when I returned to the truck. And in front of it stood Benjamin Willard III.

I looked for Zeus, assuming that he had finally shown up for work, but he wasn't there. Maybe, I thought, he had grabbed his carry can out of the back of the pickup and gone ahead, leaving me to pull up the truck, "What's up, Mr. Willard, sir?" I asked.

"Just checking in to see how you are doing." He looked relieved to find me still ambulatory, no limbs missing and the truck still intact and not stuck in a ditch.

"Heard anything from Zeus?"

The boss shrugged his shoulders. "He hasn't shown up yet," he said. "I went by his house and knocked. No answer."

I nodded with a look of concern, but I was secretly pleased that I could continue the driver game, one I thought I was playing like a pro. Like Pickles, Grits, Billy. Or, better yet, like Zeus. I planned to change into one of his clean T-shirts after lunch. He wouldn't mind, not since I was doing his work for him while he was off doing whatever the hell he was doing. And what was he doing? Despite my delight in getting to drive a route, I had a nagging sense of uneasiness about Zeus' absence. I dropped the barrel on its side to the edge of the trough, and Benjie winced. "Careful there son, those cans cost good money."

Irritated by the reprimand, I stared at Benjamin Willard III, channeling Zeus, waiting for the boss to either say what was on his fat mind or leave, and hoping for the latter. Staring at him, I thought, not like a summer helper but as the almighty Zeus would, as Tippy Toes the driver should.

"You alright? Everything going OK?" the boss asked.

"Everything's just fine, Benjie," I said. He looked hard at me. He was used to me addressing him as "Mr. Willard" and he wasn't sure what to think about this sudden familiarity.

"OK then." He smiled nervously and turned to return to his pickup when he stopped and lifted his pig-like nose into the air. "What's that?" he said. "I smell something."

If Zeus had been there, I knew exactly what he would have said: "Of course, you smell something, Benjie, this is a goddamn garbage truck. And you smell goddamn garbage."

I started to say I didn't smell anything. Then I stopped. I could smell it, too. It was a sharp, acrid, whispering, wavering but fast growing stronger smell.

Smoke.

"Where is it coming from?" I said. I looked up and down the road hoping to see someone burning lawn debris. Benjie looked too, and we stood there behind the garbage truck turning in slow circles, snouts to the air, sniffing and looking again. As I turned I realized that the smell was strongest when I faced the rear of the truck. I looked inside and I could see three small, white-and-gray tendrils of smoke working their way past the compacted trash and the great compactor blade. I remembered the six barrels of ashes that I had picked up earlier at the hunt club—the six barrels of ashes that I had decided to check for embers by patting them on top instead of sticking my arm inside.

I was screwed and I knew it.

Benjie was unnerved by the thought of one of his precious trucks going up in flames. "These machines cost a lot of money," he chided the crew with regularity at the Greasy Wrench. "They aren't machines—they're trucks," Grits had answered just the other day. And Pickles had added, "Actually they're pieces of crap, Benjie. My truck's older than your grandma."

"My grandmother passed away 15 years ago," the boss replied.

"My point exactly," Pickles said.

But on this day, one of the boss's trucks was burning, and we stood and stared at the smoke trails. "Hose," the boss finally said. "We gotta find a hose." He peered down the long driveway that led to the Packington house. "Can you back this truck down there?" he asked

I looked. The drive was narrow, just a few feet wider than the truck. "Yes," I lied. "No problem."

The boss crossed the road and started lumbering the Packington's driveway, moving at the speed of a man who wanted to run but hadn't for decades and couldn't remember how. "I'll go ahead and have a hose ready," he shouted.

"I know the woman who lives at the house—her name is Anita," I yelled. "She is in the backyard picking tomatoes." Benjie turned his head, gave me a fleeting look of puzzlement and then slowly, painfully bounced his way up the driveway, gravel grinding under his polished work boots.

I got into the cab of the smoldering truck and looked in the rearview mirror, expecting to see flames. None. Yet. I jammed the gearshift into reverse, and the grinding then settling clunk was somehow reassuring. I needed reassurance. I had never backed a garbage truck more than the dozen yards or so it took to reach a grocery-store dumpster, and even then maneuvering a garbage truck in reverse was a slow, awkward and uncertain chore unless you were Billy, who could navigate backwards with as much ease as he could go forward. Zeus was a natural, too. He could back up the Green Goddess while dishing out profound social commentary and sipping hot coffee from a Styrofoam cup with one hand.

But Billy and Zeus weren't here; I was. And the garbage in the back of my truck was slowly, inexorably burning—burning its way toward those thick rubber hoses that carried the flammable hydraulic fluid that gave the compactor its power. I didn't know what would happen if those hoses melted through, but I knew from listening to drivers that you shouldn't be anywhere near if they did. I'd heard cautionary tales of rolling balls of flame. Shreds of burning garbage drifting into the sky. Of drivers incinerated and the charcoal remains of their hands found later clutching the steering wheel. I looked into the two large rearview mirrors and began to back up, turning the wheel sharply to align the truck with the start of the driveway. It looked like a close fit. No margin for error. Pull this off, I thought, and all will be forgiven and Benjamin Willard III will be singing my praises tomorrow morning at the Greasy Wrench.

A branch brushed the driver's side mirror and then a larger one smacked the passenger side, cracking the glass. There was only one thing for it—more speed. I put my foot on the gas, and the truck barreled backward up the Packington's driveway toward what I prayed would be the boss waiting with a garden hose. Then the truck reached a wide spot in the driveway just before a sharp, narrow bend where it swung left—the last bend before the Packington's house, and I braked. There was, I knew, no way the truck could make it around that corner. Not even Billy or Zeus could negotiate such a turn.

In the rearview mirror, I could see Benjie running hoseless toward the rear of the truck, bobbing up and down in his flesh-stuffed fatigues. He was pointing at the back of the truck and shouting, but the only word I could hear over and over was "hydraulic, hydraulic, hydraulic."

Benjie reached the back of the truck, and I could see him flailing at the turnbuckles that drivers loosened and unhooked before dumping trucks at the dump. Smoke was pouring from the rear of the truck. I thought I saw flames, but it might have been Benjie's bright red forehead as he yanked back the pull-down lever that raised the truck bed and prepared to dump several tons of burning garbage on the Packington's driveway.

I opened the truck door and stepped onto the running board. "No," I yelled over the noise of the still-rising and now sharply tilting truck bed. "Not here. We can't dump it here."

Benjamin Willard III looked up as the truck reached its maximum tilt and I could hear the compacted garbage inside begin to slide.

"Get in the damn truck and pull it forward," he yelled. "Dump this load. Now!"

Paul Neville

    I got back in the truck, put it in first gear and popped the clutch. The truck was carrying close to a full load, and the nose of the truck lifted off the ground like a pawing horse. I could see branches on each side, and I could hear the garbage whooshing down from the great metal box and sliding onto what had been the Packington's driveway but was now a mountain of burning, smoking, steaming, and stinking garbage. Benjie ran to get clear of the growing mound. Ten yards behind him I saw Mrs. Anita Packington standing with a stunned look on her face and both palms uplifted in the universal gesture for "What the hell?"

    I stepped out of the truck and looked at Mrs. Packington and waved. "So sorry, Anita," I yelled. She cocked her head and cupped one hand to her ear. I yelled again, "So sorry, Anita," but this time my voice broke on "sorry" like a pimpled 15-year-old boy auditioning for the church choir. It was not the voice of a goddamn knight in the service of goddamn Willard Sanitation Service.

Chapter 31: Mount Packington

The Packingtons took the flaming garbage incident surprisingly well. After Mount Anita, as neighbors took to calling it, had been thoroughly saturated by the Rivergreen Rural Volunteer Fire Department, the firefighters and Mr. and Mrs. Packington posed for pictures in front of the hill of wet garbage. A reporter for the local weekly, the Freedom Courier Journal, took a picture and ran it on the front page, along with a story that misspelled my first and last names but got Benjamin Willard III's name and Roman numeral right. The reporter got the story mostly right, too, except for the part about me not sticking my arm into the barrels of ashes to see if they were still hot, which I didn't tell her about because she didn't ask. The truck was undamaged, thanks to the sanitation company owner's "lightning quick thinking" and, as the reporter put it, his "bold and decisive action." On the back page of the section was a full-page color advertisement for Willard Sanitation—"Humpin' to Please"—complete with a coupon for $5 off the first month's service.

Benjie rented a backhoe, and put Billy and me to work cleaning up the mess. Billy worked the heavy machinery, and I had shovel duty, but it wasn't bad. I got 10 hours of overtime and the honor of buying the crew breakfast at the Greasy Wrench, where I caught surprisingly little flack for setting Zeus' truck on fire. Billy was thrilled with the chance to play around on a backhoe and collect his overtime, which his wife Serena used to buy school clothes for Susie, Sandy, Sara and Sally. Pickles told me about the time he had set the boss's new diesel truck on fire and how he thought the boss was going to have a stroke and be permanently debilitated—but how could you have told the difference if that had happened, anyway? As for Grits, it was clear he knew exactly what had happened—how I had ignored his and every other driver's warnings and dumped ashes without first properly checking them. But Grits already held me in such low regard that he apparently decided not to waste his breath by sharing that knowledge.

But by far the most interesting outcome of the burning garbage incident was the letter I received from Lyla, who had mercifully been away at the time at her college orientation. The letter came in a blue onionskin envelope, and I recognized the handwriting—a graceful, lilting script that enticed me to read it as soon as I saw it in my apartment mailbox.

Iris was still at work, but I didn't feel right about reading Lyla Packington's letter in the apartment. So I took the short dirt path that led to the boat ramp next door, walked out on the small dock next to it, sat on the unpainted wood and opened the envelope. The paper inside was a matching soft blue, and I smelled it because I thought that was what a guy who gets a letter from an exotic and beautiful woman is supposed to do, even if he doesn't have a clue yet what the exotic and beautiful woman has written to him. But it didn't really matter; the only fragrances I could smell were my work clothes and the dead fish under the dock.

"My Dearest Jesse," the letter began, and the words made me woozy with remembrance and a roiling lust, and I instantly knew beyond any doubt that I would still crawl on my hands and knees all the way to Hiram College in Ohio if that's what Lyla Packington asked me to do. And never look back.

"I trust that you are well, my friend," it continued. I am well, I thought. Quite well at the moment, thank you.

"Anita informs me that you paid a visit to our home last week and left behind a gift—a fragrant offering. You might want to consider just leaving a calling card next time."

I smiled, and the smile went from my head down to my gut before sprinting back to my face. Good Lord and God almighty, Lyla Packington actually thought about me, enough to write a letter to her "dearest Jesse" on blue onionskin paper.

Then there was a postscript: "I hope you stay well and that when you peruse a letter such as this that you pause to hear the wind behind the words. Soon it will be time for you to fly. Make certain you do. Your old comrade in literary arms, Lyla."

The wind behind the words. I could feel it—a low September breath riffling off the lake that made me, at least for the moment, completely forget about Zeus, Iris, and Willard Sanitation. I sat on the edge of the dock, took off my filthy sneakers, rolled up the legs of my jeans, and put my feet into the faintly cool green water. I read the letter three more times, pausing each time at the phrase "pause to hear the wind behind the words." Then I carefully put it back in its envelope, and slid the envelope in the back pocket of my jeans. I looked out on the lake, which was empty of boats and humans, and thought about Lyla and the swirling possibilities that her letter suggested and what to do about them. Should I write her back? Should I quit my job and drive to Hiram College and seek a prize that might—or might not be waiting? Or should I just keep moving forward, one step at a time, waiting for another sign that might tell me what to do?

Iris wasn't home yet when I got back to my apartment. I opened the door and walked inside. The room felt cold, dark, empty and still, and I saw a lopsided chocolate cake that Iris had left on the kitchen table. Next to the plate was a note that read, "Go ahead and laugh, but I tried." I was stricken with guilt about the letter in my back pocket and my ability—and complete, mindless willingness—to be caught up and carried away by it.

Zeus, I thought. When my friend Zeus returns from wherever the hell he's gone, he'll help me figure this out.

Then I heard Iris' beater VW pull into the parking space in front of the apartment and come to a sputtering stop. I quickly slipped the letter out of my back pocket and pulled the poetry anthology from Mr. Elmer Schmidt's class out of the cardboard box next to the bed. I slid the envelope inside and stuck the book back in the box.

The door opened and I sat back on the bed, putting my hands behind my head, as if to clearly indicate they had not been busy doing anything they shouldn't be doing. Like reading a letter from Lyla Packington.

"Well," Iris said. "So what do you think about my cake?"

Chapter 32: The Quarry

A Liberty Township fire truck and ambulance, their flashing red lights startling even in the noon glare, were parked on the highway shoulder next to the quarry pond and Ernie's Snake Pit. I was running behind on Zeus' Wednesday route, but I'd been craving a bowl of chili and a cheeseburger all morning and planned to run inside the bar for a quick lunch after emptying the truck at the dump. I was also eager to walk into the bar for the first time as a driver, however fleeting that status might be—and however much goading I was sure to get from other companies' drivers for setting Zeus' truck on fire. It doesn't take long for news to travel in Garbageville.

As I approached the Snake Pit, I could see a cluster of people in the parking lot. They were mostly drivers from the bar, and some kids who fished the pond from its banks. I spotted Ernie, looking incongruous in his ankle-flapping black wool pants, white socks, a wrinkled white shirt, and thick black suspenders.

It was unusual to see emergency vehicles next to the Snake Pit. In my time at Willard Sanitation, I never saw a fire truck, cop car or anything resembling an official vehicle near the place. The bar seemed to exist off the official grid, with authorities apparently ignoring the joint in the hope that it would eventually collapse on all the felonious souls inside and save the township the cost of having to someday raze the place.

I pulled Zeus' truck into the parking lot, flipped off the transistor radio that I had dared not move from last tuning—an all-jazz station from University of Chicago—WGRV. Zeus called it W-Groove and liked that it was heavy on Coltrane, whose sacred tones Zeus had told me required not just a listener's silence, but reverence as well.

I got out of the truck and walked to the edge of the quarry where the onlookers had gathered.

"Hey, Ernie, what's going on?" I asked. The old man turned to see who was talking. I was surprised how worn he looked in the daylight, and I realized it was the first time I'd seen him outside the cavern darkness of his bar. His scrawny, creased neck looked like a snapping turtle's, and his eyes narrowed as he remembered who I was. "You're the kid who's working with Willard Sanitation this summer, right?" he said after a couple seconds.

The Garbage Brothers

I nodded yes. He looked back at the parking lot and saw Zeus' truck. "Are you driving his route today?" Ernie asked.

I nodded again.

"Well, fuckin' hell," he said, lifting a long boney arm and pointing toward a circle of men in uniforms standing around a body lying near the edge of the pond about 20 yards away. "Hate to tell you this, son, but there's a dead man over there, and I think it's Zeus. A Mexican kid found the body this morning. I came out and had a look-see and called the cops."

Ernie's words made no sense, and at the same time they made perfect, terrible sense. I felt numb and cold, even in the late summer heat. The shoreline was muddy, and the weeds were trampled where the emergency workers pulled the body from the water. Ernie walked over to talk to one of the cops, a short, stocky man wearing a rumpled brown uniform and black Wellington boots caked with mud.

Ernie pointed in my direction, and the officer motioned for me to approach. "You know him?" he asked, nodding toward a body lying on a black plastic tarp spread unevenly in the mud and weeds. My eyes moved in slow motion. I could see a man wearing white Converse sneakers, blue jeans and a sodden T-shirt. His eyes were half closed and their light was gone. The skin was a pale blue and his long, tangled wet hair and beard clung to his shirt. His head was turned to the right and his mouth was partly open as if he were in mid-sentence, and the welt on his forehead was a terrible dark purple.

I looked away and tried to think. But there were no thoughts, no words. Just the image of a muddy, lifeless body that both looked exactly like Zeus and yet looked nothing like him. A northbound diesel freightliner roared past and then a gaggle of cars, all of them slowing, drivers gawking. I looked up at the noon sky. It was a deep, brilliant blue. I could feel the cop watching me and waiting with barely concealed impatience.

"Answer the man, goddamnit," Ernie said.

"Yes, sir," I said to the officer. "That's Zeus—his real name is Jake Callahan. He drives for Willard Sanitation."

"When's the last time you saw him?" the cop said.

"I think it was the end of work last Wednesday," I said. "He didn't show up for work after that. That's his truck up in the lot—I'm working his route."

As I spoke I remembered Zeus sitting in the cab of the Green Goddess in the Snake Pit parking lot and smiling when I asked him what had prompted the attack in the bar. "Oh, we were just havin' us a lively debate about the origins of life on planet Earth," he'd said.

I gave the police officer my boss's name and phone number—and walked back to Zeus' truck. This time I got in the passenger seat, and I put my head between my knees, listening to the sound of trucks rolling past. I tried to cry, feeling like that's what I should do. What was expected of a friend. But nothing came. I felt stuck, frozen, just like I'd felt when I saw Zeus being held on the floor of the Snake Pit. Then I looked up and saw Ernie staring at me through the open driver's window.

"You OK, kid?" he asked.

"Yeah," I said. "I'm OK."

"Come inside and I'll get you a shot of schnapps to help you get back on your feet," he said.

I sat up. "Thanks," I said. "But I gotta get back to Zeus' route."

"Looks like it's your route now," Ernie said.

I nodded. After he'd gone I got out of the truck, walked around the cab and got into the driver's seat. I turned on the transistor. WGRV was playing "Magic Man" by Grover Washington Jr., one of Zeus' favorites. I looked at the picture of "Miss Lily" and turned on the ignition and pulled onto the highway.

About a mile up the road I spotted a phone booth in front of an auto parts store. I got out of the truck, stepped inside the phone booth and called Iris at her work. I told the surly man who answered that I needed to talk with Iris and that it was important. As I waited for her to come to the phone, I read the "for-a-good-time-call" graffiti scratched on the booth, closed my eyes and saw Zeus' pale blue face. I listened to my breath, and Iris came to the phone.

"Jesse?" Iris said. "What's happening? My manager said it was urgent."

"Zeus," I said. "Fucking Zeus."

"What about Zeus?"

"He's dead. Police just pulled his body from the quarry pond next to the Snake Pit."

"Do you need me, Jesse? I can come to where you are—right now."

"No," I said. "I've got to finish the route. I just wanted to let you know."

"I'm sorry," she said. "Oh, I'm so sorry."

She hung up, and I looked at the receiver and said it one more time: "Fucking Zeus."

Chapter 33: Garbage Waits for No Man

When I walked into the Greasy Wrench at 4:30 a.m.—opening time—on Monday morning, Billy had yet to arrive, and Pickles was sitting alone in the crew's booth, his massive form bathed in yellow diner glow. He sat in his usual place, leaving space for Zeus' memory on his right and for roughly half of me on his left. The big man's shoulders were hunched forward, sheathed in a flannel shirt a couple of sizes too small, as all his shirts were. His elbows were on the table as he cradled a thick ceramic coffee cup in his palms, absorbing the warmth, as he stared, oblivious to my arrival, at the Union Pacific calendar on the wall.

The door closed behind me with the jingling of bells, and Delores stepped from behind the counter to intercept me, putting a strong, thin hand on my arm. "Jesse, honey, how are you?" she said in a soft voice.

I shrugged and avoided her eyes. "OK," I said. It was a lie. I hadn't slept. Every time I had tried to close my eyes I saw Zeus' body on the muddy tarp at the quarry's edge. I saw his wounded face, his open mouth, his bloodless lips.

"Honey, I knew it was you who identified Zeus at the quarry for the police," Delores said. "A cop who came in yesterday told me what happened."

I said nothing, and yearned to put my head on one of her bony shoulders and sob like a child in his mama's arms. But that could not happen. Not at 4:30 a.m. on this September workday morning at the Greasy Wrench Cafe in Freedom, Illinois. Not with Pickles sitting in the booth and the other drivers soon to arrive. Not when I was the one who might have to bear witness to the crew about what I'd seen. I hurt, but I didn't know what to do about the slow burn in my chest. Iris had tried to loosen the logjam of my sorrow after coming to my apartment the previous night. But I'd turned inward, just as I wanted to do now with Delores.

Delores squeezed my arm again, and for a moment it felt right, warm and reassuring. I wanted her to keep holding me steady and warm, and I wanted her to keep saying mother words. She leaned forward and gave me a soft kiss on the uppermost part of my cheek, and I smelled the bracing, brassy aroma of her drug-store perfume and the lotion on her strong hands.

"It's gonna be alright, Jesse," she said. "You just sit down. I'll bring you coffee."

I shuffled into the booth, and Pickles gave me a sideways glance and the barest of nods. I thought about sliding into the empty seat across from Pickles until Billy and Grits arrived. But then I squeezed in as usual next to Pickles because it felt like the right thing to do and because I didn't want to move again or say any more than I had to this morning. I wanted to breathe the incense of the coffee and bacon and eggs and hash browns that Delores would soon bring to the table, and I wanted to be with the drivers in all their greasy, smoky stink and stubble. I needed it all on this sad, dark morning.

"How you doin', Pickles?" I asked.

No answer. Just a low grunt, and I nodded as if my benchmate had just delivered a profound soliloquy. Delores brought my coffee, with plenty of room for cream and sugar, which I added in comfort excess as the other crew members arrived, first Billy with Grits right on his heels. Billy looked even more ragged than normal. He stared at Pickles—an unusual occurrence; this was not a group of men who believed in eye contact. Then he shook his head. "Jeethuth. Chritht, Pickleth" he said. "Fuckin' Theuth. Can you believe it?"

Pickles nodded. "Yeah, I believe it," he said softly, exhaling a plume of Marlboro smoke and raising his eyes to the train calendar.

Grits lit his cigarette and stubbed it out in the black plastic ashtray. Then he lit it again, and looked at me across the table with something less than his normal reptilian indifference.

"So I hear that you was there when they found Zeus," he said.

"No, I got to the Snake Pit after they'd pulled him out of the water. I just ID'd the body for a cop."

"No need for you ever to be talking to no police," Grits said.

"Leave the kid alone," Pickles said.

"Bet you've never seen a dead man before, have you?" Grits asked.

"I saw my dad on the living-room couch after he died of a heart attack. But this was different."

"Goddamn right it was different," Grits said.

"Well, what the hell happened to Theus?" Billy asked.

Pickles' eyes dropped from the train calendar, and he stared at Billy.

"No need to ask," he said. "You know."

Billy looked down and nodded. "Yeth," he said. "I gueth I do"

The bells on the cafe door jangled. "Well, here comes Benjamin Willard the turd," Grits said. "This should be a load of 'ain't-it-just-the-saddest-thing-that-happened-to-Zeus?' horseshit."

But there was none of that. Just the big boss, looking redder and shakier and morning drunker than usual. He stood sweating at his normal place at the end of the booth, pressing his clipboard into his soft gut. "Gentlemen," he said, looking down at the clipboard as if he'd written down something to

The Garbage Brothers

say. But he could go no further and he choked and heaved slightly forward, swallowing the sounds until he could swallow them no more. He opened his mouth to speak, but there were no words. Just a low moan.

Everyone in the cafe, even the cook in the kitchen, stopped and watched as Benjie began to shake, tried to stop, and then gave up and sobbed like a grade school kid. The drivers stood one by one—Billy was the first and then Grits, who stubbed out his cigarette in his half-eaten hash browns and walked with the foreman out of the cafe. I followed, and at the door I looked back and saw Pickles rise and pause next to Benjamin Willard III. Pickles lifted a great paw and pressed lightly on the boss's right shoulder, patted it once and then walked toward the door.

"Garbage don't wait, Benjie," he said.

"Ain't none of you payin' today?" Delores asked from behind the counter.

"Give the checks to Benjie," Pickles said.

Delores nodded. Then she reached for two of the snow-white Styrofoam cups that she used to fill every morning for the youthful driver with the great flowing beard and the even greater flowing charm that melted the ladies. She filled them with coffee, added a dollop of creamer to each and then handed them to Pickles as he passed. "One for you, one for Jesse," she said.

Chapter 34: Farewell to a Friend

The Wilton Daily Independent reported the next day that the body of one Jake "Zeus" Callahan, 34, of Freedom, had been found by a child fishing in a quarry pond near the Liberty Township dump. Authorities said the cause of death appeared to be drowning, but added that a head injury suggested the possibility of foul play. "The county sheriff's office is investigating the death," the article said, adding that Callahan was survived by his wife Totina and daughter Lily of Carbondale, and brother Darnell of Las Vegas.

"Police are investigating—that's one big bucket of bullshit," Grits said over breakfast at the Greasy Wrench. By now everyone at Willard Sanitation knew about Zeus' bloody encounter with one of the Renegades at the Snake Pit. Pickles had mercifully not mentioned my failure to come to Zeus' assistance. But while Billy, Grits, and Benjie didn't know, I did. And my inability to help my friend was an unbearable burden.

The look on Pickles' face made clear he thought—no, he knew—that Zeus hadn't drowned and that he'd been killed by Largo and his drug-dealing gang. Grits said he'd stopped by the Snake Pit and that Ernie told him Zeus had returned to the bar after work the same day as the pool-cue attack. Ernie said Zeus ignored his advice to "Just get the fuck out of here and go home," and had instead approached Largo. "Ernie said the two talked like nothing had happened, played pool and even walked out together at closing time," Grits said. "Just like they were two old buddies."

"You know that's when they did it," Pickles muttered, looking first at me and then at Grits and Billy. "Zeus must have owed that son of a bitch money for drugs, so Largo and his buddies dragged Zeus' skinny ass into that quarry and stepped on his fuckin' beard until he couldn't breathe nothin' but mudwater."

Billy leaned forward and spoke in a quiet, firm voice. "You don't know thath what happened, Pickleth," he said. "Not for thertain. Tho maybe we thould all jutht thtay away from the Thnake Pit for a few dayth."

"Don't tell me where I can go or can't go, Billy," Pickles said.

Billy pursed his lips and shrugged, and then looked at me. "Well, it lookth like you'll be drivin' Theuth' routeth until Benjie hireth a new driver," he said. "Think you can keep from turning the Green Goddeth into a blowtorch again?"

"I think your asshole's the only blowtorch we need to worry about," Delores said, as she leaned over the table to fill our coffee cups. I loaded my cup with cream and sugar and then leaned back and listened to the drivers speculate on who the boss should hire to replace Zeus.

Billy thought Benjie should hire his cousin, Sammy, who did roadwork for the county. "Thammy'th a good Polak—workth all day, even if he'th drunk. We call him Turtle Head. Lookth like a big thnapping turtle with a mouth that goeth out like thith." He took the greasy forefinger of each hand, inserted one in each corner of his mouth and pulled back hard.

"Jesus Christ," Grits said. "I couldn't look at that every morning. Goddamn turtle head." Grits thought the clear favorite should be his older brother Titus who had recently moved to Freedom from Tennessee and who, like Grits, had served time for assorted crimes against humanity. Unlike Grits, Titus sailed on home to Jesus during his prison voyage, and recently took the job as associate pastor of the Tabernacle of the Holy Winds, which met in the old Freedom Grange Hall and which Mary Rose and her kids attended on Sundays.

"Yeah, thath jutht what we need at Willard Thanitatihion—a pathtor who thpeakth in tongueth and bringth the Gothpel glory to all thothe thweet ladieth on Theuth' routeth," Billy said.

Billy was right about Benjie's decision to have me drive Zeus' routes for the time being. Until the boss hired another driver, he didn't have another choice unless he wanted to do Zeus' work himself, which he had no intention of doing. To both Benjie's and my considerable relief, I did the job in the days that followed without wreaking much havoc, and there were no more truck fires. The work was grinding and exhausting, but I welcomed it. It left me with little time or energy to think about what had happened to Zeus, or my future. It was a relief to stagger under the weight of stuffed-down-and-filled-to-the-top carry cans, haul them to the truck to flush their contents and then head to the next house and the next. When the day was done, I went home and ate Iris' makeshift meals—usually bologna and cheese sandwiches and tomato soup—and watched Iris draw in her sketchbook.

Iris tried to get me to talk about Zeus, saying I would feel better if I did. I resisted, but then the memories started flowing and it was easier to let them out than hold them back. She listened as I told her how Zeus used to stare at the picture of Lily on the truck dashboard. About the time Benjie had tumbled backwards in horror when Zeus heaved the flying mummy dog missile in his direction. About Zeus' spot-on imitation of the rich asshole customer who hurt his arm "playing poh-low." About the time we went swimming during an early morning pickup at the Wilton City Pool and nearly choked with laughter thinking what Benjie would say if he caught us backstroking in our skivvies on company time. And then I told her about that terrible day I stood frozen in place watching Zeus dazed and helpless on the concrete floor of the Snake Pit, the red-and-purple welt already the size of a penny roll on his forehead.

"You would have helped him if you could have," Iris said. "And it looks to me as if Zeus' problems ran a whole lot deeper than needing someone to help him stand after he got hit in the head by a drug dealer swinging a pool cue. Pickles took care of that, and he was the right one to do it. If you think you could have saved Zeus, you're wrong, Jesse, and you're giving yourself too much credit. Just like I was wrong as a little girl to think I could have saved my father from driving drunk and running into a tree, and my mother from going to prison. And my little sister from going into foster care. Sometimes all you can do is just watch when bad things happen to people you love."

Iris pulled me next to her on the bed and held me. I began to cry and then to sob. And she held me until I was done and had fallen asleep in her slender arms. And she was still holding me in the morning.

~ ~ ~

Zeus was laid to rest on a sunny Saturday afternoon 10 days after his body was found at the quarry. The service was at the Wilton Memorial Chapel, which was fitting since it was the third stop every Monday and Friday on one of Zeus' routes, and I knew it well. There was a big green dumpster in the back behind a brick enclosure, and when we lifted the heavy lids Zeus liked to warn me that there might be trash bags inside filled with intestines. Once Zeus spotted a box that contained a garbage disposal and read the specs on the back of the box, noting the extra-heavy-duty motor and high-intensity stainless steel blades needed, he said, to properly blend human remains.

A small group of mourners gathered shortly before noon. The word among the drivers was that Zeus left Totina flat broke, and that her father, after waiting a week in the hope that some other relative would step forward, bought the cheapest, no-frills funeral package for his son-in-law, so cheap that Billy whispered to me in the lobby that Zeus would have to hold together the sides of his cardboard coffin from the inside.

The chapel was nearly empty except for his family, which huddled shoulder-to-shoulder in a front-row pew. Totina was there along with her daughter Lily and her parents, Vernon and Irene Rutkowski, whom I had met at the family reunion at Flat Rock Lake. Vernon, his flat-top landscaped to hedge perfection, kept glancing back at the lobby, as if irritated by the Willard crew's noisy and ragged presence, and eager to get the service over and done.

The Garbage Brothers

The Willard Sanitation crew stood in conversational clumps in the mortuary lobby. Grits slumped, yearning for a smoke and wearing a brown suit that hung shapeless off his wire-hanger shoulders. Mary Rose was next to him in her floral print Sunday church dress. She watched the parking lot through a window, waiting for Iris to arrive. Iris had spent the night before at her house and told me she planned to come to the service, so I was surprised she wasn't there yet.

Nearby and blabbing away at his normal Greasy Wrench volume was Billy, who wore a surprisingly sharp-looking black suit, string tie and a campaign button on his lapel that read "Billy B for Supervisor," which he showed off to me by turning his lapel in my direction.

Standing next to Billy was his wife Serena and his daughters Susie, Sandy, Sara and Sally, looking glum and not happy to be at a funeral on a warm, sunny day. They were all wearing matching brown knit dresses with Billy B campaign buttons prominently displayed, and looked to me like a Girl Scout troop on a field trip to a funeral home.

Benjamin Willard III, wearing a tweed sports coat that made him sweat, stood close to Billy, wincing at his foreman's unmuted observations and frequent lapses into profanity. Benjamin was accompanied by his silent, eye-darting spouse Delilah, whom I'd heard the drivers called "Devilina" because she took the calls and recorded customer complaints on the blue slips that the drivers despised.

Pickles was the last of the crew to arrive. He ambled through the front door just a minute or so before the recorded music started. He wore a deep purple, red and green Hawaiian shirt that he had retrieved a few weeks earlier from a dumpster at the Ramada Inn, and a pair of baggy khakis. Delores wore a floor-length green dress that might have made her look like the classiest person in the room if it weren't for her vibrant purple high heels, matching fingernails and lipstick, and a side slit on her dress that made a daring and revealing dash up her right thigh.

The mortuary director herded the crew inside the chapel, and we all sat in the back rows, as if Zeus' death and Totina's grief—she was sobbing inconsolably—were contagious. The minister, a short, fleshy man in a baggy black suit with dark bags under his eyes, stood and began what he promised would be a short message "because I know you are all heavy-hearted" and "there is nothing I can say to ease your sorrow, except. . ." I tuned out what turned into a dismayingly long message, which included the minister's speculation that Zeus would be rejoicing at this moment if only he'd known that the message of the Gospel was available to all who seek "Him," and about how he would have wanted us to "take this opportunity to repent of your many sins and to ask your Lord and Savior to come into your hearts." Billy picked his nose and waved off Serena's attempts to hand him a hanky. Benjie fell into a sound, sweaty and head-nodding slumber, and Grits stared through a stained-glass window and looked as if he might have been transported to a wood-planked chapel back in some Appalachian holler.

The minister was still talking when I saw Pickles, whose eyes met mine as he was in the act of standing. Delores reached to pull on the tail of his Hawaiian shirt, mouthing the words, "No, no, no." But it was too late. Pickles stepped into the aisle, adjusted his vibrant Hawaiian shirt and strode to the front of the church, where he stood towering over the minister who had paused in mid-altar call. "Padre," Pickles said in a voice that carried to the furthest corner of the furthest coffin in the mortuary. "We would all appreciate it if you would shut your big yap and give me that mic."

The minister stared at the man-mountain towering over him, and promptly handed the microphone to Pickles and took a seat. Pickles paused for a few seconds before beginning, and I knew what was coming. "Totina, my dear," Pickles said with a nod to Zeus' wife. "This is for you and your sweet Zeus." He lifted the mic, cleared his throat, and crooned in his best Sinatraesque voice: "I'll be seeing you in all the old familiar places. . ."

No one on the Willard Sanitation crew was surprised that Pickles had decided to seize the moment and, as he liked to put it, "Frankify" the room. But the Rutkowski clan was clearly taken aback. Vern started to stand in protest, but then sat back down in grudging admiration as soon as Pickles launched into a pitch-perfect chorus: "I'll find you in the morning sun and when the night is new, I'll be looking at the moon and I'll be seeing you."

When the big man was done, he winked at Totina and handed the microphone to the still-shaken minister who wisely jettisoned his plans for an altar call and instead led the mourners in singing the first and final verse of "How Great Thou Art."

After the service, we all trailed from the chapel and into the glaring September sunlight. A soft, fat hand plopped on my shoulder. It was Benjie, with his wife Delilah at his side.

"And how are you today, young man?" he asked.

"Well, Benjie. I've just been to a funeral," I said, reflecting that Zeus would have been proud of my sarcasm.

"Billy says you aren't going to college this fall. Is that right?"

"Looks that way," I said.

"Young man," Benjie said, "have you considered staying on and becoming a full-time driver for Willard Sanitation? As you know, we currently have an opening, and my wife and I think you would be an excellent choice to join the Willard Sanitation family.

"I appreciate you thinking of me, especially after I set one of your trucks on fire," I said. "But I need to think about it."

"Take as long as you want and give it some thought, son. We'd love to have you join the Willard Sanitation garbage family," Benjie said. Then Benjie and his wife swiveled as one very large person and walked toward the parking lot.

It was then that I saw—and heard—Iris' beater VW pull into the parking lot. She emerged from the car in a short black dress, looked at the people leaving after the service and walked across the mortuary's manicured front lawn. She made a beeline for Lily, who was sitting cross-legged and alone, pulling out blades of grass by the fistful. Iris knelt next to Lily, put her arms around the little girl and gave her a long, tender hug. I'd never seen Iris look so soft, so open, so warm and so comfortable. She looked liked home.

Chapter 35: Coming Soon

One week after Zeus' funeral, on a Saturday morning, I came home from the commercial run that I used to work with Zeus and that I appreciated for its absence of residential stops that required trudging up driveways with carry cans. It was my favorite run before Zeus died because Benjie gave us overtime for working an extra half day—and because Zeus brought a red-plaid Thermos filled with coffee that Delores had loaded with cream and sugar, and a bag of day-old muffins that she had squirreled away for us. We took turns tossing out conversational topics.

Zeus' contributions ranged from rock 'n' roll—he was certain that the Big Bopper was a deity—to his daughter Lily's insatiable demand for scary bedtime stories. I liked to talk baseball—I insisted Richie Allen had the sweetest swing in the majors, and the beat poets, whom Zeus had never heard of but took to immediately when I read him poems by Ginsburg, Corso and Snyder that I brought on our Saturday runs.

But this Saturday was slow, and time dragged because I missed my friend. It was late morning before I got home. Iris' car was out front, the curtains were drawn on the front windows, and when I walked inside it was dark and she was still in bed. I took a quick shower, hoping to slide into bed with her. But when I emerged from the bathroom, she was sitting up, wearing a blue terry cloth robe, pillows propped behind her, knees drawn to her chest and her thin arms wrapped around them. There was a heaviness in her expression I hadn't seen before.

"Hey," I said. "How are you?"

"I'm pregnant," she said. "That's how I am."

"You're going to have a baby?"

"Yes. That's what happens when you get pregnant."

I nodded, searching for the right thing to say for a situation that—considering our sporadic use of birth control—I had given little consideration. I wanted to tell her that I was delighted by the news and that I was ready and eager to embrace fatherhood. But that would be a lie, and I knew she would see it. I thought about saying sorry that I had gotten her pregnant, but I knew that might be the worst thing to say at the moment.

I took a deep breath. I closed my eyes, and I saw a flickering home movie in which I was standing next to Iris as she held our newborn baby at the hospital, both of us blissfully happy. I watched myself heading off to work as a driver at Willard Sanitation and coming home at night to a happily waiting mother and child. Then I was standing on the boat dock at Diamond Lake reading the letter from Lyla that exhorted me to consider the wind behind her words. And then I saw Zeus, standing in front of the mummy-dog house exhorting me to seize the first chance I had to "get the hell out of Freedom."

Iris studied me as she awaited my response. "Well?" she said.

I pulled on a pair of jeans and sat next to Iris on the bed, reaching for a limp, unresponsive hand. I felt tangled, conflicted and blurry. I needed time to think, and time was a luxury I did not have at this moment. So I squeezed her hand and said: "Tell me everything."

And that's what she did. She told me about her visit a week earlier, the morning of Zeus' memorial service, to the public health clinic in Wilton. How a nurse had given her the pregnancy test results in a beige room with too-close walls that made her feel claustrophobic. How when she stood to get up and felt so dizzy she thought she was going to fall and would have if the nurse hadn't grabbed her arm.

Iris told me she'd had a sudden vision of our baby at that teetering moment—a vision so instantaneous there could be no doubting its validity. It was a boy, she was sure of it, and he had a big flop of brown hair just like mine and the tiniest fingers and toes she had ever seen. So small they looked as if they belonged to the ceramic salt shaker that looked like Tom Sawyer that her Aunt Mary Rose kept on her kitchen counter. And that vision, so perfect and precise, made her realize the fragility and holy gift of this child—her child, our child. Formed like a burst of flame from a nothingness that now was something real.

She said the nurse gave her a brochure about nutrition, and talked to her in a medical monotone about options available to single mothers who decided they didn't want their babies—options that included adoption and abortion. Iris said she'd lifted her hand like a crossing guard stopping traffic for school children. "I am having this baby and I am keeping it, thank you very much," she told the nurse. Then she drove to Zeus' service, where she sat alone at the back of the room. She said she took a full week to digest the news and didn't tell me or her family because she needed time to think.

Iris watched me intently as she talked, and I smiled because I didn't know what the hell else to do. And just when I thought I couldn't smile any longer, I realized what I needed to do, what my father in one of our rare father-son conversations had called "The Right Thing." And I knew I needed to say the words before I thought about them, before doubt or hesitation stopped me. "Then we will have to get married," I said. The words felt noble, true and clarifying. Then I waited for what I knew would be her delighted response.

"Have to get married—have to?" Iris said. The words were cold, distant, serrated, and I dearly wanted back inside her earlier vision, the one with the glowing light and the baby with miniature toes and fingers that looked like mine.

"Get to get married?" I said. I suddenly felt less certain, less gallant, less everything, and the moment was sliding away from me and there was nothing I could do about it. Iris looked hard at me, and I could tell she knew everything, that she had divined my entrails like Old Testament prophets probed the intestines of dead pigeons. She walked into the bathroom and locked the door. "Iris," I called. "Please come out. Let's talk." But she didn't come out, not for a long time. When she did she hastily and wordlessly put on her clothes and left the apartment, ignoring my pathetic "Let's-talk" pleas. Then she got into her VW and rattled down the lake frontage road toward her home.

I tried calling Iris several times that afternoon and the next day, but she didn't answer. I wasn't sure what I was going to say, but I knew it had to start and end with "I'm sorry." Part of me wanted to add "and please marry me." But the hard truth was that a craven and real part of me hoped that she would refuse and that I'd be free to wander the world. Free to chase Lyla. Free to resurrect my fast-fading dream of going to college and becoming a writer.

I hung up twice when Mary Rose picked up the phone. I couldn't talk to Iris' aunt until I'd resolved things with her niece, and the last thing I wanted was to be invited over to Grits' house, where I was pretty sure everyone already knew about Iris' pregnancy and where I knew there was a Louisville Slugger leaning against the wall in the family room.

I left my apartment and walked around Diamond Lake—partly because I wanted to be away if Grits came to call but also because I needed time. Around 2 p.m. I stopped at Lucky Sid's Tavern, where I tried to call Iris from a payphone next to the restrooms. I ordered a cheeseburger, fries and a beer—the waitress didn't bother to ID me—in a dimly lit bar on a brilliantly sunny Midwest summer day.

I took a swallow of cold beer and then another, contemplating a backlit Hamm's Beer sign hanging on a wall over the bar. It depicted a rippling blue river and a big-bellied bear in a baseball cap paddling a canoe toward a waterfall hidden around a bend. And I wondered how it was going to turn out for the bear.

Chapter 36: The Wrath of Grits

Usually, Billy was the first crew member to arrive at the Greasy Wrench. When I walked into the cafe on Monday morning, Grits was sitting alone in the Willard Sanitation booth, his slit eyes fixed on the cigarette that he held between the forefinger and the middle finger of his left hand.

Delores had a cup of coffee poured and waiting for me on the table at Zeus' old seat across from Grits. She put a menu next to the coffee. "It's OK, Jesse," she said, giving my shoulder a little squeeze. "Sit there—it's time."

I nodded, and as I slid into the booth Grits surprised me by pulling a pack of Camels from the pocket of his work shirt and holding it in my direction.

"No thanks," I said, "Don't smoke."

"Maybe it's time you start," he said with a tight-lipped smile that was no smile at all.

I closed my eyes. The man knew. Everything. And he might already have that damn hunting knife on his belt unsheathed under the table. And I yearned for my old seat hanging halfway out of the booth, ready for a swift getaway.

"So," Grits said in a slow, slicing voice. "I hear you're gonna be a daddy. At least, that's what my little niece tells me," Grits continued.

I was silent. The rest of the cafe also was silent and Delores, Larry the fry cook and every one of the half-dozen customers seated in other booths and at the counter were hanging on every word of our conversation.

"Now, suppose you just tell that sweet girl's uncle how that little baby happened," he said. I looked outside the window and I could see Billy gesturing in our direction as he talked with Pickles, and I realized that our solitude was a setup. Grits and I were alone on our island booth for a reason, and everyone knew it.

The bells jangled on the cafe's front door, and Benjie strode inside, his piggy eyes focused on the clipboard and a sheaf of blue complaint slips clutched in his right hand. He stopped and looked around, puzzled at the absence of normal cafe chatter and clatter. Then he looked at the Willard Sanitation booth and caught Grits' burning eyes. He glanced at Delores, who gestured toward Billy and Pickles still talking in the parking lot, and then the boss executed a precise U-turn and exited the premises.

Delores delivered a plate of scrambled eggs and ham, hash browns and toast that I had not ordered and set it in front of me. She gave Grits a meaningful have-mercy-on-this-child look. "I'll be back with some coffee in a few," she said.

Grits ignored Delores. "I asked you a goddamned question," he said to me.

I took a deep breath and pushed my plate to the side. I knew there was nothing I could do except tell the truth. Well, a bare-minimum truth: "We made love six weeks ago," I said, figuring that was a safer response than the full truth, which was: "We've had sex a few hundred times—so many times I think I've lost count."

"I know you had sex with my niece, you moron," Grits said "What I want to know is why you did what you did after I warned you not to do it."

I looked up at Grits and his penetrating eyes and greasy, swept-back hair. My only option—at least the only one that might keep a knife out of my rib cage—was a thorough, unqualified grovel.

"I'm so sorry, sir," I said. "It never should have happened."

"You're sorry?" Grits said. "You're sorry you piece of shit? Now what do I do with sorry? What do I do with 'It shouldn't have happened'? What does my niece do? What does my family do?"

I was silent; I had no answers and Grits knew it. "Well, son," he said, his words chopping the air between us. "I think you know what you have to do, don't you?"

I nodded, both heartened and disheartened that Grits had just called me "son." "I have already asked Iris to marry me, sir," I said.

Grits arched his eyebrows and pursed his lips and considered my response, which appeared to be news to him. "Well, that's a fuckin' start," he said. He stuck the cigarette in the side of his mouth and pointed a long, thin finger at me and then in the direction of the Tabernacle of the Holy Winds church across the highway. "We ain't nearly done, not until the day you walk down that aisle with my niece. And even then you and me ain't done. You understand?"

I nodded, and my heart sank as I did. "I don't know if Iris wants to marry me," I said.

"Don't matter now what she wants. Don't matter now what you want." He pointed again at the church. "Two of you gonna be walkin' and her aunt and uncle are gonna be watchin'. That's all you need to know."

He leaned forward and smoke wafted from each nostril. "You hear me?"

"Yes sir, I hear." I knew I sounded to the raptly interested people in the room like the scared puddle-pissing puppy that I was, in fact, at that moment. I didn't care. I just wanted to survive my session with Grits.

The Garbage Brothers

He leaned back and gestured with his cigarette hand to Delores. She went to the door and gave the "all-clear" sign to Billy and Pickles, who had been joined by Benjie. They filed through the door, trooped down the aisle to the Willard Sanitation booth and took their usual seats, looking at me with wide-eyed curiosity.

"Look at you thitting in a big-boy theat," Billy said. "That left butt cheek of yours won't know what to do with a benth under it."

Billy beamed as Delores set down his plate of biscuits swimming in a sea of gray and butter-yellow gravy. "Welcome to our thweet little family, Tippy Toeth," he said. "I'm thure you will be a lovely addithion."

"He ain't one of us yet, Billy. But he's gonna be—ain't that right, son?" Grits said.

I stared at my plate, which I'd yet to touch. "Yes," I said.

"Yes, what?"

Pickles lifted his huge left hand and pointed the fork it held at Grits' face. "You said what you had to say. Now back off, and leave the kid alone," he said.

Chapter 37: Billy's Big Secret

Iris didn't come to my apartment after work that night, and she didn't answer when I called her uncle's house. This time I didn't hang up when her aunt picked up the phone, and Mary Rose mercifully avoided the bristling reality of her niece's pregnancy, asking how my job was going. "Be patient," she added at the end of a very short conversation. "Iris just needs some time to rest and think," she added.

"Will you tell her I need to talk with her when she is ready?"

"I will do that," she said. "Now you have a good night and sleep well, son." She put just enough emphasis on the last word to let me know that she knew. And to let me know what both she and her husband expected.

I heard a knock on my apartment door and winced, fearing Grits had come to chain me to the back of his truck and drag me to the Tabernacle of the Holy Winds. I peeked through the front curtains and was relieved to see Billy's beat-to-shit Ford pickup.

"Good evening, Mithter Tippy Toeth," Billy said with a big grin when I opened the door. "I have come to conthult with my motht exthellent campaign manager."

I stared at Billy and then remembered the township supervisor election. After all that had happened in recent weeks—the truck fire, Zeus' death, the revelation that Iris was pregnant and Grits' grim summons to the altar—I had forgotten that Billy was running for supervisor.

"The election's just a few days away," I said. "I don't think there's enough time now for a campaign, Billy."

Billy held out a crooked, greasy finger and beckoned. "You juth come with your ol' friend Billy," he said.

As we drove, Billy sang "Ring of Fire" in an aggravatingly high key and kept time by tapping his thick fingers on the steering wheel. Whenever I looked at him, he grinned and arched his thick, furry eyebrows, as if we both were in on the same unspoken secret.

We drove toward Freedom. When we passed Grits' cul-de-sac I looked to see if Iris' car was parked in front—it wasn't. "Don't worry, your little girlfriend'th not goin' anywhere—not when thee ith carrying' a little-bitty Tippy Toeth in her tummy," Billy said.

"How did you find out Iris was pregnant?"

"Your friendly foreman Billy knowth everything that happenth in hith kingdom," Billy said. "It may thurprithe you to learn that your next-door neighbor ith my wife'th great aunt. And Great Aunt Elthie thayth you two keep her up all night coin' the hokey-pokey. Tho I knew it wath jutht a matter of time."

I nodded, and looked in silence out the window as we drove into Freedom and past the Jaguar Gentlemen's Club that Billy liked to call his "happy plathe." Pickles told me there was a chair next to the stage that the waitresses reserved for Billy, who shed tips like an old dog sheds fur. While Billy had a deep appreciation for what the club advertised as "harmless visual stimuli," the dancers valued his service as an unofficial bouncer. I'd heard stories from crew members about how Billy dragged grabby customers into the unpaved parking lot and hurled them several car lengths, leaving them to pick cinders out of their exposed parts

But something was amiss at the Jaguar on this night: The lights were out on the rooftop billboard, which proclaimed that the club's stage was home to "The Most Beautiful Girls in Northern Illinois" and included the neon outline of a buxom woman in a purple bikini to prove the point.

"They forgot to turn on their sign," I said.

"Oh, I'd better stop and remind them," Billy said, pulling into the Jaguar parking lot. Before I could answer he was out of the cab and running for the front door. And in about 30 seconds the billboard appeared fully lit. But instead of an advertisement for the Jaguar there was a huge, blown-up photo of Eldon Kersnocki, emerging from the restroom at the Greasy Wrench, cigarette drooping from his lips, clutching a folded newspaper in one hand and buttoning his drawers with the other. He was bug-eyed from the flash of Billy's camera. In big black letters across the top of the picture were the words: "DUMP ELDON. VOTE BILLY BARTKOWSKI FOR SUPERVISOR."

"Well," Billy said. "What do you think?"

I stared at the billboard, remembering the morning several weeks earlier when Billy had taken the picture of Eldon exiting the shitter at the Greasy Wrench. I turned to look at Billy and held my hands out in wonder. "Why?" I said. "Why did you think this was a good idea, Billy?"

Billy looked amused at my inability to see the obvious.

"Becauthe he'th a dithguthting old man who doethn't even know how to uthe a thocket wrench. And becauthe Townthip Thupervithor Billy Bartkowthki will keep the truckth running, plow the highwayth when it thnowth and build a beautiful park with a playground and thwimming pool for the kidth."

It was a warm night, and Billy was perspiring from the power of his vision. There was no arguing with him. "OK, Billy," I said. "It's a profound political statement. Now take me home. I'm tired."

We drove for a minute in silence—probably a record for the time I'd spent in Billy's exuberant company. Despite my misgivings about Billy's campaign sign and how Eldon might react, I felt bad about my negative response. I needn't have worried. I watched out of the corner of my eye as the fingers of Billy's right hand began to twitch. Then I heard him singing—softly but growing in volume—"I fell into a burning ring of fire, I went down, down, down, and the flames went higher." I joined in, and soon we were bellowing as we rolled down the road singing. "And it burns, burns, burns, that ring of fire, that ring of fire."

I was surprised to see Iris' car when Billy dropped me off in front of my apartment. Inside, the lights were off and I could see her in the glow of the street lamp that seeped through the branches of an old maple. She was in bed with the covers pulled high—the way I already knew as a young man—or thought I knew—that women pull the covers when they are upset.

I walked quietly to the side of the bed. "Are you sleeping?" I whispered.

There was a slight turning of the shoulders and a return whisper. "No," she said.

I sat down on the edge of the bed and put my hand on her shoulder. "How are you?" I said.

"Still pregnant," she said.

"Anything I can do?" I said.

"Yeah," she said. "You can start by asking me again to marry you. And this time do it right."

I had already given the matter some thought, having rehearsed before each time I'd called her in recent days. "Iris," I said. I knelt next to the bed and held both her soft, warm hands, which were even softer and warmer than I remembered. "Will you marry me, Iris? It's what I want, and it's what I need."

The last sentence was a spontaneous addition that surprised me as the words fell out. And after I said them I couldn't help but wonder if they were true, if I really did want to marry Iris and if I really needed her. No matter; it was too late. The bell had been rung. And there was no unringing it.

Chapter 38: Eldon's Revenge

The lights glowed inside the Greasy Wrench when I arrived a few minutes before 5 a.m. the next morning. I saw through the front window that none of the other Willard Sanitation crew members were there yet, which was unusual. It was the rare morning that Billy wasn't already well into a second breakfast by that time. And Grits wasn't sitting glumly smoking and staring at his coffee cup.

I parked the Corvair, walked to the entrance and pulled on the glass front door. It wouldn't open, but there were customers inside, regulars I recognized who were drinking coffee and shoveling forkfuls of potatoes and eggs into their mouths. I tried the door again. It wouldn't move. Clearly an oversight, I thought, or a practical joke. Delores wiped down the counter and I knocked on the glass door. She looked up, and then looked down again.

I knocked again, this time harder. Delores put down her cloth and walked quickly over to the door, unlocked it and then opened it just far enough for a brief, whispered conversation.

"You can't come in, Jesse," she said.

"Why not?"

"Eldon doesn't want anyone from Willard Sanitation in the cafe. Not after he saw that billboard this morning."

She gestured across the highway. There it was, looking even larger and harsher in the emerging daylight than it had the night before. From this angle, it looked as if Eldon were looking ruefully at me as he buttoned his woolly trousers on top of the Jaguar Gentlemen's Club.

"So what are we supposed to do for breakfast?"

"Pickles said he was going to run over to the Grab and Go and get something to eat for the crew," she said.

"I'll tell you what you can goddamned do for breakfast—you can eat a bucket of horseshit!" The grating voice belonged to none other but the star of the billboard, Eldon Kersnocki. He stood a few feet behind Delores, holding a folded newspaper and wearing the same wool pants and suspenders pictured in the billboard. His suspenders were out of kilter, pulling one side of his pants higher than the other, and it looked as if the incumbent Liberty Township supervisor had just made his morning pilgrimage to the Greasy

Wrench's shitter.

Eldon pulled the front door shut and I could see him through the glass jawing away at Delores, who was trying to ignore him. He turned and stepped to the counter, grabbed something—I couldn't see what—handed it to Delores and then shuffled stiffly back toward his office.

Delores opened the front door and handed me the object that Eldon had taken from the counter. It was a maple bar that had been squeezed into a ball. I could see Eldon's fingerprints on the moist, fragrant frosting.

"He says Billy's campaign manager—I guess that's you—should stick this up his ass," she said. She handed it to me with a wink and a smile.

I looked at the doughnut, which despite its intended mission and Eldon's fingerprints, looked pretty good. I was tempted to take a bite but handed it back to Delores.

"Give it back to Eldon," I said, returning her wink with one of my own. "He might need something to wipe with." I knew it wasn't a great comeback, but I was pretty sure it would play well with the crew—if I could find them.

Turned out they were easy to find. I walked down the gravel driveway leading to the garage, and I could see the great wooden doors on the garage had been pulled open. Inside, sitting on overturned carry cans, were Billy, Pickles and Grits. They were drinking coffee out of paper cups and there were two open boxes of Pop Tarts and a carton of orange juice on the ground next to Billy. Pickles sat with his shoulders slumped and hands on his widespread knees, staring intently at the dirt floor and looking as if he were plotting Billy's demise.

"How long do you figure on keeping that billboard on top of the Jaguar?" Grits asked.

"Jutht ath long ath I pleathe, thank you, Gritth," Billy said, taking a delicate bite from a strawberry Pot Tart and then licking the jelly off a grease-stained forefinger.

Pickles lifted his head and stared at Billy with a look devoid of warmth and humanity.

"Take. . . that. . . fuckin'. . . sign. . . down. . . or. . . I. . . will. . . take. . . a. . . chainsaw. . . and. . . climb. . . up. . . there. . . and. . . take. . . it. . . down. . . mythelf," Pickles said.

"Mythelf?" Billy said, raising an eyebrow.

"That'th right," Pickles said. "You heard me."

Chapter 39: A Chance Encounter

Iris made clear in nearly every conversation that she thought I should accept Benjie's job offer, and she regularly inquired why I had not yet done so. "With the baby coming, it's not your decision to make—it's our decision," she said. It was a presumption that I found both unsettling and aggravating, but true. I never had given much thought to my future, as evidenced by my ass-bumping skid through high school, but I resented being informed that the choice of where to work and live was no longer mine alone to make. Meanwhile, our rosy vision of the two of us living in Paris and of me writing novels while she designed fashions had been jettisoned and replaced by talks about me taking a full-time job with benefits at Willard Sanitation and finding a house where we could raise our family.

But I also understood why Iris was pushing so hard to prepare for the baby, why she was right that we needed to find a place better than my cramped, chronically damp studio—a place she could sing lullabies to put the baby to sleep instead of relying on the theme song to the Andy Griffith show drifting through the wall from Elsie Mondenhoofer's TV.

Still, I put off telling Benjie I was taking the job. Something was holding me back, and that something included Zeus' grimly prophetic warning to get the hell out of Freedom while I still could. I intended to marry Iris and be a proper father for our baby. But I was struggling to reconcile the consequences to my dreams of becoming more than a closet writer, of going to college despite Mrs. Manlove's "bottom-quartile" curse, and of having a meaningful life, even though I didn't have a clue what that meant or how to find it. The prairie winds of precarious change seemed to have blown every half-concocted dream I had from my horizon.

Despite my silence, Benjie seemed to assume that I would accept the job, and so did the other drivers who dialed down the verbal abuse and stopped referring to me as their summer bobo. Grits eased up on his menacing stares and threats, apparently convinced that his niece and I were making our way to the altar. One day he handed me a complaint slip on the back of which he'd scribbled the phone number of his brother Titus, who was now the associate pastor of the Tabernacle of the Holy Winds Church, and told me to call him to set the marriage date. But I was well aware that he was still keeping a close eye on me, looking for any sign that I was planning to leave Freedom—and his pregnant niece—behind.

After a few weeks of driving Zeus' old routes, the novelty of driving a garbage truck full time began to wear off. There were the small pleasures of Gary the Backhoe guy presenting me with my first nudie mag and of Ernie greeting me by my first name and a thumb-flavored bowl of chili waiting for me on the bar at the Snake Pit. But the days quickly became a mind-numbing blur broken only by the inevitable complaints of customers who had the audacity to give Benjie a holy earful if I crushed one of their garbage cans by driving over it or failed to pick up their trash long enough to allow maggots—Zeus used to call them "live rice"—to create fragrant, swarming universes inside their garbage cans.

On the last Wednesday in September, I drove the Rivergreen route and was jogging, a half-full carry can slung over my back, down the Packington's winding gravel driveway where a few weeks earlier I had dumped a mountain of burning garbage. I heard the grind of car tires on the gravel behind me. I moved to the left side of the driveway to let the car pass and nodded hello as the car pulled even, assuming the driver would be Anita Packington. But when I glanced to my right it was Lyla. She slowed, then stopped her family's lime green Ford station wagon and rolled down the window. I heard Bob Dylan singing "Girl From the North Country" on the tape deck in her car. She turned down the volume and smiled, which seared my gut like a summer lightning strike.

"Hey, Jesse," she said. "How are you, my old friend?" She stopped the car and got out, moving with a liquid lightness that was all Lyla. She wore tight jeans and a beatnik black turtleneck that revealed the small, taut breasts that I'd fantasized about for my entire senior year. I would have stared at them if it weren't for the swirling, searching blue pools that were her eyes. Good God, Lyla was beautiful, and here she was, reaching out to me with a hand and touching my filthy right arm as I stood next to her car.

"Look at you, Jesse," she said. "You look like a real honest-to-God workin' man. I do believe this life suits you."

I was undone by Lyla's wind-chime voice. Speechless.

She sat cross-legged on the hood, studying me with those bottomless eyes. I realized I was still standing with a partially filled carry can of garbage slung over my shoulder. I let it drop to the ground with a splatting thud, and she looked down at a crescent of garbage juice droplets on her leg and used the sleeve of her turtleneck to wipe them off with an untroubled grace.

"So did you get my letter?" she asked.

I nodded yes.

"Why didn't you answer me?" she asked.

"I meant to," I said. "But I didn't know what to say."

"Well, do you know what to say now?" she asked.

I paused, wondering how to answer. Since I'd last seen Lyla, I'd gone to work as a summer helper at Willard Sanitation and I had learned more, seen more, known more, felt more, laughed more, touched more, smelled more, tasted more and heard more than I'd known was possible. I had grown strong, and I had at least a prayer of holding my own in a cafe booth filled with garbage felons—men who, with the exception of Grits, had become my friends. I was the neglectful campaign manager for a politically ambitious apeman. I had counseled a middle-aged man-mountain on his relationship with a diner waitress and taught him a Robert Burns poem. My closest friend in the garbage universe had coldcocked me and two months later had been found dead in a gravel pit. I had disinterred a mummy dog in a cellar filled with garbage. I had flown down an airport runway on top of a garbage truck. I'd become a driver with a fine green Chevy garbage truck of his own. And, oh yes, I had met a girl named Iris who was going to have our baby and who I had asked to marry me.

"I don't really know where to start," I said. "How about you? How are you and Brett doing?"

Lyla shrugged. "I don't know. Haven't seen him for a while. He followed me out East for summer orientation at college. We had a big fight and he left. Walked out of the dorm bone naked howling poetry into the night. Left his car with all his belongings parked at my dorm. Last time I heard he was somewhere in Colorado—Boulder, I think—but I haven't talked with him."

I felt a pang of envy at the grandness of my old friend's parting. "I'm pretty sure he's fine," I said.

She studied me for an uncomfortable period of time in even more uncomfortable silence. Finally, she nodded to herself with amusement. "You've changed," she said, "You've lost that hungry look. Got yourself a little girlfriend now?"

"Yeah, her name is Iris," I said. And as I spoke I felt a sense of betrayal, knowing that Iris deserved better than to be the object of Lyla's speculation.

Fuck it, I thought. Nothing to do now but tell the truth. I took a deep breath, closed my eyes, and spoke the words that needed to be said.

"Iris is going to have a baby—our baby. And we're going to get married," I said. "I'm not going to college—I'm probably going to stay in Freedom and take a full-time job humpin' garbage."

Lyla studied me before speaking, and I could feel her X-ray vision all the way down to the end of my spine. "Why?" she said. "Why would you give up your writing, your future—your everything—because you got some little girl pregnant?"

I looked down at the gravel on the driveway and then off into the woods. Lyla was beyond beautiful, and I could picture myself chasing after her to Hiram College and then the beaches of Martinique, the plains of Argentina. Wherever. But Iris was here and she was going to have our baby.

"She's more than 'some little girl,' Lyla," I said.

I started to say more, but didn't. Lyla brushed my forearm with a forefinger that a minute earlier would have sent an electrical current coursing through me but that now felt like, well, just a finger. "I need to get back to work," I said, hoisting the carry can over my back.

"Well, it was lovely seeing you," Lyla said. She swung her legs off the car. Then she got behind the wheel and drove down the gravel path to the main road, disappearing as quickly as she had reappeared in my life. And I was alone with my thoughts and a carry can half filled with wet garbage.

Chapter 40: Election Night

On election night, the two candidates for township supervisor and their supporters gathered inside the township garage, which served as Election Central in Liberty Township. Eldon Kersnocki had his workers park the trucks outside and sweep the trash and mouse droppings that had built up since the last election. Then they taped crepe paper and balloons to the cinder-block walls, where they stayed put for an hour or so before drifting to the floor, where they would remain until the next election. Billy arrived after work and set up two card tables with metal folding chairs and a red plastic salad bowl filled with pretzels. Eldon left word with his crew for Billy to place his tables at the front of the garage, a gesture I suspected was because Eldon wanted everyone in attendance to watch Billy's humiliation as the vote count progressed.

Billy invited the entire Willard crew to watch what he was certain would be his glorious victory. But by the time Helen Ventura, the septuagenarian township secretary—and rumor had it, Eldon's longtime love interest—posted the first results at 7 p.m. I was the only driver who had shown up. The rest had made it clear they didn't want any part of "Billy's bullshit election." Iris and I made conversation with Billy, his wife Serena and their four daughters, Susie, Sandy, Sara and Sally. Serena was an intense woman with ruddy cheeks, long dark hair swept back in a bun and a medicine-ball torso that was a scaled-down version of her husband's. And the four girls, all brunettes with identical pony tails, purple dresses with lace collars and patent leather shoes, looked like scaled-down versions of their mother.

The early results confirmed my expectations that Billy's candidacy was doomed. They showed Billy trailing by more than 300 votes. Billy shrugged it off. "Jutht you wait and thee," he told me. "Motht of the prethincth haven't reported yet," Billy said, and I nodded in agreement, thinking, as almost everyone not sitting at Billy's tables did, that the contest was already over.

"Quite the party," I whispered to Iris.

Benjie and his wife Delilah arrived at 8 p.m. just as Helen Ventura walked to the front of the room to post the latest election update. She was carrying a metal clipboard and a laundry basket filled with ballots that she toted with her, even when she went to the restroom, for what she called "reasons of election security." Serena said she suspected that Helen might be using her bathroom time to stuff the ballot box, but Billy shook his head no. Helen, he said, was an honest woman despite her years of proximity to Eldon, and he didn't want Thuthie, Thandy, Thara and Thally to hear any "untheemly dithperthionth" against her character.

I looked at Billy with surprise. "Unseemly dispersions?" I said.

He grinned and thumped his forehead with a thick index finger. "You know, Tippy Toeth, you're not the only perthon in the crew who can read." I considered reminding him that his favorite publication was "Nude Volleyball, U.S.A," but thought better of it when I remembered that his daughters were at the table.

Benjie wore the same sharply pressed khaki uniform pants, shirt and hat that he wore to work and that I now believed he wore to bed. He approached Eldon's long line of folding tables at which were seated every Greasy Wrench employee with the exception of Delores. Eldon was seated next to a punch bowl, filling Dixie cups with a precise half ladle each. It was clear he was still nursing his billboard wound and he snuck occasional glances at Billy, who seemed oblivious to the numbers on the tote board, stuffing his mouth with pretzels and spewing crumbs as he chatted up his small cluster of supporters.

I watched as Eldon left his post as punch-bowl monitor and approached Billy from behind like a lamprey weaving in for the kill.

"So how is everyone in this cozy little group of losers doing?" Eldon said. He paused, savoring the sweetness of the moment, and his power over all those gathered in the garage that belonged to the once and future township supervisor. And here was his foe, already wounded by early returns on the field of battle and surrounded by his homely wife and children and his stupid campaign manager.

Billy ignored Eldon, but I stood, unsure what I was going to say but certain that I needed to do something to defend my friend, my co-worker, my tormentor, my foreman—the man who taught me that it was possible to eat pound cake and grapefruit from the dumpster and survive. I squared myself between Billy and his tormentor. "Go away, Eldon," I said. "Leave Billy alone."

Eldon ignored my intercession and pointed at Billy. "You're going to lose and you know it, Billy," he said. He pulled a Kodak Instamatic from the pocket of his pants and took a picture of Billy, the flash lighting up the front of the township garage. "Now I'm gonna frame this and put it on a billboard over the Greasy Wrench. It will have just one word—loser," he said and then shuffled back to his stool next to the punch bowl.

Helen Ventura walked to the front of the room to post another update. She stepped away from the blackboard, and the room watched her pause for a moment and exchange a look with Eldon before she wrote. The new results showed Eldon was still in the lead but now by only 156 votes. Three precincts had yet to report their votes—all of them in Wilton.

Iris reached over and squeezed my hand. "I don't feel well," she said. "I think I need to go home."

Her hand felt warm, and her face looked pale. "Sure," I said. "Want me to take you to my apartment or your home?"

"My home," she said.

I leaned over to Billy. "Got to take Iris home. She's not feeling good," I said. "You're doing great, Billy."

It was a well-intentioned lie, and Billy knew it. "You don't think I'm gonna win, but it's gonna happen. And three people know it—me and Eldon. And Helen Ventura."

I nodded and we stood and headed for the door. We passed Benjie who had found Eldon's back-up punch bowl and was sitting alone, elbow braced on a long table as if waiting for someone to engage him in discourse. Our eyes met, and he smiled. "Can I buy you a drink, young man?" he said.

"That's Eldon's punch," I said. "Unless there's rat poison in it, I don't think he'd want me drinking it."

He nodded his ruddy and shiny piggy face, his eyes curiously moist. "And who is this beautiful young lady?" he said.

"This is Iris," I said. "She's Grits' niece. You met her at Zeus' funeral."

The boss beamed as he stared unabashedly at Iris' short black dress. "Really?" he said. "I don't recall. Such a lovely young woman." Then he reached out and gripped my forearm with surprising strength and drew me uncomfortably close. "We still need to talk about your future, young man," he said.

I pulled away, and headed for the door. "Iris doesn't feel well—I gotta take her home, Benjie," I said over my shoulder. "See you in the morning."

Iris was quiet and withdrawn as we walked out of the township garage and to my car. I turned on the radio and dialed it to my favorite late-night radio station, one that played airline music and where the announcer talked in a hushed voice about faraway places, tropical women and lingering regrets. We drove past a field of ragged corn stalks, and there was a rising coolness in the air, much like that night we had sat together on a log on the Fox Breath River and she had set me on fire with a kiss.

"I'd guess you could have food poisoning, but I don't think you could have gotten anything from Billy's pretzels," I said. "Did you sneak over to Eldon's table for shrimp or anything?"

She smiled and shook her head. "I'm loyal," she said. "I wouldn't sell out Billy for a shrimp."

"I would. Probably so would Billy," I said, drawing a small laugh that made me think she was feeling better

I kissed her goodnight, gave her a hug and slipped away before Mary Rose or Grits saw me at the front door. And when I reached the top of the hill that led to their cul-de-sac, I saw a large orange, red and yellow half orb on the horizon two or three miles to the south. The edges were ragged, and it looked like a fire. A big one.

I considered what might be burning. I traveled that stretch of highway most days on my routes and thought it might be a fire at the dump—that happened now and then and I had seen it before. But dump fires tended to be low, smoldering affairs that would not be so visible at night from such a distance. Then I realized that it was the Snake Pit. There was nothing else on that stretch of highway big enough to send up flames like those.

I turned off the radio, and when I reached Freedom I turned right onto Highway 40. As I drove south the fire grew in size and intensity. There was something otherworldly about the flames and the black tendrils that wove up through them and into the night sky. The flames surged and rose and then surged and rose again. In a few minutes I neared the Snake Pit and I could see several fire trucks, lights flashing, and a gaggle of milling, useless firemen wearing bulky asbestos gear and big-brimmed red helmets that made them look like warriors preparing for a siege. But the fortress had been engulfed by flames and there were only flashing glimpses of the walls, doors, windows and the raggedy flat tar roof that made the flames dance with an obscene glee. It looked as if the firefighters had started deploying hoses but, after realizing the hopelessness of their task, stopped and now were relegated to the role of conflagration witnesses. There was no need, no hope, nothing to be saved and the heat was so intense that no one could approach closer than 20 yards. The acrid smoke made my eyes and lungs burn, and I could see this was a fire that would not last long. The Snake Pit was going, going, going and soon would be gone.

I felt dazed and in a dream. I had eaten lunch at the Snake Pit earlier in the day, and Ernie had inquired if my testicles had dropped yet then walked away cackling. God, I hoped the old man was OK. I left my car on the dump side of the highway and walked over to the firefighters. "Was there anyone inside?" I asked. Partly because I wanted to know about Ernie. Partly because I wanted, needed to break the spell of the flames that were sucking the oxygen from my lungs and heart.

One of the firefighters, a tall man in his 30s with a big drooping mustache and a look of bemusement at my stupidity, answered. "Kind of fuckin' hard to tell at the moment," he said. We stared at the fire, and he spoke again. "It was past closing time," he added. "I doubt anyone was in there. But we don't know for sure."

I walked back to my car and got inside. I looked ahead through the windshield at the entrance to the dump, and there was Pickles' pickup parked behind a scraggly oak and out of sight of the firefighters. Then I saw the big man. He stood behind the truck watching the fire in the same crazy Hawaiian shirt he'd worn to Zeus' funeral. His ruddy face looked even more flushed in the light of the flames, and he was holding a cigarette in his right hand. Pickles lifted it to his mouth, revealing what looked like a dark streak of something—was it grease?—on the underside of his forearm.

Pickles knew I was watching him. As I put my car in gear, he turned in my direction and lifted his left hand, and his fingers moved up and down below his chin as if they were combing an imaginary beard. Just like Zeus had done incessantly when he was alive. Then Pickles turned back to the fire and watched the Snake Pit burn.

Chapter 41: Victory and Loss

The front door was propped wide open at the Greasy Wrench the next morning, and as I parked my car I could see Delores through the cafe window. She was delivering a tall stack to Billy and refilling Grits' coffee cup. Still unsettled by the late-night Snake Pit fire, it took a few seconds for me to realize that the election was over and that Eldon must have decided to be magnanimous in victory by reopening the cafe to Billy and the rest of the Willard Sanitation crew.

"G'mornin' little thleepy head," Billy said as I slid into what the crew now referred to as "the Zeus seat" facing Billy and Grits and next to the window.

"Good mornin', Billy," I said. "How are you holdin' up after last night?"

"I'm peachy," Billy said. "Why wouldn't I be?"

"Well," I said, speaking slowly as if addressing a small child, "you did lose an election last night. I'm sure it didn't feel good to watch Eldon do a victory dance." I felt bad as soon as I had spoken. I was being condescending, and Billy deserved better.

He reached down to the seat next to him and pulled up a copy of The Wilton Daily Independent and slid it across the table. "Happen to thee a newthpaper today, Mr. Thmarty Panth?" he said.

I looked down at the front page and the top headline. "Bartkowski upsets incumbent in supervisor race," it said. And I saw, just above the fold, another headline that read, "Fire destroys Snake Pit Tavern."

"Jesus Christ, Billy," I said. "You won?"

"Of courthe, I won," Billy said. "Wilton voterth love their hard-workin' garbage man, and thothe were the latht prethincth to come in after my campaign manager went home to do the bonkydonk with his girlfriend. I beat that thithead Eldon by 123 goddamned voteth."

"I can't believe you won, Billy," I said, sneaking a quick glance at Grits to see if he was riled by Billy's "bonkydonk" comment. If he was he didn't show it. Grits stared out the window and, as usual, tuned out the breakfast conversation.

"You better believe it, Mithter Tippy Toeth," Billy said, leaning back in the booth and savoring his opportunity to expound on his victory. "By the way, my lovely wife Therena read that book you got from the library, and we thpent every Thunday going door to door in Wilton with my girtlh Thuthie, Thandy, Thara and Thally. Like I thaid latht night, they love their garbage man and hith thweet little Polak family in Wilton. Thath why I alwayth check thothe canth for the tithueth. But if you really want to know what made the differenthe it wath my billboard."

I glanced over my shoulder but didn't have a clear view of the Jaguar Gentlemen's Club. "Is that damned thing still up there?"

"Abtholutely," Billy said. "I thought Eldon might want one more day in the thpotlight."

He reached down to the bench and picked up the library book I'd loaned him at the start of the summer, "So You are Seeking Office—a Guide for Women With a Vision." "You thould take it back—I think it'th a little overdue," he said, sliding it across the table to me.

"So you're really the next township supervisor?"

"Won't be thupervisor till January when Eldon'th term ith up," Billy said. "I'm thtill goin' to be your foreman until then," he said. "Tho you better not give me any bullthit."

Grits looked at me for the first time since I'd walked into the cafe. "So you gonna tell us what you was doing at the goddamn Snake Pit fire last night?" he asked.

Grits unfolded the newspaper and pointed to a picture of the fire that showed a cluster of firefighters—and me—watching the fire burn. I realized the photo must have been taken at about the same time I was asking if anyone had died in the fire.

"I was just watching," I said. "I took Iris home, and then I saw the fire and drove down to see it. That was one monster fire. Does the story say if anyone died?"

"No," Billy said. "But two copth thtopped in here for coffee thith morning and told uth the plathe burned to the ground. They found some crithpy human remainth, but they haven't been identified. The copth said it wathn't Ernie—he and the cook got out in time. I gueth Ernie got thome mild burnth when he ran back inthide to get hith teeth from the cup where he keepth them behind the bar."

"I bet the insurance money Ernie's goin' to get will make those burns feel better," a rumbling voice to my left said. I turned and it was Pickles, sliding into the booth and giving me a glance that sent a clear "keep-your-yap-shut-about-seeing-me-last-night" warning.

"Jeethuth Chritht, Pickleth," Billy said, shaking his head. "Fuckin' Thnake Pit gone up in fucking flameth."

"And Billy Bart gets elected supervisor—the world is going to goddamn hell," Pickles said.

"Snake Pit fire kind of stole the thunder from your dumb-ass election, didn't it?" Grits observed as he studied the front page, flicking cigarette ash onto the tabletop next to Billy.

The door of the Greasy Wrench jangled opened and Benjie entered. He paused, complaint slips and clipboard in hand, watching the bent, elderly man shuffling his way from the hallway that led from his office-bedroom to the cafe's bathroom. It was Eldon, worse for wear from his election night defeat.

"Fuck you, Benjie, and fuck your idiot foreman," Eldon said. "Fuck the whole sorry-ass lot of you. Now get out of my way, I have to take a shit." He stopped and glared at Billy and lifted a gnarled forefinger of his right hand as his left worked the buttons on his pants. He opened the bathroom door and the entire diner listened to him slam down the seat on the commode.

"Why did Eldon let us in the cafe this morning if the billboard's still up and he lost?" I asked.

"He didn't let us in. Delores did, and I guess Eldon figures he might as well make money off Billy's bottomless belly while he can," Pickles said. "But if I was you I'd take a good look at my eggs before I put any in my mouth."

Benjie turned to face his crew and Billy climbed onto the seat of the booth, ape arms extended. "Come thay good morning to your nexth townthip thupervithor, Benjie," Billy said, puckering his lips and sending a smacker so loud in the direction of the boss that Delores turned from the kitchen window to see if it had been intended for her.

Benjie walked to the booth, and he smiled at Billy, looking genuinely pleased for his foreman. "That was a great night, wasn't it?" he said. He turned to Pickles and Grits. "Why weren't you fellas there?"

Grits shrugged. "Maybe it was 'cause I didn't give a shit, Benjie," he said.

"And I was otherwise occupied with a certain waitress friend of mine," Pickles said. Then, as he lifted his coffee cup, pinky extended toward the now seated Billy, he added with a British accent: "But all the best to you, my dear Mr. Supervisor. All the best."

Benjie delivered his normal recitation of customer complaints, and the drivers gave the owner their normal complete inattention. "So who is going to take your place when you become supervisor?" Pickles asked Billy as Benjie bent to pick up the complaint slips from the floor where Pickles had shoved them when the boss wasn't looking.

"I dunno—maybe Mr. Tippy Toeth here. He'th a bright young man. It thure won't be you or Gritth," Billy said

"First time anyone ever used the word 'bright' talkin' about Tippy Toes," Grits said.

When Benjie was done, the drivers walked from the Greasy Wrench to their trucks. The morning air was cooler now as fall had begun to arrive and the oak canopy over the garage showed whisperings of yellow and red. There was an uneasiness in the air, brought on in part by the events of recent days—Billy's election victory and the great conflagration at the Snake Pit. And I had the unsettling feeling there were more changes to come, and not necessarily good ones.

Grits walked stiff-legged, hands stuffed in his front pants pockets, ahead of me. I paused to talk with Pickles, who trailed several yards behind me, his right hand lifted to his mouth working a toothpick that he held daintily between his forefinger and thumb.

I stopped and waited for him, and he offered a sad, knowing nod. "We're gonna miss that dump of a Snake Pit, ain't we?" he said. "Where am I going to get my morning shots and beers?"

"Pickles," I said. "Tell me who died in that fire."

He said nothing and kept walking. "Pickles," I tried again, "Who died in that fire?"

Pickles stopped and he leaned down and cocked his head toward me and gripped the top of my arm near the shoulder so hard I couldn't move and could barely breathe with the pain. When he spoke, it was with a voice that was soft but held my complete and unswerving attention. "You know goddamn well who died in that fire. Just like you know goddamn well who killed your friend Zeus."

Pickles was right. I knew.

"Listen to me," he said. "If anyone asks, you didn't see me last night—I wasn't there. And you never tell anyone otherwise. This is the last time we are going to talk about this. Understand?"

I nodded. Pickles released my shoulder and walked into the garage. He turned and looked at me with a smile as if nothing in the world was amiss. "C'mon," he said. "Like our lovely boss likes to say, the garbage waits for no man."

Chapter: 42: The Tabernacle

Iris didn't return to my apartment after work, but that wasn't unusual. Often she stopped by the house to see Mary Rose and the kids, to do laundry and devour a dinner that actually included vegetables. But she always called to let me know she was staying the night at her place, and there were no calls from her that night or for the next two nights after that. I tried phoning her after work, but Mary Rose answered and informed me in an uncharacteristically distant voice that Iris couldn't come to the phone. "But I'm sure she will be in touch soon, Jesse," she said.

"What's going on, Mary Rose?" I asked after the third night of Iris' absence. "Why won't Iris talk to me? Did I do something wrong? Did I say something? Is she OK? Tell me what's going on."

"She's all right, Jesse. I'm sure she'll call."

Grits, as usual, was no help. He ignored me over breakfast at the Greasy Wrench, and when I approached him in the garage while he was sweeping out his cab with the stub of a whisk broom after work. "I got nothing to say to you. Just stay away from my niece, and my house."

I stopped by the clothing store where Iris worked, and the manager said she had called in sick. I drove past her house several times, and her car was parked off the driveway in the yard, and the curtains on her bedroom window were drawn. I considered parking on the highway shoulder and sneaking down the hill through high weeds to tap on her bedroom window, but I thought better of it.

I was pretty sure that Iris would get in touch when she was ready—but ready after what and from what and how long it would take—remained a mystery. I didn't have a clue. We hadn't argued. We were, at least the last time we talked, in agreement about getting married, although we hadn't yet set a date and I hadn't called her Uncle Titus at the Tabernacle of the Holy Winds Church to make arrangements. She wasn't feeling well the night of the township election, but she'd said it was just an upset stomach.

Then, as I was pulling into the company garage after a day at work on the fourth day of Iris' absence, I remembered the letter. Lyla's letter. The one that opened, "My Dearest Jesse." The one that was written on delicate onionskin and exhorted me to hear "the wind behind my words." The one that said

The Garbage Brothers

"soon it will be time for you to fly." The one that I'd tucked into my poetry anthology on the same page as the Robert Burns poem I'd once memorized in the hope of getting Lyla to shed her reservations. The same page that on which, as a love-forsaken senior in high school, I'd crossed out the title of the poem, "O, My Luve's Like a Red Red Rose" and written next to it in painfully earnest blue ballpoint ink—and underlined it three times—"Lyla's poem."

As soon as work was done, I raced home to see if the letter was still in its hiding place. To my dismay, the book—and Lyla's letter—were gone.

"Damn it," I howled. And then I yelled it again, loudly enough that Elsie knocked on my door a few minutes later bearing two Dixie cups filled with pudding and a look of grandmotherly concern—and intense curiosity.

"I heard sounds," she said. "Are you and Iris all right?" Without invitation, she inserted her head inside the apartment and peered around. "And where is Iris by the way? I haven't seen her for days."

"We're fine, Elsie," I said, taking the pudding from her and starting to close the door. "I just stubbed my toe and yelled. Sorry I disturbed you. And thanks for the pudding."

"Well, I'm concerned," she said, retreating not one inch from the doorway. She looked at me without saying anything for a few moments and then said, "Iris is a nice girl, Jesse. If you did something wrong then you should make it right. And you should do it sooner rather than later."

"Yes, ma'am," I said.

"Well, good," she said, and she turned and slipper-shuffled back into her apartment, leaving her door cracked open for surveillance purposes.

"Good night, Elsie," I called after her. Then I grabbed my car keys and drove to the Tabernacle of the Holy Winds.

~ ~ ~

A stocky man in an ill-fitting brown suit slumped in a chair with a Bible open in his lap and the heels of his scuffed black wing-tips on a desk in the church lobby. There were two signs above his desk. One read "Receptionist" and the other "Associate Pastor."

"And how can we help you today, friend?" he asked, lifting his head with a start that made me suspect that he'd been studying The Word in a state of prayerful slumber.

"We?" I said. I looked around the lobby and into the sanctuary, which was the former grange hall's meeting room and was filled with metal folding chairs.

"By we, I am referring to the Holy Spirit Wind, God the Father, and my Lord and Savior Jesus Christ," he said. "And" he added, "yours truly, Pastor Titus Japes." His accent was deep-holler South and I could see the family resemblance to Grits, although the elder brother was at least 50 pounds bigger and several inches taller than his younger sibling.

"My name is Jesse Wheeler and I am engaged to your niece, Iris. You must be her Uncle Titus."

"I know who you are," he said. "The Lord told me you were coming, and I have been praying for you."

"I need to see Iris."

"Yes, you do, my son," he said. "Let us see what we can do. Wait here and we will give her a call."

Pastor Japes stood. His hair was slicked back with a Jerry Lee Lewis hump in front. There was no phone on his desk. He stood and walked into Head Pastor Rolly Rawlins office—the name and title were on the door along with a plastic placard with clock hands that indicated he would be back at 10 a.m. the next day—and closed the door behind him. As I waited, I tried to remember what Iris had told me her Uncle Titus had done to serve time, as his younger brother did, in the Tennessee State Penitentiary. I couldn't remember, but his social skills were certainly better than those of Grits, so I guessed that whatever crimes he'd committed were more in the grifting line rather than homicide.

I heard Pastor Titus talking in a low voice in the office but couldn't make out what he was saying. I looked around the church—it was austere but not unfriendly. Hanging on the far wall of the sanctuary was a big wooden cross made of two unpainted 4x4s tied together with fence wire. Two spikes had been pounded into the bottom of the vertical post, and one spike on each side of the horizontal. On the far wall, just above a walnut-stained plywood lectern, was a framed color portrait of Jesus, the same picture that a Sunday school teacher had once presented to me for memorizing the books of the Old Testament after, in an act of Christian grace, overlooking my omission of Habakkuk.

Iris' uncle stepped out of the office in a couple of minutes, saw me standing in the entrance to the sanctuary and stood with his hands folded in front of him at his waist like a funeral home director. I noticed that he had had JESUS tattooed in rough black letters just below the knuckles of each hand. "My niece will be here shortly and you two may talk in private in the sanctuary," he said. "We're leaving for the night, so lock the door when you leave."

He turned to leave, then stopped. "Do you require prayer, my son?" he asked.

I didn't answer right away, trying to think of a nice way to say. "No, thank you, I just want you to leave as soon as possible so I can see Iris and tell her I didn't cheat on her and see if there is anything else going on I don't know about."

The Garbage Brothers

Pastor Titus took my silence as assent. He walked back to me, took my hand and started praying in a language I did not understand and one in which the same phrase was repeated every few seconds. "Hafu harranjah aseemah halloo hafu harranjah aseemah halloo."

"Are you speaking in. . .," I started.

"Yes, son, we're praying in tongues—it's our direct line to the Father," he said, tightening his grip and intensifying his prayer. And, despite my discomfort at Pastor Titus squeezing my hand and praying in tongues for God knew what, I felt a curious easing of my anxiety. And, it had to be my imagination, a faint stirring of the air in the sanctuary.

He finished his prayer with one last emphatic "Hafu harranjah aseemah halloo," then smiled and fished a loose cigarette and a matchbook from a pocket of his suit jacket. I recognized Grits' smoker mannerisms, the tap of the cigarette tip on the back of his wrist and the way he bent the match and lit it still attached to the matchbook. Must be a Japes family tradition or the way inmates did it in the Tennessee state pen, I thought.

~ ~ ~

Iris walked into the lobby, and Pastor Titus looked at me. "The Lord hath indeed heard our entreaties—Oh, he hath indeed," he said and he turned with a flourish to leave. "Now trust in God, my son, and all shall be revealed."

Iris walked past her Uncle Titus without acknowledging him, looking as if she was determined to get our meeting over with and leave. She looked pale—paler even than she looked that night in the car when I'd driven her home from the township hall.

Iris sat down in the front row of the sanctuary, and I pulled up a chair and sat across from her, my back to the cross.

"Iris," I said. "I'm so sorry about the letter from Lyla. You have to know that I never answered it. Never called her. Never wrote her. Never saw her. Well, actually I did see her a week ago when I was doing the Rivergreen route—that's where she lives. And I knew that day that there was nothing between us."

Iris was looking down at the floor as I spoke. "I don't care about the letter or you and Lyla now—I did at first, but now I don't."

"Then what's going on? Why did you disappear? Why haven't you returned my calls? What did I do? Just tell me."

"You didn't do anything," she said. "It's the baby."

"What about the baby?"

She pressed the palms of her hands to her eyes and was silent. "The baby's gone," she finally said. "The night you took me home. I went to the bathroom. There was blood. I went to the emergency room in Wilton and they said I'd had a miscarriage. The baby is gone."

At first her words passed right through me unheard and unheeded.

"What?" I said.

"I had a miscarriage, Jesse. There is no baby anymore."

I heard myself breathing, as her words drifted to the earth like leaves blown by a passing truck. Pastor Titus closed the front door of the church behind him and pulled his car out of the church's gravel parking lot. I breathed in and breathed out and looked out a window. I saw an elderly woman with snow-white hair walking out of Gary's Grab and Go with a shopping cart. It was early fall. and the evening light had a particular sharpness, as if atoning for darker days to come.

"How are you now?" I asked.

Her eyes pooled. "I'm tired and my heart hurts. But I'm alright. The doctor told me to rest and stay in bed. Mary Rose has been taking care of me. She drove me here. She's waiting in the parking lot."

"Why didn't you tell me before? I should have known. I should have been at the hospital with you."

"I needed to be alone," she said. "I needed time."

"I should have known," I said. And as I spoke the reality of Iris' words began to penetrate the fog inside me. I closed my eyes and could see a tumble of images—the rear of a garbage truck, and its hopper filled with broken furniture—a high chair with its stainless steel legs twisted and bent. A kitchen table. Fence slats from the fixer-upper house we'd talked about finding after the baby was born. Lawn chairs from the front porch. The percolator I'd taken from my grandfather's kitchen after his death, the one with an art deco design that reminded me of the Empire State Building. It was all in there in the hopper, the blade lowering to crush and compact it for deposit at the county dump.

"What do we do now?" I asked. "Do we have a funeral?"

Iris shook her head no. "There was hardly anything there," she said. "The baby was a speck, and now it's gone. And I couldn't handle a funeral—all the people watching."

I took her hand. It was warm and soft, but when I squeezed it there was no response.

"So what do we do?" I asked again.

"We talk, I guess. Try to figure it out."

"Do you still want to get married?"

"I don't know—it's too soon."

"I still want to get married," I said quickly. Too quickly. It might have been a lie, or it might have been the truth. I didn't know. I just thought it was the right thing to say.

She smiled. It was a sad, knowing smile devoid of blame or recrimination.

"I don't think you know what you want right now. And I'm not sure what I want."

"I still want to marry you."

She sighed. "We need time to figure it out," she said. "We both have choices to make, and we need to make sure we do the right thing. I read the letter from Lyla—I borrowed the book to read poetry, and there was her letter. It made me realize that you have things you want to do, places you want to go, maybe even other people to love. Maybe I do, too."

I nodded, my head and heart roiling. Despite my sorrow about the miscarriage, I could feel a stirring, a sudden, unseemly in-pouring of warm, swirling possibilities. Of being unbound, unencumbered. Free. Free to go. To pursue Lyla. To find a college that would accept me. To go anywhere that wasn't Freedom and Willard Sanitation. But at the same time I was free to stay and make things right with Iris, whose hand felt so small and vulnerable in mine. Free to marry. Free to find the little rat's nest house in the country we'd talked about and fill it with kids and weedy gardens and dogs and pots of soup.

"You know it would break Grits' heart not to have me as a son-in-law," I said. Iris laughed—it felt good to hear—and she brushed the tears from her eyes.

"You'd be surprised to know that he's actually beginning to like you," she said. "He says you're a tough little son of a bitch. He didn't think you'd survive the summer. But here you are."

"Here I am. For whatever that's worth," I said. And we walked out of the Tabernacle of the Holy Winds Church, and I hugged her. Mary Rose was waiting in Grits' pickup with both hands on the steering wheel, as if she had been negotiating traffic inside her as we talked inside the church. She lifted the fingers of one hand in a partial wave, which I returned before walking to my car. I got inside my baby blue Corvair, turned it on and drove off into the dark, cold, and shimmering night.

Chapter 43: Go West, Young Man

When I got home, the absence of Iris and all the "what-might-have-beens" descended on me like muddy floodwaters cascading over a dam. The apartment was empty and dark. I opened the curtains on the front window, sat on the bed and stared at a pictureless wall and the picnic table topped with a cup that Iris had bought in the gift shop at the Chicago Art Institute. On the side it had Vincent Van Gogh's "Self Portrait," and the string of a four-day-old tea bag dangled down the side over his wounded ear. So quiet. So devoid of hope. Even Elsie's apartment was still, and there was no traffic on the frontage road.

I walked outside to check the mailbox, half hoping I'd see Iris' car in the parking lot but knowing I wouldn't. There was one letter—it was from the University of Oregon, whose writing program had caught my attention when I was desperately scanning college catalogs for potential schools.

Oregon was the first school to inform me that my application was rejected, followed by all the others in an ominous drumbeat of impending failure. I slit the envelope using a dirty steak knife left on the kitchen counter and unfolded the cover letter, running the heel of my right hand over the folds. At the top of the page was the green-tinted outline of fir trees and a snow-covered mountain peak. "Dear Mr. Wheeler," it read. "We were sorry to inform you in July that the University of Oregon had rejected your application for admission. But we are now pleased to report that you have been accepted for one of a small number of openings that we have for the winter term."

I looked out the window and cleared my throat, as if the sound might ensure that I was awake and this was not a cruel dream. Then I looked down and re-read the first sentence. Then I read the rest of the short letter, which advised me that, based on personal circumstances that I'd described in my application essay, including a recent parental death and family financial setbacks, that I might qualify for a hardship scholarship.

I felt a brief jolt of electricity run through my core. Given my high school counselor Mrs. Manlove's "bottom-quartile" curse, I had never expected the University of Oregon—or any of the schools to which I'd applied—to accept me. I'd picked University of Oregon on a whim, remembering that was where the novelist Ken Kesey had studied. His descriptions of Oregon—a land of snow-covered mountains and rampaging rivers and towering Douglas firs and verdant valleys and high deserts—struck me as the exact opposite of the Midwest, where I'd spent much of my life moving from suburb to suburb, all of them looking the same. And here now was a letter informing me that I not only had been accepted as a student in the winter term, but that there might be money available to help pull off my miraculous deliverance from Freedom.

My apartment was nearly dark. I sat, still in my work clothes on the unmade bed, holding this lightning-bolt letter from far-away Oregon and all the glorious, wind-blown possibilities that place contained. I remembered my talk with Iris and the deep-water sadness in her eyes. Then I put the letter on the bed, lifted my hands to my face and wept.

Chapter 44: The Fall of Pickles

Billy, Grits and Pickles were already seated in the booth when I arrived at the cafe the next morning. Billy greeted me with a sly, head-cocked grin, which usually meant that I was going to get a crappy special job that no one else wanted. Grits ignored my presence as usual, extinguishing his cigarette on the scarred tabletop and looking out the window as a black-and-white state police cruiser with two troopers in it slowly pulled into the lot and took up three parking spaces by the front door.

"Fuckin' police—can't even park a damned car," Grits growled, leaving unspoken the gaping question of why two state troopers were at the Greasy Wrench at 5:20 a.m. That was the question considered by most of the dozen diners in the Greasy Wrench, several of whom looked as if they might have outstanding warrants. Pickles either didn't see the troopers or ignored them, taking a deep drag on a Newport he'd bummed from Delores and cocking his huge head back and exhaling one of the finer smoke rings I'd ever seen, holding its form until it reached the asbestos-tile ceiling.

I felt Delores' hand on my shoulder. "What would you like to eat this morning, sweetie?" she said. She wasn't looking at me as she talked. She was watching the troopers, a tall and thin young man with a pencil mustache and a short, bulky older man, as they entered the jangling front door. Their eyes swept the cafe, looking not for empty seats, but for someone.

Delores walked to the troopers who stood still wearing their tasseled Smokey the Bear hats in the entry across the aisle from the cash register. "Can I help you, boys?" she asked. "The booths are full up, but there are some seats at the counter."

Pickles took a casual sip of coffee, eyes fixed on the Union Pacific calendar. Grits watched the troopers without moving. Billy, eyes riveted on the troopers, slowly wiped his mouth with a paper napkin, an unprecedented act of hygiene. The bells on the cafe door rang, and Benjie strode inside, head down and oblivious to the presence of the state troopers.

"Startin' to rain, fellas," Benjie announced to the room. Puzzled by the silence, he looked up and saw the two troopers directly in front of him. The younger trooper pulled a photo from the left front pocket of his morning-crisp blue uniform shirt. He looked closely at Benjie, held the photo up for

The Garbage Brothers

him to see and then turned and showed the same picture to Delores, who stiffened and put a hand on the counter behind her.

"We're looking for this man—his name is William Peterman. Do you know him?" His partner, a veteran with sergeant's stripes and a gut that suggested he'd rather be ordering pigs in a blanket than executing an arrest warrant, watched the room as his partner waited for an answer.

Delores was silent, and she leaned away from the trooper asking the question. I saw Benjie's right hand, the one holding his ever-present clipboard, start to gesture to our booth, but then the slow-moving tumblers in the boss's brain clicked into place and he lowered his hand. Then Grits spoke in a high-strung nasal twang, every syllable ratcheting the tension in the room. "Ain't no William Peterman in this room, so you boys get your doughnuts and just keep movin'," he said.

The young cop glared at Grits and took a step toward the Willard Sanitation booth. "So you're sayin' the name William Peterman doesn't ring any bells?" he said.

"I'm not tryin' to ring no goddamn bells," Grits said. "Just tellin' you there ain't no William Peterman here."

"I believe you two fine gentlemen want the stupid-looking giant who's sitting in the booth across from the loudmouth hillbilly." The grating informant's voice belonged to Eldon Kersnocki, who had a newspaper folded under one arm, slippers on his feet, and was en route to his morning constitutional.

I'm not sure whether I moved out of the booth on my own—or whether Pickles lifted me out. But suddenly I found myself standing in the aisle and watching Pickles stand and turn to face the approaching troopers. Pickles extended his wrists, pressed together and arms straight. "Gentlemen," he said with a slight bow. "William Peterman. At your disposal."

The younger cop stepped toward Pickles with handcuffs that looked as if they would never fit around Pickles' wrists. But they did, closing with dismaying ease in a click that resonated through the cafe.

"William Peterman, you are under arrest for arson and the murder of Largo Fuscaldo at the Snake Pit Tavern on Nov. 4. You have the right to remain silent. Anything you say. . ."

"What's happening, William?" Delores asked in a shattered-glass voice that caused most of the cafe's customers to look away.

Pickles drew back his shoulders, lifted his head and looked at Delores. "Don't worry, my sweetness—it's just life unfolding the way it's supposed to," he said. Then the officers walked Pickles out the door, one in front of the big man and one in the back. The bells jangled on the door as the three men departed. The room was silent. And then everyone and everything moved at once, heads turning, eyes meeting, forks descending, a spatula scraping and clanging in the kitchen. Everyone moved—except for Delores, who stood motionless watching the troopers load Pickles into the back of the squad car, his great head bowed to avoid hitting the frame around the car door.

Eldon proceeded with his morning shuffle to the bathroom. As he opened the door, he paused to look at the Willard Sanitation booth where we were staring at each other, waiting for someone to break the silence.

"Lemme know when they come for the rest of you sorry sons of bitches," Eldon said.

Chapter 45: Bailing Out the Boss

After the patrol car carrying Pickles pulled out of the Greasy Wrench and onto Highway 40, the Willard Sanitation crew, or what was left of it, sat in stillness. Grits gave me a hard stare, and I realized I was sitting in Pickle's massive sinkhole on the cushioned bench. I slid into Zeus' old seat next to the window and looked at the empty parking spaces where the state police car had been just a few minutes ago. Billy lifted a forkful of pancakes to his mouth and then returned it uneaten to the plate—another unprecedented occurrence.

"Jeethuth Chritht," he said. "I can't believe they jutht arrethted Pickleth."

"Well, I goddamn believe it," Grits said. "Truth is we all knew that asshole Largo needed to pay for what he did to Zeus. And Pickles was the only one here with the balls to do it."

Billy pushed his plate away and rubbed his eyes with his palms, as if hoping that when he opened them Pickles would be back in his seat, eyes fixed on the wall calendar. "What are we gonna do now without Pickleth? Tippy Toeth ith already coverin' for Theuth, but who'th gonna do Pickleth' goddamn routeth," he said.

No one had noticed that Benjie had quietly left the cafe and walked back to the garage after the troopers departed with Pickles. But everyone in the cafe lifted their heads when the boss walked in the door wearing one of Pickles' old uniform shirts and work pants that, despite the boss's considerable girth, were so large that he had to use a safety pin to keep them from falling. And he topped off his outfit with a Chicago Bears stocking cap with a bobbing fuzzy orange ball at the peak.

Benjie plopped himself next to me. It felt wrong that he was wearing Pickles' uniform and taking his still-warm seat—and even more wrong that the boss looked as if he actually intended to do his route. Billy hunched over his syrup-streaked plate, holding his coffee cup with both hands. "Jethuth Chritht, Benjie," he said. "You thurely don't think you're going to do Pickleth' route, do you?"

The boss's face pinked with indignation. "And why not?" he said.

Grits took a long drag and exhaled. "Benjie, when is the last time you actually did any work—I mean besides listening to customers bitch and signing short paychecks?"

The boss held up the clipboard. "Got all the addresses right here," he said. "How hard can it be? And how else is his work going to get done until I can find someone to replace Pickles, who isn't gonna be gettin' out of jail any time soon?"

Grits started to make another pitch for hiring his preacher brother Titus. Then he looked up, and there was Delores standing at the end of the booth, order book in hand. She looked dazed, as if she'd just staggered away from a fatal car accident.

"I'd like three eggs over easy, four strips of bacon. Make the bacon brown, extra crispy," Benjie said, his enthusiasm for the food that he had watched his drivers devour for years overcoming whatever, if any, discomfort he was feeling for Delores.

She wrote down the order without speaking, turned and walked to the kitchen while Benjie gazed at her polyester-sheathed hindquarters. "My God, Benjie, what do you think Pickles would do right now if he saw you staring at his girlfriend's little heinie?" Grits said. Benjie shrugged.

"Benjie, much as I like to think about you having a heart attack doing Pickles' route, you just can't do it," Grits said. "There's a bunch of 50-gallon drums you sure can't lift. And you haven't done any real work for. . .well, hell, Benjie, you've never done any real work."

Benjie leaned back in his seat with a hurt look on his face "I can do the same work any of you men do," he said. Then he appeared to realize that his declaration lacked the requisite profanities. "I goddamn hellfire guarantee I can goddamn do it," he said.

"You don't even know how to cuss, Benjie," Grits said. "Don't say we didn't warn you."

There was a crash behind the counter, and I looked over to see Delores staring at the floor, which was covered with eggs, toast and bacon. She crouched and started picking up the broken pieces of the plate, but then dropped them and stayed low, hugging her knees and swaying and shaking her head. I nudged Benjie to get out of the booth so I could help her. But just as I took my first step she stood, untied her apron, dropped it to the floor and walked out the door. She stopped outside, looked at me through the glass door and held her hand up to let me know that she did not want to be followed.

I returned to my seat, and Benjie slid in next to me. "Jeethtuth, Benjie," Billy said. "Hope you're not hungry—I think that wath your breakfatht.

~ ~ ~

It was a few minutes after 3 p.m. when I pulled into the company garage. The day had gone smoothly—or as smoothly as any day humping garbage can go. There were no irate customers, no barrels of ashes with buried embers, no truck breakdowns, no blocked alleys and no extra pickups. Best of all, there were no roving blue pickup trucks containing Benjamin Willard III. And while I was worried about Pickles, my fears were offset by the satisfaction of knowing the boss was working his fat ass off for a change like the rest of us.

Billy and Grits had already finished their routes and were in the garage. Billy was at the final stage of what he called "thanititithing my cab," which meant he sat on the running board and studied the latest nudie mag provided by Bruce, the backhoe guy at the dump. Grits stood by the garage door, staring into space and emptying his third pack of Camels of the day.

"Well, Tippy Toeth," Billy said, looking up from a black-and-white photograph of amply bosomed middle-aged women playing badminton. "And how wath your day? Anyone give you any bouqueth?"

"My day went just fine, Billy," I said. "Anyone heard anything about Pickles? And has anyone seen the boss?"

Billy shook his head. "No on both counth," he said. "I didn't thee Benjie at the dump or on the road all day. Did you thee him?"

"No."

"Gritth?"

Grits shook his head.

"Well, I checked when I got back, and there are 49 callth on the anthwering mathine in the offithe," Billy said. "They're all cuthtomerth thaying their trahth wathn't picked up today—cuthtomerth from Pickleth' route."

Grits spit on the dirt floor. "Guess that shows you can't send trash to pick up trash," he said. "Maybe Benjie got his dick caught in that clipboard of his."

"Oh thit," Billy said, ignoring Grits' comment. "Whath the firth thtop on Pickle'th Monday route?"

"Why don't you tell us, Billy? You're the foreman who's supposed to know everything," Grits said.

"I know his first stop—it's that liquor store-lounge bar in a shopping center off Prairie Road—I think it's called The Office," I said.

Billy and Grits looked at each other. "Oh, thit," Billy said.

Billy turned to me. "Drive over there and thee if Benjie ith there," he said.

I could see Pickles' blue Ford garbage truck parked in front of the liquor store, which had a lounge in the back. I entered, conscious of my work-fragrant jeans and filthy T-shirt, and the cashier, a thin man with a satanic goatee, nodded in the direction of the lounge as if he'd been expecting me. "Your boss is in the back," he said. "Hope you brought a wheelbarrow to haul him out."

Benjie was slumped, head in his arms, in a fleshy heap at the bar. The Chicago Bears cap was still on his head but was pushed back to the point that it was ready to fall off. He was sitting, barely, on a bar stool, and there were at least a half-dozen empty shot glasses and a half-empty glass of piss-yellow beer on the bar next to him.

"Mr. Willard, sir," I said. "Are you awake?"

There was no response, and I thought for a moment he had passed out. But there was elbow movement—a definite sign of life. Benjie lifted his head "Willard Sanitation," he said. "How may we help you?"

The bartender, a middle-aged woman with curly blond hair, paused from drying a bar glass. "Well," she said, "you can start by closing your tab and picking up our garbage. The dumpster's so full the lids won't close."

The big boss turned and looked at me with his narrow, sweating eyes, first seeing and then not seeing and then seeing again.

"It's my friend Tippy Toes," he said. "What are you doing here?"

"Billy sent me," I said. "We got a shitload of complaints off Pickles' route and couldn't figure out what happened."

"No," the boss said. "I mean what are you doing here? At Willard Sanitation? You should be doing more than just humping garbage. You should be the new foreman when Billy leaves—goddamn him for leaving, anyway."

"Yeah," the bartender said. "Who'd want to leave a boss like you?"

"I don't have hardly any experience, Benjie," I said. "You don't want me to be your foreman."

"Well, you're not a goddamned felon, so you got that goin' for you," Benjie said. He paused and leaned back on his stool, exhausted from the exertion of expressing a thought. For a moment it looked as if he was going to fall over backwards. "I was once a young man like you," he said.

Then he closed his eyes as if picturing young Benjamin Willard III in all his youthful glory.

"Will you please get him out of here?" the bartender said, looking at me with the eyes of a woman who had endured an entire working day in the company of a morose drunk.

"I am fully capable of removing myself from your premises," Benjie said. "And I have a route to run." He stood, steadying his weaving self against the bar. I asked the bartender if I could use the phone. She put it on the bar and slid it in front of me. As I watched Benjie weave his way toward the front door, I called the garage and told Billy that the boss was shitfaced and heading off to begin Pickle's route. "Well, thit," Billy said. "You go with Benjie and try to keep him from killing you both, and we'll start on the back end of Pickleth' route and meet you in the middle."

I hung up the phone and thanked the bartender who had her right arm extended to me, palm open. "Your boss's tab is $24," she said. I took out my wallet and saw I had one $20 bill. I pulled it partially out of my billfold and

The Garbage Brothers

then stopped, realizing that was all the money I had until payday.

I was about to tell the bartender that Benjie would pay her the following week, when I noticed that she had reached into my wallet with her long fingers and plucked out the bill. "That's all I've got," I said.

"It comes out of your pocket or mine," she said. "I pick yours."

I thought about arguing, but the money was already in the till. I looked outside and Benjie had somehow managed to climb into the truck and pull it in front of the liquor store, where he was honking the horn.

I walked out of the store and looked at Benjie through the open driver's window. "You're in no shape to drive, Benjie," I said.

Tippy Toes," he said. "If I couldn't drive drunk I wouldn't go anywhere. Get on the back—we've got some goddamn hellfire work we goddamned shit hell have to get done."

~ ~ ~

It took the entire Willard Sanitation crew, or at least what remained of it, just a couple of hours to run a route that usually took Pickles a full work day. Somehow Benjie managed to avoid flattening any pedestrians or ramming a building. He also managed to hit every stop despite his inebriated state, which he nursed with a six-pack of Stroh's on the floor next to the gearshift that was covered with a pink wool cozy knitted for Pickles by Delores. It was a glorious cool fall evening, and the work felt effortless. I lifted every barrel, even the heaviest, with ease. I loped from house to house, carrying 80-pound loads as if I had done it all my life. More than once in the evening light, I could see Benjie's sweaty moon face betraying something close to admiration at my unrelenting pace. I felt as if I could hump garbage all night and the next day, and never break stride.

Billy and Grits met us near the middle of the route, and our satisfaction at seeing each other eased the sense of loss that we had for Pickles. "Mithter Livingthton, I prethume," Billy said, extending a gloved hand to me from his driver's seat when the two garbage trucks pulled nose to nose.

Grits reached behind the driver's seat of his cab and pulled out their last remaining tall boy of Schlitz and handed it to me. "Here ya' go, numbnuts— it's our last so pass it around," he said. I accepted the gift with a nod, pulled the tab, drank the first lukewarm, fumey swallow and handed it back to Grits, who took a sacramental swig and handed it to Billy. Benjie was slumped forward in the driver's seat of his cab, and his forehead was resting on the wheel and his eyes were closed. The boss was sound asleep.

Billy, Grits and I stood like dirty scarecrows behind the truck. I took a seat on the steel edge of the trough and Grits sat on the curb, his bony knees extending toward the dimming sky like church steeples. Billy turned his orange carry can upside-down and sat on top of it, squashing it nearly in half with his bulk and looking like an emperor seated on a pumpkin throne.

There was a whiff of a breeze, and the sweet stench of decay from our trucks drifted in the evening air. Billy raised the communal beer in a toast, and we waited to hear his offering. "To the hardetht-working thonth of bitheth I ever had the pleathure of humpin' garbage with," he said. "And here'th to Pickleth, may God keep hith thorry ath off the electric chair."

Billy passed the can to Grits, and when he handed it to me there was barely a swallow left. I let it dribble down my throat, the sweet, bitter ambrosia of the garbage gods.

"Amen and amen," I said.

Chapter 46: The Highway

When I opened my apartment door that night, I knew what I was going to do. Knew with a certainty I'd never had before in all my 18 years.

I stuffed my clothes, including a torn jean jacket I'd salvaged the day before from the garbage, into black plastic trash bags and carried them to the back seat of my car. I added my box of books, which included the blood red Revised Standard Version Holy Bible that a Sunday school teacher had given me along with the story of how a ray of sunlight had landed on him and him alone in a packed stadium at a Chicago Bears game one frigid December day, and how at that moment he had understood God's grace for the first time. I added a notebook filled with scrawled poetry. I pulled the blanket and sheets off the bed along with two pillows and stuffed them into another trash bag. I picked up the letter from the University of Oregon and stuck it in my back pocket.

I closed the door behind me and thought about saying goodbye to Elsie. But I knew if I told her what I was doing she might call her son-in-law, Billy, to let him know I was leaving and that Billy, in turn, might tell Grits that I was skipping town. More importantly, it was nearly time for the Andy Griffith Show, and even at 18 I knew there are some rituals in life that mustn't be interrupted, and Sheriff Andy, Opie, Aunt Bee, Barney and Floyd the barber were at the top of Elsie Mondenhoofer's list.

The streetlight cast a soft glow over the frontage road and leaves from the nearby oak tree that were strewn across it. I closed the door to the apartment behind me, got in the car and headed for the county jail in Wilton.

The sheriff's deputy at the front desk was a plump middle-aged man with a crew cut, a small sharp nose and eyes just a shade too close together. He closed the Playboy he was reading, inserted a thumb to keep his place and raised his head with a look of "who-the-hell-are-you-and-why-are-you-here?" irritation.

"Yeah," he said. "What do you want?"

"I need to see William Peterman," I said.

"No visiting hours after eight," he said.

He waited for me to leave, but I didn't budge. "Mr. Peterman is my father," I said, reflecting as I said it how easily I lied after five months in the company of felons.

"How nice for you," the deputy said. "Come back tomorrow."

"Tomorrow's too late. I'm leaving town tonight, and I need to say goodbye." He was silent, unpersuaded; it was time to up the lie ante. "Look," I said. "I won't be back for a long time. I'm going into the Army and am probably headed off to 'Nam. I need to say goodbye."

"Your father's been in here plenty, and I've never seen you before."

"Well, I'm here now."

He could see I wasn't going to leave—and that my presence stood between him and the sweet mysteries inside the magazine. "Look," he sighed. "I can take you back to see him for 10 minutes—no more."

"Ten minutes works," I said.

"I need to see what you've got in your hands," he said.

I nodded and handed him a manila envelope I had brought with me. He looked inside and handed it back.

"That for your old man?" he said.

"Yep."

He got up from his desk, locked the front door of the jail, gave me a quick pat down, and then unlocked the steel door that led to the cells behind him.

The inside smelled like an uneasy blend of dirty socks, food and disinfectant. The fluorescent lights shined blue and bright on the cages below. When we got to his cell, Pickles was slumped on his bunk, his back against a concrete wall, one leg on the bed and the other on the floor. There were a couple of other prisoners in the lockup, both looking as if they were either asleep or so bored they couldn't move.

"Hey, you got a visitor, Bill," the deputy said. "It's your kid. Says he's leaving town. You've got 10 minutes."

Pickles said nothing, and turned to face us, putting both legs in front of him on the gray-painted concrete floor. "Can't let you inside," the deputy said to me. "But you can stand here in front of his cell and talk. I'll be back in ten. Understand?"

"Got it," I said.

The deputy left, and Pickles and I stared at each other for a few seconds. "Well, sonny boy," he finally said. "How are things at home?"

"Mother got stuck today at the office and the kids had to do all the housework," I said.

"So Benjie never made it past the first stop?"

I nodded.

"I've gotten hung up there a few times myself," Pickles said. He cocked his head. "Why are you here, Tippy Toes? It ain't to give me the latest installment in Benjie's miserable life. Is Delores OK?"

"It's not about Benjie. And Delores is sad but OK—she left work today after the cops hauled you out," I said. "But she stayed long enough to drop Benjie's breakfast on the floor."

"So what is it then—is Grits still twisting your dick over that niece of his?"

"No," I said. "Anyway, his niece and I might be history. She lost the baby, and I'm not sure where that leaves us."

Pickles brushed his thinning hair back with his fingers, and he looked at the floor. "I'm sorry," he said. "That's a hard loss."

I nodded, aware our time was nearly half gone. "I'm leaving town, Pickles," I said. "Like you and Zeus always told me to do. A school in Oregon was foolish enough to accept me as a student."

Pickles leaned back on his bunk and smiled. I was moved that he was happy for me, even though his own circumstances had taken such a precipitous turn for the worse. "Well," he said, "fuckity fuck felicitations to you, my good sir. I always thought there might be a brain somewhere in that skull full of dogshit."

I paused as I searched for the words, wanting to make sure I found the right ones. "I'm glad I met you, Pickles. You're a friend. And you taught me a ton—you and Zeus both."

"Looks like we at least taught you to know when it's time to get the hell out of Freedom," he said. "Having both of us gone will put Benjie in a hell of a bind, won't it?" He leaned back against the wall and savored the thought.

I looked behind me. No deputy, at least not yet. Then I asked the question we both knew I had come to ask.

"Pickles, what happened at the Snake Pit?"

He sat up, and then he stood and took two steps to the front of the cell, and he seemed even bigger in a steel cage than he had seemed that first day I walked into the Greasy Wrench. He rested both arms against the bars and leaned forward, as if we were having a casual chat at the cafe.

"You don't need to know, and it ain't pretty," Pickles said in a low voice. "Let's just say the world has one less son of a bitch and Ernie gets to retire from soaking his thumbs in chili every day," he said. "That's what happened."

I heard a door open and then footsteps. "Time's up, kid," the deputy said. "Got to get out of here. Right now. Or I'll get in deep shit."

"You live in deep shit, Carl," Pickles said to the deputy. Then Pickles squeezed a huge right hand through the bars, and we shook hands. "Keep a good grip on those numbnuts of yours, Tippy Toes," he said.

"Keep a good hold on your own," I said.

"Not much else to do in here," he said.

Paul Neville

I started to leave and then remembered the envelope I was carrying and turned back and handed it to Pickles. He opened it, looked inside and pulled out the calendar with a picture of a gleaming silver train rolling into a mountain tunnel. He pulled it out and held it against the wall of the cell.

"This will do just goddamn fine," he said.

~ ~ ~

After leaving the county jail, I drove through Wilton, remembering where the dumpsters, burn barrels, garbage cans, potholes and cranky customers were located and feeling a perverse satisfaction that these were the things I'd learned while my high school classmates were off at college pondering philosophical paradigms and congruence theorems. I drove past the Wilton Country Club where the head chef, a stocky Chinese guy who guffawed when Zeus called him "Cookie," left us greasy paper plates stacked high with crisp bacon strips on Saturday mornings. We'd dine on them in the alley, nibbling gently, elbows cocked and pinkies extended.

Just past Wilton's city limits, I turned north and drove down a rural road past a pullout that was Pickles' favorite napping spot and where he insisted that a big oak tree sheltered us from Benjamin Willard III's prowling eyes, even though the garbage truck stuck out on all sides like an elephant hiding behind a telephone pole. A few miles down the road I passed the charred, sad remains of Ernie's Snake Pit Bar and Grill with yellow police tape still draped across what remained of the building's facade. I pulled off in the parking lot next to the quarry and tried to say a prayer for Zeus but no words came. I pulled back onto the highway and kept going.

By the time I reached Freedom, night had descended. The Greasy Wrench Truck Stop and Cafe was dark. Across the street the parking lot at the Jaguar Gentlemen's Club was full, and Gary's Grab and Go was still open for evening shoppers. I pulled into the Greasy Wrench parking lot, scrounged a pencil stub in the glove compartment and wrote a note on the back of a crumpled blue complaint slip. "Benjie," it said. "Leaving town to go be a college kid in Oregon. Sorry to leave you in a fix. Jesse." Then I walked back to the garage, my feet grinding on the gravel that had once swallowed my Corvair, and slid the note under the garage door so Benjie would find it in the morning.

I got back in the car and a minute later pulled off on the shoulder and looked down on Grits' ramshackle residence. The lights were on in the kitchen, and I could see Mary Rose sitting at a table, probably reading or praying for the salvation of Grits and her sad, lovely niece. The kids were probably in the family room sprawled on the Naugahyde sleeper sofa, with Grits dozing off on the duct-taped recliner. The lights were off in Iris' bedroom.

I sat in my car, and then I turned off the engine, got out of the car, eased the door shut, and walked down a narrow, weedy path. I looked in Iris' window, and in the moonlight I saw her asleep on her bed. I put my hands on the filthy window glass and pushed up, and it opened with surprising ease.

"Hey," I whispered. "Iris, it's me, Jesse." She stirred, then lifted her head and looked around with the wide, confused eyes of someone just waking up from deep sleep.

"Why are you here, Jesse?" she asked.

Before I could answer, the door to Iris' room opened, and there was Mary Rose, standing in the doorway and holding a laundry basket filled with clean clothes. She scanned the room taking in everything: Iris in bed, the open window and me standing in front of it frozen in the headlights of her searching and all-knowing eyes. Then she put the laundry down, as if everything were perfectly normal, nodded at me and put a hand on Iris' leg. "Love you so much, sweetheart—blessings on both of you children," she said in a soft voice that was as much a sigh as a statement. Then she left, quietly closing the bedroom door behind her.

"Iris," I said. "I'm leaving town and driving out West. I got accepted at the University of Oregon." I pulled the letter from my back pocket and held it up as if it were a historic document.

"They must have been impressed by your summer job," she said with a smile.

"Come with me," I blurted.

We both fell silent. I hadn't known I was going to ask her to come to Oregon with me. The words just tumbled out, but I wasn't sorry I'd said them, even though I knew she would say no. She sat up and brushed the hair from her sweet, sad face. I thought I had never seen a more beautiful girl in all my life, and I wanted her to come with me—wanted it more than anything I'd ever wanted.

She paused and then shook her head and said what I expected. "I can't leave," she said.

"Sure you can. We'll call Mary Rose in the morning and tell her what we're doing."

"Jesse," she said. "This is my home."

"I know," I said. "Let's go find a new one."

She slipped silently, wordlessly out of bed, slipped on jeans and a stretched-out red T-shirt, and turned on a bedside lamp. I watched in disbelief as she laced on a pair of blue tennies and then took the basket of clean clothes that Mary Rose had brought, added a sweater and a jacket from her closet, and then handed the basket to me. She looked around the small room and took a small framed picture of her and her little sister sitting at a picnic table next to their mother. Then she picked her purse off the floor and crawled gingerly out the window.

Paul Neville

I carried the laundry basket with one hand and held one of her hands with my other. We walked slowly, silently up the weedy hillside path. When we reached the car, she stood on the shoulder of the road as I shoved her belongings into the crowded back seat. I got in the car and checked the rearview mirror to see if Grits was striding up the road with the Louisville Slugger in his hands.

"Wait," Iris said. She stood outside the car and turned to look down at the house below. I heard a muffled choking, and I knew she was crying. And I knew with heart-squeezing certainty that Iris had changed her mind, and that I would be driving to Oregon alone. I waited for her to turn, retrieve her belongings and say goodbye. Then she lifted both of her small hands, the tender palms turned up to the sky the way she'd once told me the faithful did at Sunday worship at the Tabernacle of the Holy Winds. She spoke softly to the sky, so softly I could not hear the words. And I knew that the true gift of tongues, if such a thing existed, must sound like Iris' sad, gentle murmuring.

She got back inside the car, left the door open, and I braced for the hard news. "Remind me what Zeus and Pickles told you about leaving Freedom." she said.

I closed my eyes and remembered Zeus' red-faced rant in front of the mummy-dog house and his finger-wagging exhortation for me "to get the hell out of town." And I recalled Pickles' admonition just a couple of hours earlier as he sat behind bars at the county jail. "They both told me to get the hell out of Freedom first chance I got," I said.

"Then let's get the hell out and never look back," she said. She pulled her door shut, leaned back in her seat and closed her eyes. Then I slowly pulled that baby blue Corvair onto the sacred highway and headed west to Oregon.

About the Author

Paul Neville is a retired award-winning journalist who worked for decades as a reporter and editor at newspapers in the Midwest and Pacific Northwest. He lives Oregon, where he is an author, whitewater kayaker and singer-songwriter whose favorite gigs are playing for the homeless. And, yeah, he once helped pay his way through Northwestern University in Chicago by working as a garbage collector.

IFD Publishing Paperbacks

Novels:
Of Thimble and Threat, by Alan M. Clark
Baggage Check, by Elizabeth Engstrom
Bull's Labyrinth, by Eric Witchey
The Surgeon's Mate: A Dismemoir, by Alan M. Clark
Siren Promised, by Jeremy Robert Johnson and Alan M. Clark
Say Anything but Your Prayers, by Alan M. Clark
Candyland, by Elizabeth Engstrom
Apologies to the Cat's Meat Man, by Alan M. Clark
Lizzie Borden, by Elizabeth Engstrom
A Parliament of Crows, by Alan M. Clark
Lizard Wine, by Elizabeth Engstrom
The Door that Faced West, by Alan M. Clark
The Northwoods Chronicles, by Elizabeth Engstrom
The Prostitute's Price, by Alan M. Clark
The Assassin's Coin, by John Linwood Grant
13 Miller's Court, by Alan M. Clark and John Linwood Grant
Guys Named Bob, by Elizabeth Engstrom
Fallen Giants of the Points, by Alan M. Clark
The Itinerant, by Elizabeth Engstrom
York's Moon, by Elizabeth Engstrom
Night Birds, by Lisa Snellings and Alan M. Clark
The Garbage Brothers, by Paul Neville

Collections:
Professor Witchey's Miracle Mood Cure, by Eric Witchey

Nonfiction:
How to Write a Sizzling Sex Scene, by Elizabeth Engstrom
Divorce by Grand Canyon, by Elizabeth Engstrom

IFD Publishing EBooks

(You can find the following titles at most distribution points for all ereading platforms.)

Novels:
The Prostitute's Price, by Alan M. Clark
The Assassin's Coin, by John Linwood Grant
13 Miller's Court, by Alan M. Clark and John Linwood Grant

Guys Named Bob, by Elizabeth Engstrom
Apologies to the Cat's Meat Man, by Alan M. Clark
Bull's Labyrinth, by Eric Witchey
The Surgeon's Mate: A Dismemoir, by Alan M. Clark
York's Moon, by Elizabeth Engstrom
Beyond the Serpent's Heart, by Eric Witchey
Lizzie Borden, by Elizabeth Engstrom
A Parliament of Crows, by Alan M. Clark
Lizard Wine, by Elizabeth Engstrom
Northwoods Chronicles, by Elizabeth Engstrom
Siren Promised, by Alan M. Clark and Jeremy Robert Johnson
To Kill a Common Loon, by Mitch Luckett
The Man in the Loon, by Mitch Luckett
Of Thimble and Threat by Alan M. Clark
Jack the Ripper Victim Series: The Double Event (includes two novels from the series: *Of Thimble and Threat* and *Say Anything But Your Prayers*) by Alan M. Clark
Candyland, by Elizabeth Engstrom
The Blood of Father Time: Book 1, The New Cut, by Alan M. Clark, Stephen C. Merritt & Lorelei Shannon
The Blood of Father Time: Book 2, The Mystic Clan's Grand Plot, by Alan M. Clark, Stephen C. Merritt & Lorelei Shannon
How I Met My Alien Bitch Lover: Book 1 from the Sunny World Inquisition Daily Letter Archives, by Eric Witchey
Baggage Check, by Elizabeth Engstrom
D. D. Murphry, Secret Policeman, by Alan M. Clark and Elizabeth Massie
Black Leather, by Elizabeth Engstrom
Fallen Giants of the Points, by Alan M. Clark
The Itinerant, by Elizabeth Engstrom
Night Birds, by Lisa Snellings and Alan M. Clark
The Garbage Brothers, by Paul Neville

Novelettes:
Mudlarks and the Silent Highwayman, by Alan M. Clark
The Tao of Flynn, by Eric Witchey
To Build a Boat, Listen to Trees, by Eric Witchey

Children's Illustrated:
The Christmas Thingy, by F. Paul Wilson. Illustrated by Alan M. Clark

Collections:
Suspicions, by Elizabeth Engstrom
Professor Witchey's Miracle Mood Cure, by Eric Witchey

Short Fiction:
"Brittle Bones and Old Rope," by Alan M. Clark
"Crosley," by Elizabeth Engstrom
"The Apple Sniper," by Eric Witchey

Nonfiction:
How to Write a Sizzling Sex Scene, by Elizabeth Engstrom
Divorce by Grand Canyon, by Elizabeth Engstrom

IFD Publishing Audio Books

Novels:
The Door That Faced West by Alan M. Clark, read by Charles Hinckley
Jack the Ripper Victim Series: Of Thimble and Threat, by Alan M. Clark, read by Alicia Rose
Jack the Ripper Victim Series: Say Anything But Your Prayers, by Alan M. Clark, read by Alicia Rose
Jack the Ripper Victim Series: The Double Event by Alan M. Clark, read by Alicia Rose (includes two novels from the series: *Of Thimble and Threat* and *Say Anything But Your Prayers*)
A Parliament of Crows by Alan M. Clark, read by Laura Jennings
A Brutal Chill in August by Alan M. Clark, read by Alicia Rose
The Surgeon's Mate: A Dismemoir, by Alan M. Clark, read by Alan M. Clark
Apologies to the Cat's Meat Man, by Alan M. Clark, read by Alicia Rose
The Prostitute's Price, by Alan M. Clark, read by Alicia Rose
The Assassin's Coin, by John Linwood Grant, read by Alicia Rose
13 Miller's Court, by Alan M. Clark and John Linwood Grant, read by Alicia Rose
Fallen Giants of the Points, by Alan M. Clark, read by Carolina Cioara

Novelettes:
Mudlarks and the Silent Highwayman, by Alan M. Clark, read by Alicia Rose